The Producer's Business Handbook

The Producer's Business Handbook

John J. Lee, Jr.

An Imprint of Elsevier Science

AMSTERDAM   BOSTON   LONDON   NEW YORK   OXFORD   PARIS
SAN DIEGO   SAN FRANCISCO   SINGAPORE   SYDNEY   TOKYO

Focal Press is an imprint of Elsevier.

∞ This book is printed on acid-free paper.

Library of Congress Cataloging-in-Publication Data.

Lee, John J., Jr.

    The producer's business handbook/John J. Lee, Jr.
    p. cm.
    ISBN 0-240-80396-5 (pbk. :alk.paper)
      1. Motion picture industry-United States-Finance-Handbooks, manuals, etc. 2. Motion pictures-United States-Marketing-Handbooks, manuals, etc. 3. Motion pictures-Production and direction-Handbooks, manuals, etc. I. Title

PN1993.5.U6 L39 2000
384'.83'0973—dc21

                                          99-087181

British Library Cataloguing-in-Publication Data
A catalogue record for this book is available from the British Library.

The publisher offers special discounts on bulk orders of this book.
For information, please contact:
Manager of Special Sales
Elsevier Science
200 Wheeler Road
Burlington, MA 01803
Tel: 781-313-4700
Fax: 781-313-4802

For information on all Focal Press publications available, contact our World Wide Web homepage at http://www.focalpress.com

10 9 8 7 6
Printed in the United States of America

Table of Contents

Foreword _____ ix

Introduction _____ xi

Chapter 1 / How the Motion Picture Industry Functions _____ 1

   Major Participant Categories and Their Functions   1

Chapter 2 / U.S. Theatrical Distributors _____ 17

   The Major and Minor Distributors   17

   Studio Integrity   18

   The Three Studio Arenas   19

   Studio Relationships with Independent Producers   20

   Producer Relationship Comparisons   22

   Worksheet: Producer's Share Analysis   22

   Share Analysis Review   22

   Split Negative Pickup Relationships   27

   Studio Acquisition of a Renegade Picture   27

   The Critical Effect of U.S. Studio Attachment   29

Chapter 3 / Foreign Territories _____ 31

   The Global Popularity of American Motion Pictures   31

   Producer Relationships with Foreign Distributors   35

   Establishing New Foreign Distribution Relationships   37

   Nurturing the Relationship   38

   Foreign Territory License Timing   39

   License Documentation   40

   Foreign Deal Memo Sample   41

   Managing Global Relationships   43

   Foreign Trends   44

Chapter 4 / Ancillary Markets and Rights _____ 45

   The Effect of Theatrically Released Motion Pictures on Other Windows   45

   Audience Sizes In Major Windows   46

   Ancillary Audience Characteristics   47

   Producers Rely on Ancillary Earnings   50

   Video Distribution   51

   Premium Cable Television   52

Network Television   53

Free Television Syndication   54

Other Ancillary Rights   55

Chapter 5 / Entertainment Banking   59

The Banking Business   59

Basis of Lending Decisions   60

The Loan Approval Process   63

Production Financing Worksheet   63

Types of Loans   65

Gap Financing   65

When to Approach the Bank   65

Chapter 6 / Completion Guarantors   67

What Completion Guarantees Do   67

Producers' Perceived and Real Value of Completion Guarantors   68

Completion Insurance Relationships   69

The Completion Bond Package   69

Completion Insurance Cost   70

Chapter 7 / Attorneys, Negotiations, and Entertaiment Law   73

Attorneys and Their Firms   73

Producers Performing as Attorneys   74

Negotiating   75

Vital Legal Aspects Relating to Story   77

Deal Memos, Letter Agreements, and Long Form Contracts   82

The Benefits Associated with the Producer Preparing
Deal Documentation   83

Deal Reviews   83

The Attorney as Counsel   84

Dispute Resolutions   85

Literary Release Sample   86

Chapter 8 / Talent, Agents, and Agencies   89

The Relationship Evolution   90

Meetings with Talent and Agents   91

Attorneys as Agents   92

Planning the Deal   92

Development Negotiation   92

Points Participation   93

Preparation of a Fair Deal   94

Agents as Creative Resources 94

Talent Reserve 95

The Participation of the Producer's Attorney 95

Chapter 9 / Development, Production, and Producing Company Structures 97

The Power of Company Structure 97

The Companies 98

Chart: Business Structure 98

Development Company Financing 100

Securities 101

Forms of Companies 101

Chapter 10 / Development Financing 103

The Essential Power of Funded Development 103

Development Funding Sources 104

The Process of Securing Development Financing 107

Worksheet: Activity Projection 108

Worksheet: Cash Flow Projection 111

Chapter 11 / The Team 117

The Complete Team 117

Corporate Structure 118

Chart: Production Company 119

Chart: Development Company 119

The Production Company's Team 122

The Development Company's Team 123

Optimizing the Teams 123

Discovering, Negotiating, and Compensating 123

Chapter 12 / Production Company's Operation 125

Defining and Establishing the Production Company 126

The Story Search 126

Development Company Emphasis 127

Preparing the Investment Offering 128

Assembling the Team 128

Producing the Investment Memorandum 129

Raising the Development Financing 129

Investment Partner Communications 130

Working the Development Plan 130

Story Selection and Initial Green Lights 133

Predirector Picture Development 134

Director Attachment 134
The Producer/Director Relationship 135
Shooting Script 136
Lead Cast Attachment 137
Preparing for Physical Production 137
Maturing Marketing Materials 138
Preparing the Production Bank Financing Facility 138
The U.S. Studio Distribution Agreement 139
The Presales 139
Engaging the Completion Bond 140
Engaging the Production Bank Loan 140
Final Preproduction 141
Principal Photography 141
Post Production 142
The Picture's U.S. Branding 142
The Global Territories and Ancillary Markets 143
Motion Picture Development and Production Checklist 143

Chapter 13 / The Producer's Business **145**
Multiple Picture Management 145
Time and Budget Economies 146
Establishing the Production Company Brand Presence 147
Sustaining Business, Artistic, and Personal Objective Balance 148
Managing Library Pictures 149
Advancing Team Vitality and Allegiance 150

Chapter 14 / Reports, Data, and Producer's Principles **153**
Entertainment Industry Statistics and Reports 153
Chart: The Most Successful Pictures Ever Released 155
Chart: Theater Attendance and Earnings by Target Audience 161
Information Sources 162
Producer Success Principles 164

Index **167**

Foreword

James D. Pasternak

This is an important book. A life-changing book. If you only buy one book on producing movies (or television), it should be this book.

This book shows independent producers, step-by-step, how to achieve fully funded development, bank production financing, and global distribution. With fully funded development, producers can make the necessary talent attachments and marketing analyses essential to packaging each movie. U.S. theatrical distribution assures global distribution. With bank production financing, producers own the copyrights to their pictures, have the greatest creative control, and receive the greatest profits.

This powerful how-to tool is structured in two parts. First, the book shows you how the 21st century film industry works from an independent producer's point-of-view. Chapters on audiences, distributors, producers, foreign markets, ancillary rights, banking, completion guarantors, attorneys, talent, and agents allow you to see inside the big picture.

The second part of the book details the producing model used by that small core group of successful independent production companies who have achieved creative independence and turn a profit on every picture they produce. This is achieved by applying seven major principles:

- Subjecting potential projects to a studio (or network) based Internal Greenlight
- Obtaining independent fully funded development
- Acquiring bank production financing
- Developing U.S. and foreign territory distribution relationships
- Planning rights liquidation
- Participating in campaign management
- Being a balanced producer

This paradigm is the map to success. You will find its treatment clear, specific, and even inspiring.

Let me tell you why I brag about this book.

As a writer/director/producer and educator for 35 years, my focus was on the creative: script, camera, actors, and editing. From the start, both students and clients asked me to help them raise the money to make their films. I realized this was a logical extension of my mission to empower them.

I came to understand how hard and often discouraging this work is. Studio executives said no for a variety of often difficult to understand reasons. Agents and managers often denied us access to their actors and directors because we could not make cash offers. Without recognizable talent, distributors were not interested in pre-sales. Even when we did get pictures made, it was almost as impossible to secure their distribution. As producers, we were stuck in a highly competitive game without a rule book.

Then I met John Lee, and I read this book, "The Producer's Business Handbook." It was life changing.

Critically important is the concept of the Internal Greenlight. This is a marketing analysis that requires you to start by first understanding and then developing each picture's endgame. By subjecting a potential project to an Internal Greenlight, you discover your audience, the marketing campaign, the above the line elements, the share of estimated global profits, the picture's earnings-to-cost ratio, and its optimum global distributors. Prior to earnest development, you discover the vital information needed to commence early relationships with each picture's most advantageous distributors.

My favorite section is the one that focuses on creating a multi-picture development company. It demonstrates how to create a mechanism that makes it attractive for private investors to invest in films; a mechanism that offers the private investor the most secure way to make a profit in the film business. This information alone is worth the price of admission.

James D. Pasternak is an internationally acclaimed screenwriter, director, and Producer, whose credits include "Cousins" for Paramount and the recently completed feature "One Hell Of A Guy," starring Rob Lowe and Michael York. His directing students include two Oscar-winners, Christine Lahti and Ray McKinnon. James produces through his production company Rogue Dreams Entertainment, is a faculty member of the Los Angeles Film School and he founded the The New School's Feature Film Production Program.

Introduction

Most of the hundreds of active U.S. independent producers operate unstable, often unprofitable businesses. Yet at the same time, fewer than two dozen independent production organizations operate solid, consistently profitable companies. The success of these companies is not attained by accident, but rather through the application of sound business principles that drive their ever advancing motion picture production craft.

The purpose of this book is to assist producers in attaining this unquestionably preferable operating position. Specifically, it discusses how the global motion picture industry works and focuses on the processes used by these independent production companies, which almost exclusively use bank production financing, release their pictures theatrically through major studios, and consistently do so at a profit.

This book is a global orientation to the relationships that the most successful motion picture producers have with the various participants in the motion picture industry. This includes how these producers direct their relationships with domestic and foreign studios, agencies, attorneys, talent, completion guarantors, banks, and private investors. The volume also contains the producer's thorough orientation to operating development and producing companies, from solicitation of literary properties, through direct rights sales and the management of global distribution relationships. Also presented is an in-depth discussion of the team needed to operate the companies, as well as how to find and attach them. Additionally, there are worksheets and instructions for the business processes of development and production, which are used by many of the industry's consistently profitable production companies.

To assist readers in a deeper understanding, and for use within their own companies, a CD-ROM accompanies this book, containing, in Excel:

1. The Producer's Share Analysis/Internal Greenlight Summary
2. The Bank Financing Worksheet
3. The Production and Development Companies' Organization Model
4. The Multiple Picture Development and Production Activity Projection
5. The Multiple Picture Development and Production Activity Projection with Live Data Worksheet
6. The Multiple Picture Development and Production Cash Flow Projection
7. The Multiple Picture Development and Production Organization Chart
8. The Production Company
9. The Development Company
10. Most Successful Picture Analysis

And in Microsoft Word:

1. A Literary Release Sample
2. The AFMA International Multiple Rights Deal Letter
3. Target Audience Analysis

This book is written to provide both instruction and worksheet support to independent motion picture producers at all levels of industry experience. Specifically, it is written to:

1. Assist experienced producers (as well as directors, writers, and other entertainment professionals), and to hone and sharpen their hard-won experience and knowledge into increasingly effective tools with which they can manage their resources. In this highly specialized field of motion picture production, often the difference between success and failure hinges on the producer's ability to dynamically engage and balance the full spectrum of business resources and relationships within his or her reach. This book opens for producers a full-aperture view of the entertainment business and provides them with the tools and instructions they need to engage all aspects of the film industry related to global production and exploitation. So it opens the way to improved industry understanding and, more important, to the capacity to operate predictably profitable production organizations.

2. Assist entry-level producers in understanding how the motion picture industry operates, plot their most promising path to achieve their independent producing objectives, and provide them documentation, as well as relationship and operational support.

Independent Producers

This book focuses on *independent producers*. These are not to be confused with attached producers (who may be executive producers, financiers, line producers, executives with a studio deal, or a star's boyfriend or girlfriend). Independent producers, as they are referenced in this text, are those who are at the creative and business helm of each of their pictures from development inception.

Many studio production-unit pictures begin their film lives in development pools. These pictures have producers, but they are often attached to perform production services and are rarely these pictures' creative genesis. Development pool pictures often have a director and one or more actors attached before a producer is attached. While these producers are typically seasoned motion picture makers, they do not have the same relationship with their pictures as do independent producers.

For instance, *Return of the Jedi* is appropriately regarded as George Lucas's picture, though it was directed by Richard Marquand. While the director is the production chief during principal photography, and is often also the supervising editor, we can be assured that Mr. Lucas's fiercely independent creative participation permeated the entire production process. It is his picture. So while creative collaboration is a bedrock quality of the best independent producers, the independent producers referenced in this book are those who are their pictures' genesis and ultimate creative authority.

Similarly, John Hughes's production company produced *Home Alone* with 20th Century Fox. Hughes was the producer and writer. Although Hughes used Chris Columbus (a respected writer/director/producer) to direct the picture, giving him the creative freedom due a director of his stature, Hughes sustained the creative dominance of an independent producer throughout the picture's creation.

In a final example, while Steven Spielberg directs most of his pictures, he generally brings in producers or coproducers. Of course, if he chooses to produce only (as he did with *Goonies*), he delegates the direction duties to someone else. Regardless, on his pictures, Spielberg is the independent producer and consequently the ultimate creative authority.

The producer definition used in this book refers to those independent producers who choose to retain their pictures' development and production authority and creative genesis, regardless of the specific functions they select in each picture.

Workbook

This is a workbook. Included are seven worksheets and several business forms. These will be most beneficial to learning and business when used with the CD-ROM that accompanies this book.

The worksheets are presented in Excel software. Each worksheet is in live sample form, allowing the most detailed scrutiny and understanding, as well as in a blank template form for their broader use in the producer's production and development companies. Central to the worksheets are the Activity Projection and the Cash Flow Projection. The production forms are presented in Microsoft Word and can easily be customized for each producer's use.

Basis for the Principles

Like most principles worth learning, the principles set forth in this book are simple and are proven by experience, as they are used by many of the industry's most successful independent motion picture production companies. The core of these principles are discovered in the answers to three questions that should be applied to all works considered for development and production:

- Is the story worth being told?
- Who are its target audiences?
- What are the production and marketing costs?

Producers who make their decisions predicated on the analysis of the answers to these questions consistently guide each of their pictures through successful development, production, and distribution.

Though motion picture producers are the reader focus of this book and theatrical release motion pictures are the product focus, the application of this volume's principles will be as beneficial to a student's first film school production as it will be to seasoned feature producers' continuing pictures.

Common Orientation

This information will likely cast some surprising light in a few dimly lit corners for seasoned producers and related motion picture professionals, and will be particularly illuminating for students of film who are preparing for careers in independent feature film production.

The following industry parable may help bring the reader to a common grounding with the information in this text:

The Forest

A squirrel and an otter agreed to confide with one another in an attempt to unravel the mysterious anomalies unique to the forest in which they lived— you know, the stuff they did not understand that frequently drove them a little crazy. The squirrel described what she saw from the trees and the otter described what he saw from the water and ground.

They met regularly to share their prevailing theories and enjoy the mutual therapy and camaraderie. This did not escape the attention of their contemporaries, and soon a broad cross-section of them met, sharing new and often fascinating perspectives. Over time, the group became secure in their mutually affirmed understandings. They settled many matters: that forest fires were caused by the sun touching the tops of the trees, and—well, almost every other problem was caused by the forest's predators.

From time to time eavesdropping eagles listened and were amazed at some of the forest animals' twisted conclusions. Pleased to dispel their bizarre notions, one of these eagles explained that he had soared over the entire forest, observing all its creations for decades, that he possessed a sound understanding of how and why things happened in the forest, and was willing to share what he knew.

It was a novel resource never before available to them. The forest animals agonized over the offer among themselves and then finally declined the eagle's proposal. They determined that they were comfortable with their understanding, and that they had scoop from sparrows and robins. Besides, the eagle was a predator and obviously an unreliable source.

There are scores of cliques within the motion picture industry, each comfortable in its peculiar understanding of how the industry functions, and why seemingly irrational anomalies regularly occur. This condition is like that of Galileo, who was forced to renounce his published discoveries of astronomy and physics, among them the stunning reality that the world was actually turning. Pressed into a humiliating public renunciation by those who were not comfortable with how these discoveries affected their understanding of life, Galileo afterward calmly declared, "And yet the world turns."

So it was with the forest animals, and so it is with many of us in the business of creating motion pictures. This is an expansive, powerful industry, with dynamics that often vault participants to the top of the heap at a given time, then dash them to relative obscurity at another. Though we may have our notions that explain why it does or doesn't work the way we think it should, it can be instructive to remember that our personal perceptions do not affect how the motion picture industry actually functions.

This volume draws upon my understanding, harvested primarily from serving as a production and distribution business affairs executive. It employs the knowledge and experience of several film industry mavens and data from the most reliable industry sources.

As an industry seminar speaker, I assumed that capacity, attendance, and aggressive participation at my presentations were a result of producers' ongoing panic about securing production funding. However, in preparation for a three-year film school commitment to teach business of film courses, I discovered that while most books were excellent in some regard, none presented a complete picture of how the industry functions from an independent producer's perspective, or most important, what the specific operating practices of the most successful production companies are. This book delivers the critical missing material.

How the Motion Picture Industry Functions

This chapter presents the ten major motion picture participant categories, reveals independent production companies as creation and production businesses with distribution capacities, and examines story as the heart of the producer's picture universe.

Major Participant Categories and Their Functions

There are ten participant categories, or basic functions and interrelationships within the motion picture industry. The most prosperous companies in each category are successful, in large measure, because they sustain a perspective of how the whole industry operates and continually sharpen their individual participation within the entire entertainment universe.

This perspective includes the view that (1) the motion picture industry is a consumer-product business; (2) that each participant is of the whole (not even the major studios participate in more than eight of the ten categories); and (3) that the various target audiences are each picture's most important participants.

In their order of importance the ten categories of players are: (1) audiences, (2) distributors, (3) producers, (4) retailers and licensed media, (5) foreign territories, (6) financing participants, (7) distributor subcontractors, (8) production talent and subcontractors, (9) ancillary media and licensees, and (10) major consumer brands.

Participant Category 1: The Audiences

Each picture's target audiences are its sources of income. Audiences are the highest priority participants in the industry, as without them, there is no industry. Producers must know the specific target audiences for each of their pictures, evaluate each picture according to its audiences, and, after committing to a story creatively, make decisions to proceed on the picture based on its target audience dynamics.

After finding a story that interests them, producers should ask two questions regarding its audiences:

1. By order of dominance, who are this picture's target audiences? This answer prepares the producer to research the leading 54 U.S. major metropolitan areas (metros), and discover the size, entertainment consumption, and media-use profile of each of the picture's target audiences. (These leading 54 are the focus of the more than 200 U.S. metros, as each of these 54 have a half-million households or more and together spend over two-thirds of total U.S. entertainment dollars).
2. How have these audiences responded to at least five pictures most similar to the story in consideration, including anticipated above-the-line creatives (story, director and lead cast) released in the past five years? The answer to this question enables the producer to project gross receipts, and the producer's share of those gross receipts, for the story being considered. Pictures with similar audiences are identified through comparing the proposed picture's dominant campaign elements and above-the-line participants with the campaign elements and above-the-line participants of previously released pictures.

Initial Feasibility Analysis of Internal Greenlight

The answers to these two questions, weighed against a picture's estimated production and distribution costs, determine if that picture will be greenlit by the producer. This is a picture's initial feasibility analysis.

If the audience profiles and picture comparisons are positive, and the income-to-cost ratio is at least two to one (in other words, the projected distributor's net income is at least twice the projected production costs), the producer should proceed with the next step in the development of most pictures. If a picture's target audiences lack dynamic consumer profiles, or are too small or difficult to reach in comparison to the picture's costs, the producer should pass rather than proceed.

The specific methods of obtaining and analyzing this information, and a complete explanation of obtaining a picture's internal greenlight, are presented in later chapters, especially Chapters 2 and 12. The following diagram demonstrates the economics of this process.

The Picture's Initial Feasibility Analysis
(in millions)

Global projected gross income (from recent historical comparisons)	$208
Less theatrical participations, distributor's fees, and expenses	$126
Distributor's net	$82
Negative cost and production financing expenses (actual estimated budget)	$31
Distributor's net income	$82
Production costs	$31
Ratio	2.6
Feasibility:	Recommend proceeding

Audience Orientation

Producers should understand and use the consumer terms used by Madison Avenue and the reporting agencies such as Nielsen Media Research, as these are the audience semantics of the entertainment industry. Utilizing this language is an especially effective tool in the producer's relationships with foreign and domestic distributors, licensees of foreign and domestic rights, product placement and premium tie-in brand representatives, advertising agencies, and public relations and promotion companies.

Audiences are categorized demographically by age as follows:

Primary Audience Age Demographic Categories	
Audience Terms	*Age Demographic*
Kids	5–11
Youth	12–17
Adults	18+
Youth and single adults	12–24
Older youth and single adults	16–24

Adults are separated into several categories, by gender, most significantly in the motion picture business by ages 18 to 24, 18 to 34, 25 to 34, 25 to 44, 25 to 54, 45-plus and 55-plus.

Audiences are also identified and evaluated by lifestyles, such as active adults, affluent adults, educated adults, working women, and so on.

There are excellent, easy-to-use consumer databases available to producers at reasonable costs, or accessible through major advertising agencies, media buying companies, and the television networks. These consumer databases allow target audiences to be identified by an extensive array of demographic and lifestyle search criteria. The lifestyle options are broad, the data is reliable, and the reports are exceptionally useful in audience quantifying and qualifying.

For example, you can sort the major metros by men 18 to 34 who are college graduates, watch a movie at a theater at least twice a month, and own a mountain bike. The requested report can reveal how many are in this audience, where their population concentrations are, what their consumption profiles for the various media are, which TV programs they watch, and so on.

Becoming conversant with this information and the databases it is derived from is crucially important, as the application of this data becomes a very powerful tool for producers who will be originating promotions, reviewing media buys, and projecting their pictures' earnings.

Distributor Pitch Preparation

Many producers are skilled in preparing the creative aspects of their pictures to pitch to distributors. However, they are not ready to pitch until they also have prepared and can present information about their pictures' audiences in the full spectrum of the distributors' interest.

Pitching their pictures to distributors, after having first fulfilled their internal green-lights, empowers producers to present information that is essential for distribution executives to evaluate their interest. This information includes these pictures' audiences, and projected gross receipts. Producers armed with this information are in the strongest presentation position possible, presenting and negotiating from a distribution insider position.

Participant Category 2: The Distributors

The major distributors are the motion picture marketing and sales companies in the global territories that establish the brand presence of each picture to their respective target audiences, and are wholesalers of motion pictures to their various media.

In the U.S. the major distributors are 20th Century Fox, Universal, Buena Vista, Paramount, Sony, Warner Bros., Miramax, Dreamworks, New Line, and MGM/UA. Each of these is a full-service studio in the traditional definition, with the exception of Miramax, Dreamworks, New Line, and MGM/UA, which lack only a studio lot. These ten majors are all-rights distributors, globally distributing every theatrical, non-theatrical and ancillary right associated with their motion pictures. And they are the prominent U.S. theatrical and video distributors for major U.S. independent producers.

In addition to the major studios there are:

1. Twenty minor theatrical distributors, five of which are owned by major distributors (Sony Pictures Classics, Fox Searchlight, Paramount Classics, Gramercy, Fine Line Features, October Releasing, and Samuel Goldwyn). Some of the largest of the remaining minors include Artisan Entertainment, Lions Gate, and First Look. The largest minors are all-rights distributors.

2. Direct foreign territory distributors. The largest of these are studios within their respective foreign territories, who produce and direct-distribute to all their territories' major media, and who also sell their pictures' rights globally. These are presented in Chapter 3.

3. Foreign rights sales companies. The largest of these organizations produce some of their own pictures, in addition to acquiring motion pictures and performing foreign market sales and distribution services for their independent producers' pictures. Some of these include Summit Entertainment, Overseas Filmgroup, J & M Entertainment, and Seven Arts.

4. Producers representative organizations. These organizations plan and execute foreign territory sales, and sometimes plan and assist in the global rights liquidation of their independent producer clients' pictures. Among these are Kathy Morgan Entertainment and International Film Distribution Consultants.

5. Television syndication companies. These companies plan and carry out sales to television stations and cable companies.

6. Product placement. These companies plan, negotiate, and manage the use, borrowing, giving, or fee earned by their producer clients for products appearing in their pictures.

7. Promotional tie-in companies. These companies originate, plan, negotiate, and manage relationships in advertising and/or promoting the release of producers' motion pictures with other consumer brands. The most prolific brand categories that participate in the motion picture industry are soft drinks and fast food.

8. Publishers.

9. Ancillary rights sales companies. These organizations, examined in Chapter 4, include companies specializing in merchandising, in-flight, scholastic, ships-at-sea, and other sales and marketing.

Establishing Each Picture's Brand and the Studio Operating Perspective

The operations and functions of U.S. theatrical distributors are presented in Chapter 2. The following section introduces the distribution phenomena of the establishment of each picture's brand, as well as the distributors' operating perspective.

Brand Presence

Each picture's value for every other U.S. rights area is primarily established during its U.S. theatrical release. American audiences are introduced to each picture during this premiere distribution window. This is where the brand, the audience perspective, and the picture's entertainment value are established.

The physical aspects of theatrical distribution are highly sophisticated. These functions include theater circuit bidding, booking the theaters that are matched to each picture, negotiating favorable film rental terms with the circuits, and staging the physical release of the picture through film exchanges. These operations substantially affect the success of each picture. For example, audiences expect the finest pictures to be at the best theaters. A good picture booked at a questionable theater sends a message to the target audiences that it may be a poor picture, potentially overturning other well executed distribution moves.

As complex and crucial as physical distribution is, however, the peerless genius in the art of distribution lies in establishing the public's opinion of each picture through paid advertising, publicity, and promotion. This is the process through which motion pictures become major brands to their target audiences.

A brand is the name by which consumers identify a product or group of products. Pepsi, Levi Strauss, and Quaker Oats have the luxury of fighting for sustained brand dominance. Theirs is a continuing and absolutely rugged battle, but it pales in comparison with motion picture brand establishment.

Every motion picture released is a separate brand. Each picture must come from absolute obscurity (with the exception of novels and sequels) to become top-of-mind with each picture's target audiences. This is typically accomplished in three to five weeks prior to each picture's opening. A television campaign may have a reach and frequency performance as high as twelve impressions (advertising viewings) by 80 percent of that picture's target audiences before the picture opens. Depending on the target audience and time of year, the cost of media alone is typically $8 to $12 million, *before* a picture's initial street date. Brand presence is so fundamental to a picture's earnings performance in every distribution category that distributors' projections of the picture's gross earnings are based on the opening weekend's theatrical receipts.

Typically the distributor manages the creation of the entire campaign, and it is the campaign, its media buys, and promotions that drive each picture's initial audiences. In fact, even with pre-screenings, the picture itself usually has little effect on the theatrical opening weekend gross, and only limited effect on the first week's earnings. Even substantial negative word of mouth will have little effect on pictures whose primary target audience is kids, and rarely has enough power to collapse any of the other audience categories until a picture begins its third week of theatrical release.

The two major campaign elements that determine each picture's opening two weeks theatrical gross are (1) how motivating the television spots are to the various target audiences and (2) the target audience reach and frequency of the campaign's television schedule. Radio, outdoor, and print advertising are important, especially during the summer, but television is the core campaign media.

Consequently, producers are most productive when they focus on sharpening the development and management of their pictures' campaigns, rather than on tracking their share of box office receipts. Besides, the producer's share of theatrical revenues is significantly diminished by the exhibitor's share (traditionally averaging 50 percent of gross box office) and the high cost of advertising and prints, among other elements examined in Chapter 2.

The picture's brand presence established during its theatrical release predicates the picture's earnings capacity in all subsequent distribution windows. These other earnings windows, especially video, premium cable, and network television, are the producer's highest earnings sources. Often those distributors who have established a strong positive brand with their picture's target audiences during the theatrical release, but have seen competing pictures, weather, or other factors keep theatrical audiences low, find that they experience a substantial audience increase during the video release.

Distributors Operating Perspective

Each theatrical screen is a unique retail environment. It accommodates only one product at a time. Consequently, distributors closely examine the earnings performance of each picture on each screen. When gross receipts fall below a screen's house-nut (the exhibitor's cost to provide and operate that screen), the picture is soon replaced with another. For example, if an exhibitor's house-nut is $3,200 and that week's gross was $2,800, the distributor knows the picture will soon be replaced by a picture with greater grossing potential.

As discussed above, each picture's opening two weeks of theatrical earnings are largely predicated on the effectiveness of its campaign. After the opening two weeks, audience opinion largely determines a picture's theatrical life. This being the case, distributors create and refine the after-opening campaigns to drive target audiences' peak attendance.

Again, campaigns are the central reason audiences buy tickets, and TV commercials and trailers are the most convincing campaign elements. This is largely so because they allow target audiences to actually sample the movie before buying a ticket. This sampling is sufficiently powerful to initially overpower negative reviews and even word of mouth. When viewing the campaign, the audience sees and hears evidence that motivates them to see the picture or not. When making their ticket buying decisions, audiences lean to their own experience, even when that experience is limited to 30-second commercials and 2- to 3-minute trailers.

These market realities motivate motion picture distributors to focus first on each picture's campaign, for this is what substantially drives each picture's earnings. Every distributor's first responsibility is to get its pictures' target audiences to theaters. Campaigns drive audiences; audiences drive box office receipts; distributors focus on campaigns.

It should be no surprise, then, that in deciding whether they will distribute a picture, distributors look first to a picture's campaign elements, then to its overall entertainment power. *Accordingly, producers should anticipate that distributors will assess their interest in distributing each picture based on a formula of 70 percent campaign integrity and 30 percent entertainment power.* That is to say that 70 percent of the decision will be based on the audience sales dynamics of the picture's elements for 30-second TV commercials and 2 1/2 to 3 1/2 minute trailers (the picture's campaign), and 30 percent will be based on how the audience will feel as they leave the theater (the picture's entertainment power).

Therefore, even in predevelopment, when producers make picture presentations to distributors, they should weight their presentations according to the above formula. The distributor must be convinced of the salability of the picture before seriously considering its production and overall entertainment values.

Participant Category 3: Independent Producers

Independent producers are the creators and manufacturers of the motion picture products. The industry's leading producers also plan and manage all of their pictures sales and distribution, and directly conduct some sales.

The final five chapters of this text present independent production company operations. This section presents the two main independent producer operating profiles, (1) creative protectionist producers and (2) balanced producers.

Considering the two prior participant categories (audiences and distributors), we can now confidently embrace a fresh independent producer orientation. Audiences pay for the producer's goods, and distributors create and motivate a market for them. These simple realities render these categories superior to the producer in every aspect of decision making. In all their operations, producers will make the most sound and profitable decisions for their pictures and their companies if they hold themselves accountable to these two categories. Audiences and distributors are the producer's most beneficial and crucial sources of business checks and balances.

Creative Protectionist Producers

Creative protectionsist producers comprise the greatest number of independent producers in the film industry. In the U.S. there are more than 800 of these production companies, operating chiefly from New York or Los Angeles.

The characteristic unique to these producers is their arm's-length, creative protectionist attitude toward distributors. These producers are so intensely focused on the creative aspects of their pictures that distributors appear to represent a threat to the artistic integrity of their pictures and are commonly blamed if their pictures financially underperform. This attitude often creates a love-hate relationship with their distributors.

If you ask these producers about the distribution of their pictures, they frequently assume a crazed expression and say, "I could tell you stories!" And they can. But so can their distributors. No matter the stories, this separatist operating style (1) promotes strained production financing, which then must come partially or wholly from private sources, (2) results in their pictures under-earning for lack of market preparation and (3) causes some of their theatrical feature films to receive no U.S. theatrical release at all.

Most creative protectionist producers fall well within the purview of the sage commentary, "They were often filled with the exhilaration of their progress up the ladder, only to find when they neared the top, it was leaning against the wrong wall."

Some of these producers are highly skilled and have industry and audience reputations for creative wizardry. Often, their pictures are released through major studios, and some even win Academy Awards. At the same time, this high-risk operating style yields high attrition among these producers, and unfortunately creates a substantial disparity between their numbers of produced pictures, distributed pictures, and profitable pictures.

The exhilaration of "climbing the ladder" occurs during production. The producer is actually producing the aspired movie, using and expanding production talents, and hopefully fulfilling his or her highest vision of the picture. The "wrong wall" revelation comes as the producer realizes that the film's audiences are too limited and the campaign elements too light to justify the distributors' production advances. In the case of too many of these pictures, they never play to a paying audience.

In most industries, this trend would correct itself, but not in the motion picture industry. Though there are far too many casualties, especially among first-time producers, the lure of fame engendered by the one success among the hundreds of failed such attempts each year is sufficient to attract new and even experienced producers back to climbing the ladder that leans against the wrong wall.

To those producing their first picture, this path is sometimes referred to as the "festival" or "Sundance path." The prescription to follow the festival path reads something like this (this is an actual encapsulation from a current private-film-school text):

> Once you have found or written a screenplay that you are passionate about, then employ all your filmmaking craft, engage production associates willing to be paid chiefly from the picture's profits, pool all the money you have, borrow

from relatives and any other sources who are willing to lend, run up your cred-
it cards for the balance of the budget, and make the film. When it is complete,
enter it in as many festivals as you can, and see how you fare.

Following this counsel, hundreds of motion pictures are completed each year by well intending producers and submitted to festivals. This past year, the Sundance Festival considered over 2,000 motion picture submissions and only about 200 pictures were screened during the festival, in all categories. Of these entrants, the industry trade papers (which rarely miss a transaction of substance) recorded three distributor pickups. These were huge wins for the three producers and their asso-ciates, but what of the estimated 195 producers who didn't obtain a distribution relationship for their pictures? Even more telling, consider the approximately 1,800 producers who didn't even get the opportunity to screen their films.

Wracked by the conflict between the thrill of producing their first feature-length picture and the reality of severe debt and disappointed, if not angry, investor-rel-atives and friends, many of these producers eventually approach distributors to screen their films, or continue along the festival path until their hopes abate.

Distributors are unquestionably willing to help new producers but are loath to receive calls from those with completed pictures to be screened. Usually, these pictures, even if clever, are simply not sufficiently marketable to warrant the essential distribution investment.

Over the course of my career, I have screened far too many of these films for dis-tributor clients. After the screening (and typical pass on behalf of the distributor), if the producer is interested, I meet with him or her and ask the difficult, essential question that can open the way to a more productive approach to filmmaking. The question is, "Before you poured your talent and resources into this film, why didn't you contact a distributor to find out if they were interested in your vision of the picture?"

At this point in the process, it is tough for producers to come up with an answer. Those who do offer an explanation generally fall into the creative protectionist category, and enthusiastically defend their position, asserting that distributor involvement would have threatened the creative integrity of their picture.

Perhaps from a purely artistic point of view, this may be true. The question is, then, are producers motivated only by their opportunity to express their vision of the story—or would they also like their vision to be shared with audiences and earn a profit?

Fundamentally, most producers want their films to fulfill three major objectives:

1. Creation: to powerfully reveal the producer's vision of the story;
2. Audience: to play the picture to as extensive an audience possible; and
3. Profits: to recoup production costs and receive a fair participation of the picture's earnings.

Balanced Producers

Balanced producers are simply that. They understand and sustain a balance between their pictures' creative, audience, and income aspects. As of this writing, there exists a small group of less than two dozen balanced producers, operating principally from New York or Los Angeles. These include Imagine Entertainment, Mandalay Entertainment, Intermedia, Phoenix Pictures, and Icon. The pictures that come from these producers and their production companies consistently receive global distribution, are profitable and attain their producers' creative visions.

Balanced producers understand the essential importance of both preparing their pictures for the global marketplace and preparing the global marketplace for their pictures. Consequently, their creation and production decisions are wholly knit together with their distribution and rights-sales decisions.

As a result of this operating style, most of these producers are able to primarily, if not exclusively, use bank-provided production financing, release their pictures through major distributors, and extract the maximum possible media and rights earnings from the various global territories.

To become a Castle Rock or Caravan Pictures, producers must employ the sound, balanced approach to production that will lead them to such success. Producers must do the work that engenders the broad, global industry relationships that these companies enjoy. Such an operating style is the result of a consistent, disciplined approach to the creation and distribution of a producer's motion pictures.

Because the operating style of these companies is low-risk, their pictures are principally released by major studios (more than 90 percent), their pictures are generally profitable (more than 80 percent), and accordingly their organizations build value, some of them becoming publicly traded.

Before committing to a picture's production, in most cases even prior to acquiring a literary property or idea (with the exception of bidding frenzies, which rarely serve even the winner well), balanced producers proceed only when they become convinced that the producer's potential gross profits are sufficiently high compared with the picture's approximate production and distribution costs. If these numbers do not proof out, balanced producers pass on the picture, even if the producer is wild to do it. Sometimes referred to as "therapy pictures," even creative triumphs are shallow victories if few ever see them and they do not earn more income than that necessary to clear production and distribution costs.

Balanced Producer's Development and Production Approach

To receive the greatest creative freedom and highest earnings, producers must sustain a balance among each picture's (1) story, (2) audiences (as affirmed by major territory distributors from earliest development), and (3) margin between cost of production and the producer's share of profits (presented in Chapter 2). This is the success wall for serious producers to lean their ladders against.

Just as balanced producers' production analyses for their pictures include script breakdowns, production boards, schedules, and budgets, so should they include liquidation breakdowns, global rights analysis, distribution window schedules, potential premium tie-in lists, and cover-shot recommendations. These processes are presented In subsequent chapters and the worksheet CD.

Understanding the intricate business of motion picture rights liquidation, for example, allows producers to plan and perform the distribution of their pictures with the same predictability as they perform the production of these films. Just as there is only one opportunity to produce a picture, there is only one opportunity to liquidate its rights.

For instance, knowing that a picture lends itself to in-flight and novelization allows a producer, while still in development, the advantage of including cover shots (necessary for some in-flight as well as foreign versions) in the picture's production plans and budgets. At the same time, the novelization of the screenplay can be planned and a publishing relationship put in play. With sufficient lead time the paperback can feature the picture's one-sheet (poster art) on its covers at retail check-out stands two to four weeks before the picture's U.S. theatrical premiere. Without the producer's involvement in these two processes, the marketing and income benefits for in-flight and novelization would likely be lost or seriously compromised.

Independent production is inherently intense. Embracing the practices of balanced producers not only assures producers the greatest possible success in marketing their pictures, but also delivers all those who are committed to the producer's success the greatest possible infusion of stability and sanity.

Even producers working under a studio umbrella are well served to remember that while most producers create one picture every six months to two years (many of these pictures passing through a before-funded development gestation of several years), each major U.S. studio releases one to three pictures a month!

The studios are masters at evaluating and extracting the greatest income from their pictures. However, producers should not expect a distributor to plan and prepare as early or as comprehensively as the producer. If the producer is the picture's parent, consider the distributors as aunts and uncles. Although a crucial part of the family, they will never care for the picture like the producer will.

Before a producer commits to a project, he or she should process it through his or her own in-house tests, as presented in later chapters, and summarily in Chapter 12. After a producer internally greenlights a picture, then it's time to bring in the rest of the family.

To sustain sanity and balance in their companies and careers, independent producers must establish and follow these basic creative and business processes to experience the artistic, operational, and compensatory benefits. When producers (the third-tier participants) develop, produce, and distribute their pictures, deeply meshed with their audiences and distributors (the first- and second-tier participants), all other industry participants (tiers four through ten), will respect and confidently participate with them.

Participant Category 4: Retailers and Licensed Media

These are the theater circuits, video outlet rental chains and sell-through retailers, premium cable networks, major free television networks, and free television syndication participants, including cable networks and independent television stations. The producer's relationships with each of these are presented in subsequent chapters. This section focuses on the larger view of how these motion picture retailers impact and contribute to the motion picture arena.

It is important to realize that each of these represents a massive, sophisticated, and separate industry. Each has separate associations and conventions and each makes its own crucial and very specialized contributions in selling to its specific and unique audiences. They are similar, however, in that they all rely on (1) producers to deliver dynamically entertaining pictures and (2) theatrical distributors to initially establish a powerfully motivating brand for each picture.

Distribution windows

Though each picture's liquidation schedule is singular to its (1) audiences, (2) marketing power, (3) time of year and date of initial theatrical release, (4) financing, and (5) distribution agreements, the typical U.S. distribution windows are as follows:

Traditional U.S. Distribution Windows

Distribution window	Time from prior window	Cumulative months
Electronic games	6–12 weeks prior to theatrical release	—
Paperback	3–7 weeks prior to theatrical release	—
Theatrical	Opening day	—
Video rental	6 months later	6 months
Premium cable	6 months later	12 months
Video Sell-through (if not originally released at a sell-through price)	6 months later	18 months
Network television	12 months later	30 months
Syndicated television	12–24 months later	42–54 months

In addition to the substantial and sophisticated campaigns mounted by theatrical distributors, each of these participants makes the following contributions:

1. Theatrical exhibitors (theater chains) plan and purchase print (newspaper) advertising in their theaters' markets. Most exhibitors have their own in-house ad agencies that manage this process. They also show trailers (movie previews) of upcoming releases and display one-sheets (movie posters) of current and upcoming pictures. Both trailers and one-sheets are provided by the distributors. Unquestionably the most motivating contribution that exhibitors make to each picture's success is providing a high-profile exhibition environment with large screens, superior sound, comfortable seating, and a theater staff who are so informed about the picture and anxious to make patrons happy that they chose to come to their theater to see it.

2. Video outlet chains rely primarily on video distributors (who are most often also the theatrical distributor for each picture) to motivate their audiences. In addition, video outlets display one- sheets, may run picture trailers on video screens in each outlet (this is really more miss than hit except for Blockbuster, which has an actual program for all its stores), and may place

local newspaper advertising, and in the case of the largest chains, even use television campaigns. As with exhibitors, most video outlets provide customers a high-tech film industry environment that advances each picture's video audience and earnings. Further, ordering an adequate copy depth (volume of copies) of each picture satisfies the early heavy audience demands and also crucially extends each picture's video audiences and earnings.

3. The sell-through video retail category is notably expansive. The highest volume of these participants are mass merchandisers, supermarkets, and music stores. These participants sell the dominant share of videocassettes, and for many titles, serve larger audiences and earn greater income than any other domestic partner. In the future, these participants will represent an increasing share of audiences and earnings. They'll be energized by the new generations of consumer hardware that offer superior performance and become less expensive over time. These retailers have the substantial advantage of high-volume consumer traffic. The most effective retail marketers place motion picture product in high-traffic areas, some screening the product on a television monitor. Many use print ads as part of their newspaper campaigns and some use direct mail. For the stronger titles, many retailers actually sell pictures at or below their cost as promotions to draw traffic into their stores.

4. Premium cable networks are uniquely important licensees, as producers often license directly with them. These licensees use the brand power of the most popular pictures to expand their subscriber base by advertising on cable systems and in a variety of magazine, newspaper, and direct-mail media.

5. Free television networks also license directly with producers. Approximately two-thirds of U.S. television households have cable television but less than half of U.S. TV households subscribe to a premium cable network. Consequently, the television network premiere often attracts the largest single viewing audience during a picture's life. The networks are masters at drawing audiences, by using their networks as the primary source to advertise motion pictures with theatrical release status.

6. Free television syndication participants, including cable networks and independent stations, deliver long-term audiences and income. Licensing to these participants is sophisticated, complex, and typically sold and managed by a television syndication company. These stations and station groups, like the networks, primarily advertise motion pictures via their stations.

Participant Category 5: Foreign Territories

These are audiences, distributors, retail media, and other rights purchasers in territories outside the United States. Foreign territories yield over half the earnings of most U.S. produced motion pictures.

The six leading foreign territories and producers' relationships with them are reviewed in Chapters 3 and 12.

Participant Category 6: Financing Participants

These include banks that provide production and distribution financing (including studios and distributors that function as "commercial lenders" for many independent producers), as well as private investors who provide development funding and, in some special circumstances, tax-sheltered production or distribution funding. Other participants in this category include law firms and attorneys and accounting firms and accountants, who advise, author, and assist in the management of securities. The roles of these participants are explained fully in Chapters 2, 5, 9, 10, and 12.

Participant Category 7: Distribution Subcontractors

This category includes sales and licensing specialists, media planning and buying companies, and campaign creators and producers, not to mention advertising agencies (some of which contribute to all three of the just-listed items). These are also manufacturers of products including videocassettes, DVD, and program duplication for new consumer technology. This category also includes CD and audiotape duplicators. Distribution subcontractors are discussed in Chapters 4, 12, and 13.

Participant Category 8: Production Talent and Subcontractors

These include a diverse and stunning array of above- and below-the-line performers and craft imagineers, producers, and suppliers. Especially included in this category are agencies, agents, managers, and attorneys who represent talent. Producer relationships with participants in this category are reviewed in Chapters 8, 11, and 12.

Participant Category 9: Ancillary Media and Licensees

These are additional retail media including pay-per-view, hotels and motels, in-flight and ships-at-sea, and other licensed free audiences, including prison systems, Indian reservations, and schools. This category also includes licensed rights, such as computer games, publishing, printing, merchandising, soundtracks and music publishing, clothing and Internet applications. These markets typically represent a small portion of a picture's income but substantially contribute to establishing its brand. These participants are reviewed in Chapter 4.

Participant Category 10: Major Consumer Brands

These are brands that link their products or name to a motion picture and advance that picture and their brand by nature of the relationship. Consumer brand relationships may take a number of forms, but generally fall into two categories.

The first and most common is the brand exposure of products used in the picture. For this, the brand either pays for the exposure or gives or lends its products to the producer.

The second relationship is a brand's use of a picture to advertise and/or promote its name or products. Fast food chains are the most active participants in these relationships. These relationships often substantially benefit their pictures through increasing their advertising campaign during its theatrical release.

These complementary brand relationships lend authenticity to pictures by using brands that create a sense of reality for the film's audiences. Such relationships often offset production costs and may even become a revenue source or powerful advertising alliance for the producer. Consumer brand relationships are reviewed in greater depth in Chapter 4.

Participant Category Summary

Having reviewed these motion picture industry participants, reconsider their order of importance.

1. Audiences
2. Distributors
3. Producers
4. Retailers and licensed media
5. Foreign territories
6. Financing participants
7. Distribution subcontractors
8. Production talent and subcontractors
9. Ancillary media and licensees
10. Major consumer brands

While traditionally viewed primarily as creatives, independent producers who operate their own development and production companies are still talent, but they are also *business owners*. In large measure their creative and financial success is reliant upon their understanding of, empathy for, and relationships with the industry participants above them on this hierarchical scale (audiences and distributors), as well as with those below them.

Story

If the creative categories were listed in priority, as the business categories have been, one creative category would clearly stand above the others. This is the ultimate art of creative genius. It is where the picture is first produced. It is the screenplay.

Story is the most essential and important, and therefore the most powerful creative asset in the motion picture industry. It is more powerful than money. Too many people with deep pockets have entered this business to establish a motion picture production empire, only to leave months or, in some insufferable cases, years later, with a monument of odd and underperforming pictures to show for their substantial investments.

Story is even more important than star power or a great director. Even "A-list" actors and directors, for money or career politics, occasionally allow themselves to be attached to pictures that should never have been made. Fine direction and acting may lift a picture somewhat, but ultimately can never redeem a weak story.

An audience-pleasing, entertaining story is the most powerful and essential asset in the motion picture business. Talent with story sense always gravitate to these pictures and want to participate in their creation.

Business operating technique, organization, planning, excellent relationships with studios, great artists, or the availability of any other assets will never offset the essential need for producers to discover, develop, and produce stories that deserve to be told. The greatest independent producers recognize great stories.

Excellence in all other producer characteristics will not compensate for failure in this one. Call it story sense, having a nose for the audience, or what you may, this is the single essential attribute, if all the other producer qualities are to even matter.

At the same time, in order to sustain the whole perspective, it's important to remember that a great story alone is not sufficient justification for a producer to greenlight its production. Great stories without sufficient audience power as compared to their production and distribution costs should not be made. But great stories are always the germ, the genesis, the foundation of every consummate picture. If the story isn't worth being told, then none of the producer's other considerations matter.

Chapter 2

U.S. Theatrical Distributors

This chapter reviews how major U.S. distributors function, and more particularly looks at the three traditional relationship categories these studios engage in with independent producers: (1) in-house studio production, (2) negative pickup, and (3) distribution agreement.

Motion picture distributors, especially the major studio distributors, are the greatest advocates of independent producers. The more producers understand how studios operate, the various relationships they may have with them, and why studios function the way they do, the more producers will be able to appreciate the studios and forge more productive relationships with them.

The Major and Minor Distributors

The ten major distributor/studios are 20th Century Fox, Universal, Buena Vista, Paramount, Sony, Warner Bros., Miramax, Dreamworks, New Line, and MGM/UA.

There are 20 minor U.S. distributors. Most of these companies release narrow target audience exploitation pictures, including foreign films. Relationships with these distributors are essential for balanced, profitable production and release of narrow target-audience pictures. These distributors are not the subject of this volume.

Each of the ten major studios is a massive, sophisticated media conglomerate. Most earn billions of revenue dollars each year.

These distributors rigorously compete with each other in all markets and every media and right, with the exception of the natural sister relationships between Buena Vista, which owns Miramax, and Time-Warner, which owns New Line.

The major studios are the ultimate motion picture entities. They have evolved to both operate completely self-contained, as distributor and producer, as well as to facilitate multiple independent producer relationships.

Each studio has the advantages of (1) global theatrical and ancillary sales power; (2) global media alliances; (3) availability of sophisticated bank, commercial, and public funds; and (4) sophisticated creative and operational checks and balances. They each have their individual committee operating styles, which in the main benefit marketing and distribution, but typically cripple motion picture development and production, often sucking the creative life from stories, through slow decision making and dulled or incongruous creative vision.

The ultimate definition of a motion picture studio is *a global distribution entity with in-house production*. Within the studio, every department and all operations in their best form are geared toward stabilizing and optimizing motion picture marketing and distribution.

The brief history of the motion picture industry reveals the tragic flaw of studios that become in-house production dominant, or fit the definition of *a production entity with global distribution capacity*.

Studios are distribution-focused primarily because (1) distribution yields higher profits per picture than production; (2) distribution accommodates a greater volume of pictures; (3) distribution connects directly with the marketplace and is consequently more stable and business powerful.

With a distribution focus, studios are naturally driven to accommodate independent producer relationships to deliver most of the motion pictures they will distribute. Studio executives enter many more picture relationships than do producers, are excellent negotiators, and are consequently exceptionally well prepared to set up relationships with producers.

Knowing this, prior to meeting with a studio, producers should thoroughly prepare, understand what they want, have *in writing* the deal points of a fair relationship for both sides, and should have consulted with (and in most cases should bring with them) their entertainment legal counsel.

Producers are classically underprepared and underexperienced. They too often leave the negotiating table without obtaining the benefits and power they should have, and with a substantially different understanding of their relationship than the documented deal points define. Contract language is precise—it is enforced in its ultimate interpretation by contract law, not by dictionary; and though most of the language is stable, definitions can literally change daily. Producers must be prepared in every creative, business, and legal aspect relative to the production and distribution relationships they negotiate. They should expect and respect that studio executives will be excellent negotiators and impeccably well prepared.

Studio Integrity

Having entered into a major studio relationship, producers may be confident that the studio—yes, all the majors listed above (I haven't audited Dreamworks, but, their executives are notorious for their integrity in this area)—will deliver an honest, complete and timely accounting for each picture. Auditing on behalf of producers,

I have found posting errors, but typically as many in favor of the producer as not. Because of the high volume of entries, allocation errors will occur, but they are honest mistakes and will be readily corrected when presented. Public producer and talent participant comments that imply accounting dishonesty among the majors represent a clearly undeserved slander. A review of the theatrical performance example below reveals that producers and other profit participants who complain that their picture has a box office of $50 million, but only cost $20 million, may conclude that the studio must have a creative accounting method. But they just do not understand how the money flows.

The Three Studio Arenas

Each studio has its own unique organization structure. However, it is important that producers be familiar with the three basic operational arenas the studios have in common: (1) the *executive arena* which consists of the ultimate studio chiefs, (2) the *distribution arena*, which is a combination of each of the distribution organizations within the studio (the most powerful are theatrical and video), and (3) the *production arena*, which consists of each studio's production organizations.

Each of these arenas has its individual presidents. Some studios have multiple presidents within each of their distribution and production arenas.

Studio Executives

Studio executives are the studio chiefs and corporate level directors of each studio: Sumner Redstone at Paramount, Michael Eisner at Disney/Buena Vista, and Edgar Bronfman at Universal, along with their teams.

Only the largest of the independent producers play in this arena. The studio chiefs make decisions relative to conglomerative studio direction, studio assets, media alliances, global market positioning, and the leaders, direction, and disposition of the various studio operating units. The studio chiefs have the opportunity to view regularly the forest and adjust their conglomerate's inner and industry participation.

All leaders of studio units report to and are evaluated by the studio chiefs. Also, all financial, accounting, and legal departments within the studio report to them.

This is the arena that ratifies, and, if appropriate, negotiates contracts with premium cable organizations, networks, the larger video chains, foreign studios, and ancillary media, among other powerful earnings sources. These relationships deliver a wonderful stability to each studio. Understanding these relationships substantially affects the deal and negotiating perception of independent producers in their dealings with the studios. These relationships will be reviewed later in this chapter.

The Distribution Unit

Distribution units include the global distribution executives and their staffs, as well as each of the sales organizations for theatrical and video, which are heart of most major independent producer's studio relationships, along with every other foreign and domestic sales organization, and the advertising, promotion, and publicity units.

This arena depends on obtaining pictures to distribute. The majority of these pictures come from independent producers, the rest from the production units within the studio.

The Production Arena

In most studios these are multiple organizations (such as Fox, Fox 2000, and Fox Searchlight at 20th Century Fox). These organizations are directed by production executives and their teams. The production arena manages a large motion picture development pool, fulfills all the production processes for in-house pictures, and participates in the development and production of independent productions that are wholly or partially financed by the studio.

Studio Relationships with Independent Producers

The studios engage in three conventional relationships with independent producers. They are (1) in-house studio production, (2) negative pickup, and (3) distribution only. Many independent producers progress in their studio relationships by evolving from studio pictures, to negative pickup productions, and then to strictly distribution relationships.

There are many crucial deal points in each of these relationships. The central deal point categories common to all these relationships are (1) creative control, (2) film negative and copyright ownership, (3) the specifics of the theatrical distribution commitment (especially minimums for advertising and opening situations), (4) the producer's profit participation, and (5) the delegation of the film's distribution rights between the producer and distributor.

In-House Studio Production

This relationship is typically engaged through the studio's production operations. The producer provides an acceptable story, plus the capacity to complete development and deliver a finished picture. The studio provides all the development and production support, financial and business (legal and accounting) resources to complete the picture, and all the distribution resources to liquidate its rights.

Though the producer has creative freedom, the ultimate creative control typically resides with the studio. Also, the negative, copyright, and all distribution rights are respectively owned by the studio. The producer is paid a production fee and typically has a net-profits participation in the film, commonly called "points."

Studio production is a good place for producers to start if their understanding is limited to the physical aspects of motion picture production. Some producers make all their pictures throughout their careers in this category, are creatively satisfied, and achieve excellent earnings.

A good example of this relationship is the early producing career experience of Andrew Davis, who brought Warner Bros. *Above The Law* and attached Steven Seagal. He entered a studio production relationship with WB that allowed him to make the picture using the support of the production department, yet giving him the flexibility to even rough-cut the picture in his home. The picture received WB's formidable marketing muscle and was successful enough to launch Mr. Davis's career as a studio producer.

Negative Pickup

This relationship is substantially more independent than studio production, and it is typically entered through a studio production unit. The producer provides an acceptable story and the capacity to complete development and deliver a finished picture and the picture's production financing. The studio provides production support, a bankable contract for all or a substantial portion of the needed production funds, and typically global, U.S. or foreign distribution, as negotiated. Negative pickup relationships commonly allow the producer almost complete creative freedom during the production process, though the studio may have the right to the picture's final cut.

Though it is a negotiable point, the picture's copyright is typically owned by the producer, and the distribution rights (as negotiated, either global, U.S. or foreign) are owned by the studio. From the gross receipts collected by the studio, the studio is paid its distribution fee for all rights it sells, recoups its direct distribution expenses, and may also have points in the picture.

An entertainment bank provides the producer with the negative pickup production financing, which necessitates that the producer have bank and completion bond relationships. The collateral provided to the bank for the production loan is one or more studio negative pickup contracts. This collateral equals or exceeds the picture's negative cost, as well as loan interest and a loan contingency. Contingency elements in the negative pickup contract are primarily that the producer will deliver the studio access to the picture's negative or a CRI (a color reverse internegative is created to make release prints) and campaign materials, on or before the contract delivery date, and that the picture contain basic above-the-line representations, including director and principal cast.

An insurance company provides the bank a guarantee (referred to as a completion guarantee or completion bond) that the picture will be delivered by the contract date with the specified creative elements intact. (Obtaining the production funding from the bank is reviewed thoroughly in Chapter 5; completion guarantees are discussed in Chapter 6.)

Distribution-Only Relationship

This relationship is typically entered through the studio's distribution arena. This is the most sophisticated relationship for producers to enter, and it delivers them the greatest overall benefits. This relationship naturally motivates the creation of the finest motion pictures, better prepares the various rights areas in the major markets, grants producers the greatest autonomy, earns the most revenues for each picture, and delivers the highest participation to the producer. Typically this is the most beneficial relationship globally for audiences, studios, producers, and licensees.

The distribution-only relationship takes many forms. Generally, the producer engages a U.S. studio to distribute U.S. theatrical and video. In this relationship the studio does not provide negative pickup, other financing collateral, or advance fees. The producer provides the finished picture, developed, produced, and financed, and in some relationships part or all of the direct distribution expenses. The studio's distribution unit provides production and campaign consulting from the picture's earliest development, along with U.S. theatrical distribution, and most commonly, U.S. video distribution.

Though the producer consults with major market distributors throughout the development and production of the picture, and is license bound to deliver the picture represented to presale participants, the producer has complete creative freedom during the production process.

The picture's copyright and distribution rights are owned by the producer. Distribution rights are licensed by the producer to U.S. and foreign studios and global media. From the gross receipts, collected by the U.S. studio, the studio is paid its distribution fee for all rights it sells, recoups its direct distribution expenses, and may also have points in the picture.

Producer Relationship Comparisons

To understand more fundamentally the three primary relationships discussed above, let us examine the individual and comparative financial performance of each, as shown in the example below.

Figure 2.1

Independent Producer Studio Relationship Comparisons

Description	Studio Producer	Negative Pick-up	Distribution Only
Gross Box Office	50,000,000	50,000,000	50,000,000
Film Rental (at 50%)	25,000,000	25,000,000	25,000,000
Distribution Fee (at 35%)	8,750,000	8,750,000	8,750,000
Direct Distribution Expense	20,000,000	20,000,000	20,000,000
Distributors Theatrical Net	-3,750,000	-3,750,000	-3,750,000
Video Gross Income	75,000,000	75,000,000	75,000,000
Video Distribution Fee	26,250,000	26,250,000	26,250,000
Video Dup & Dist Expenses	5,952,381	5,952,381	5,952,381
Distributors Video Net	42,797,61	42,797,61	42,797,619
Premium Cable Gross	5,500,000	5,500,000	5,500,000
PC Distribution Fee	1,375,000	1,375,000	
Direct Distribution Expenses	150,000	150,000	150,000
Distributors PC Net	3,975,000	3,975,000	5,350,000
Network Gross	7,000,000	7,000,000	7,000,000
Network Distribution Fee	1,750,000	1,750,000	
Direct Distribution Expenses	200,000	200,000	200,000
Distributors Network Net	5,050,000	5,050,000	6,800,000
Major Foreign Territories	75,000,000	70,000,000	70,000,000
Foreign Sales and Distribution Fees	33,750,000	33,750,000	33,750,000
Foreign Sales and Dist Expenses	2,000,000	2,000,000	2,000,000
Distributors Foreign Net	39,250,000	39,250,000	39,250,000
Total Distributors Net	87,322,619	87,322,619	90,447,619
Production Financing Expense	4,500,000	2,250,000	2,250,000
Negative Cost	20,000,000	20,000,000	20,000,000
Producer's Gross	62,822,619	65,072,619	68,197,619
Studio Burden	11,308,071		
Talent Participation	9,423,393	9,760,893	10,229,643
Producer's Net	42,091,155	55,311,726	57,967,976
Studio's Share	37,882,039	27,655,863	0
Producer's Share	4,209,115	27,655,863	57,967,976

Worksheet for the text "The Producer's Business Handbook."

Included with this text is a computer CD-ROM that analyzes this example. Instructions for using this file are with the CD. The cells are formula driven, allowing the user to perform "what-ifs" and to analyze specific pictures. As you move the cursor to each cell, the formula reveals its performance relationship to other cells. The example below is the same as that found on the computer CD. Each relationship example is for the same picture, earning the same from each distribution and rights area.

The following definitions will help those unfamiliar with the terminology.

Theatrical Distribution

Gross box office is the total box office receipts collected from theater attendees for a particular picture. This example uses $50 million. Oh, that this were typical! Of the leading 100 pictures released in the summer of 1998 (May through August), only the leading 25 earned $50 million or more. More telling is that only four of the remaining 75 pictures topped $25 million.

Film rental is the share of the gross box office due the distributor. The *film rental agreement* is the document setting forth the terms between the exhibitor and the distributor. The terms of these agreements commonly allow for higher earnings for the distributor early in the picture's run, when the box office is highest, and lower as exhibition continues and the receipts are lower. The example uses the commonly applied percentage of 50 percent each for exhibitor and distributor.

The *theatrical distribution fee* is earned by the distributor and calculated as a percentage of the film rental. The percentage is typically 35 percent of film rental, unless the producer provides most or all of the direct distribution expenses and negotiates a lesser fee. Producers are comfortable with the fairness of this fee if they consider (1) the distribution fees charged manufacturers in other industries, (2) the high distribution costs the distributor advances in behalf of the producer, (3) the sophisticated process and organization the distributor delivers and must sustain, and (4) the low probability that the picture will be theatrically profitable.

Direct distribution expenses (DDE) are the expenses incurred by the distributor in the process of distributing a picture, which are recoupable by the distributor from the picture's remaining gross receipts. These expenses are principally advertising (often $12 to $20 million) and prints (for example, $3 million for 2,000 prints at $1,500 each). Together these are commonly referred to as "P&A" (prints and advertising). However, direct distribution expenses also include campaign creation and production, promotion and publicity, film exchange costs and festival expenses, among many other out-of-pocket expenses.

The *distributors theatrical net* is the film rental less the distribution fee and direct distribution expenses. The application of fees and expenses are the same for all three distributor relationships, yielding the same amounts each. Consider how difficult it is for pictures even to recoup their distribution expenses. With a $50 million gross box office, this typical picture is $4 million away from recouping its distribution expenses.

Video Distribution

Video gross income. Video is typically the single most profitable motion picture earnings category. Each picture has its own earning dynamics in each category and changes substantially, depending on the success of the theatrical campaign. Many pictures are nevertheless served conservatively well when their picture's projected video earnings are configured by using a ratio of three times the picture's film rental. This ratio was used to derive the projection used in the example.

Video distribution is very sophisticated, but not nearly as much as theatrical distribution. Videos are marketed at either a rental or sell-through price. Because the studio does not participate in video rental revenue, the wholesale cost of rental videos in general is approximately $63.

Sell-through priced videos are the biggest growth area in video distribution. Aspects of this area, including price-point and every aspect of marketing, are still being redefined. The *video distribution fee* is negotiable, but for all three relationship examples shown below, it is 35 percent.

Video duplication and distribution expenses. Video duplication is very competitive. The largest and most respected duplication company in the film industry is Rank Video Services. If the duplicator performs all aspects of printing the sleeve, duplicates the product, and manages the inventory and shipping, the typical 120-minute movie is still not more than about $3 each, only about 5 percent of a $63 rental-priced video. The additional advertising, promotion, publicity, and other expenses vary widely picture to picture, with the ad budgets of major sell-through titles rivaling their theatrical budgets. The projection in the example uses 12 percent of the video gross income, a conservative percentage that will be higher than most actual expenses and lower than some.

Distributors video net is the video gross income less the video distribution fee and duplication and distribution expenses. The application of fees and expenses is the same for all three distributor relationships, yielding the same amounts to each of these categories. The video gross income exceeds all other domestic earnings categories. Even more impressive is that the distributor's video net is over half the gross. Again, a picture's brand power is established in its theatrical release, but the greatest U.S. earnings and profits area is in the video release.

Premium Cable Distribution

Premium cable gross. Premium cable companies are those television networks that are commercial-free and earn their income principally through viewer subscriptions. The major premium cable networks are HBO/Cinemax, Showtime, and Starz/Encore.

The major income follows the major audience tune-in, which occurs during the picture's premium cable premiere period. The license for the premiere of a picture with a $50 million gross should be at least the $5.5 million used in the projections.

The *premium cable distribution fee* should not exceed the 25 percent used in the projections. Because the market for these rights is limited, and the licensing is comparatively unsophisticated, it is common for balanced producers to sell these rights direct from their production companies, and preserve the distribution fee expense.

The *premium cable direct distribution expenses* are primarily legal fees and trade-show representation. They should not exceed the $150,000 indicated in the projections.

The *distributors premium cable net* is the premium cable gross income less the distribution fee and direct distribution expenses. The application of fees and expenses is the same for all three distributor relationships, except the distribution fee retention for the distribution-only category.

Network Television Distribution

Network television gross. The networks that purchase motion picture premiere free-television motion picture rights are those non-subscription television networks that are broadcast in every market where television programming is available. These networks are principally NBC, CBS, ABC, and Fox. Other "netlets" now broadcasting in major and medium metros that may soon become competing rights purchasers in this category are UPN, WB, and the cable network TNT.

The *license income* for the free television network premiere of a picture with a $50 million gross should be approximately the $7 million used in the projections.

The *free network television distribution fee* should not exceed the 25 percent used in the projections. Because the market for these rights is limited, and the licensing is comparatively unsophisticated, balanced producers frequently sell these rights direct from their production companies and preserve the distribution fee expense.

The *free network television direct distribution expenses* are primarily legal fees and trade-show representation. They should not exceed the $200,000 indicated in the projections.

Distributors free television network net is the network gross income less the distribution fee and direct distribution expenses. The application of fees and expenses is the same for all three distributor relationships, except the distribution fee retention for the distribution-only category.

Foreign territory gross. Most American-produced pictures have higher earnings from all the foreign territories combined as compared to U.S. earnings. Chapter 3 reviews foreign territories in depth. The projections use a foreign territory earnings figure equal to 60 percent, compared with a U.S. theatrical gross of 40 percent. The simplest equation that can be used to arrive at this foreign earnings amount is 150 percent of the U.S. theatrical gross.

The *foreign distribution fee* used in the projection is 45 percent. Because balanced producers sustain a close working relationship with the primary distributors in each of the seven major foreign territories, many of them have a foreign distribution department as part of their organizations, thus preserving the distribution fee.

Foreign direct distribution expenses include the relationship development meetings that continue throughout development and production, as well as participation in the major foreign sales events, legal fees, and preparation and delivery of elements to the foreign licensees. The projection uses the flat expense amount of $2 million.

Distributors foreign net is the foreign gross income less the distribution fee and direct distribution expenses. The application of fees and expenses is the same for all three distributor relationships.

The *total distributors net* is an accumulation of the net income from all five major earnings categories set forth above. In this example there is less than a 4 percent difference between the studio relationship categories.

The *production financing expense* is the producer's cost of the money used to produce the motion picture. Because the studio is a commercial lender rather than a bank, the financing is more expensive, typically 3 to 5 percent over the prime rate. Further, because the distributor allocates all the funding at the time the motion picture documentation is engaged, it is common for interest to be charged on the entire amount from the first day of this relationship. Depending on the producer's credit history with the bank, the ratio between the collateral pledged and the loan amount, among other factors, the bank may charge an interest fee of one-half to 3 percent. It's important to note that most of these bank financings are lines of credit, drawn down by the producer in increments as needed, and accumulating interest only on the total amount drawn rather than the whole loan. The example is for a motion picture costing $20 million. In this example, the two advantages of bank interest and charges on only the amount actually in use save the negative pickup and distribution-only relationships half of this expense.

The *negative cost* of this picture is $20 million. Though such expenses are not reflected here, studio relationships sometimes carry the financial burden of using costlier studio facilities or departments.

The *producer's gross* is typically the distributor's net less the production financing expense and the picture's negative cost.

A portion of *studio burden* is a common expense for studio pictures. This expense is a portion of the studio's total distribution arena overhead (this does include direct distribution expenses). Each picture's expense formula is set forth in the agreement. It may be a picture's percentage of the studio's total earnings for the year. (Considering theatrical earnings only, if a studio earned $750 million during the year and your picture earned $25 million, your studio burden expense would be 3.3 percent of the total).

A motion picture's *talent participations* are those points in the film's profits that are owned by key participants, possibly the director and one or more key cast members. This projection applies 15 percent of the producer's gross to talent participations.

The *producer's net* is the producer's gross less any other distribution, production, or profit participant expenses. This indicates an advantage of 27 percent for a distribution studio relationship rather than an in-house studio relationship and a 24 percent advantage for a negative pickup studio relationship over an in-house studio relationship.

The *studio share* is that amount of the producer's net in which the studio participates for its share as a partner of the producer in making the production and distribution of the picture a reality. For the in-house producer, this is the whole remaining amount except for the producer's points, in this example 90 percent. For the negative pickup producer this is 50 percent for the studio. For the distribution-only producer, the studio is not a further participant.

The *producer's share* is the amount remaining for the producer after all production, distribution, and financing expenses and participants have received their portions.

The in-house and negative pickup producer's shares are 7 percent and 48 percent, respectively, of the distribution-only producer's share. This is why balanced producers have the capacity to establish major businesses with greater creative and financial freedom.

As you become familiar with the performance of these three studio relationships, it will become clear that there are, in fact, no poor studio relationships. It's easy to see why producers spend their entire careers in studio/producer relationships. They produce motion pictures in the powerfully sophisticated and immensely savvy confines of the studio, receive excellent producer fees, share in the pictures' profits, and have none of the operational distractions of a full service independent production company.

Split Negative Pickup Relationships

Negative pickup relationships are traditionally with one studio, for all rights, globally. However, occasionally, there are U.S./foreign split negative pickup relationships. An example of this is Icon's (Mel Gibson and Bruce Davey's independent production company) financing for *Braveheart*. Though they covered a portion of their budget from Ireland's Section 35 funds, their financing substantially came from Paramount (the lead studio), for acquiring U.S. rights and 20th Century Fox foreign rights.

Studio Acquisition of a Renegade Picture

Let us now explore more deeply the studio's common economies and operating styles by examining how an independent producer's freshly completed motion picture offered them for pickup. *Renegade pictures* are those pictures developed and produced without studio participation or knowledge; they are most commonly privately financed. The picture in this example was produced for a trim $12 million. As is common, the picture's investors are now anxiously looking for their investment's return.

The studio screens the picture and discovers that it has strong cross-over target audiences and motivating campaign elements and is studio quality. The studio is interested (and amazed, as this is an unfortunately rare experience) and asks for a meeting with the producer.

Typically the producer comes to the meeting motivated to seek the return of the $12 million production cost and to obtain a distribution commitment. But the meeting is a little different from what the producer anticipates. The studio admits it likes the picture and that it is considering making a substantial distribution investment in it. It then reveals that if the campaign elements come together and the test audiences respond well to the campaign and the picture, it could invest $8 to $12 million or more in prints and advertising in the film, an investment close to or even exceeding the picture's production cost.

At this point it may not seem fair to the producer to ask the studio to return part or all of the production cost, as well as commit to such substantial distribution expenses. In this case, however, the producer explains that the investors are leaping up and down for their capital, and asks the studio for help.

Three business days later the studio and producer meet again. The studio presents an agreement granting the producer a $12 to $16 million deal. It sounds, and in many respects is, a dream come true for the producer. The studio executive explains that the studio is committing to the major theatrical release of the picture it had discussed, and may advance $8 to $12 million in theatrical distribution expenses alone. Plus the studio will pay the producer an advance against the producer's earnings of $4 million, and 50 percent of the picture's net profits. For this, the studio will receive all the picture's distribution rights globally and the other 50 percent of the picture's net profits. The producer is typically pleased with this offer, for the advance is sufficient to sate the investors' return-of-capital appetite, especially when it is combined with the good news of the studio's distribution commitment.

Before examining the studio's perspective, it is crucial to understand that most renegade pictures offered to the studios do not have sufficient earnings potential to warrant a distribution investment. Distribution is expensive, and these pictures are classically out of audience focus.

Motion Picture Output Relationships

Every studio (even studios that own or are media sisters with foreign, premium cable, television network, and video chain entities) has motion picture output contracts with premium cable entities, the major networks, major video chains, and foreign entertainment entities. To simplify yet keep this transaction well within the bounds of current studio media relationships, let's consider that this picture meets this distributor's premium cable contract criteria.

The studio's output deal criteria are typically simple, driven principally by a minimum television media expenditure during the picture's theatrical release and the potential of the picture to earn a minimum theatrical gross. For this example we will use a studio output base license fee of $5 million for each picture the studio delivers and assume that the studio will deliver at least, but not exceed without mutual consent, ten pictures per year. These agreements typically have escalator clauses that allow higher license fees to be paid for pictures exceeding a minimum gross box office. For instance, if a picture's gross box office exceeds $30 million, an additional fee will be paid, for example, $100,000 for each additional $10 million in box office, not to exceed a total license amount, for instance, of $12 million.

Studios may also have multi-picture license relationships with the major television networks. For this example we will use a base per picture amount of $3 million.

The video chain relationship, though substantially different, is fairly predictable. For instance, for a given picture, it may be apparent that it will be rental priced and sold to the leading three retailers in at least a 25,000-unit quantity. If the wholesale per unit price is $63, this is $1,575,000 from each retailer.

If the picture in consideration lends itself to be exercised in these studio relationships, the studio will earn these revenues as it becomes the distributor of the picture:

Premium cable	$5 million
Network	$3 million
Video (after product cost)	$4.5 million

If the picture is strong enough to generate theater circuit bids, most or all of the direct distribution expenses may be advanced by the major circuits from the bidding process. Though it varies dramatically from picture to picture, it should also be considered that the average picture earns more than half its revenues from foreign territories.

Given the above studio perspective, let us revisit the motion picture in review. If the studio is able to offset most of its theatrical direct distribution expenses from circuit bids, that leaves $12.5 million in ancillary output income to offset the producer's advance of $4 million. Additionally, the studio will receive distribution profits from the rest of U.S. video market (the three leading chains represent less than one-third of the total U.S. video revenues), foreign territories, and all other ancillary rights.

By nature of its media and theatrical relationships, the studio could have acquired this picture for a $4 million advance and hefty distribution commitment to the producer and actually started its relationship with this picture substantially in the black. Renegade picture pickups are typically negotiated through a studio's distribution unit.

The Critical Effect of U.S. Studio Attachment

For the producer, the studio's U.S. theatrical commitment is the central element that affects the picture's preproduction sales, financing, and global earnings power.

One of the first queries by all other potential global licensees is: "Is a major studio attached?" U.S. studios have a powerful reputation for releasing pictures with substantial earnings power. Though every U.S. and foreign licensee internally assesses each picture, they are substantially attracted to or wary of each picture depending on the picture's major U.S. studio relationship.

C h a p t e r 3

Foreign Territories

Immediately following each picture's internal greenlight, producers should begin comprehensive coordination of these pictures' foreign creative, marketing, and sales planning. Just as producers identify each picture's U.S. distribution windows and liquidation breakdowns, they should also prepare these pictures' major foreign territory marketing and releases with the support of their foreign territory distributors.

This chapter presents (1) the six dominant foreign territories; (2) how to begin and sustain the relationships within each of these territories that are necessary for pictures to perform at their global peak; and (3) the process of negotiating and licensing these territories.

The Global Popularity of American Motion Pictures_____

U.S. gross box office earnings exceed $6 billion annually. Foreign-territory produced pictures as a group, rarely approach five percent of the annual U.S. gross box office. This includes the foreign-territory motion pictures that are English language. Consequently, U.S. producers who have not done their research may not appreciate the pervasive popularity of U.S. pictures in the major foreign, English, and non-English speaking territories.

With the relaxation of foreign government regulations of media and commerce, U.S. motion pictures continue to expand their global consumption dominance. It isn't the quantity of motion pictures coming from America that appeals to global audiences; producers in some foreign territories produce more feature films per year than those produced in the U.S. The foreign popularity of U.S. productions is more due to either one or a combination of (1) the entertaining presentation of great stories, (2) the ever-increasing spectacle, and (3) an amazing fascination with American culture.

Global and Foreign Box Office Statistics

Because the global box office reports best demonstrate U.S. dominance in foreign markets, we will (1) review the performance of the top ten box office hits in each of the largest entertainment-consuming foreign territories and (2) compare the global to the foreign-territory box office earnings of the top 30 motion pictures ever released.

A review of the charts below and on the next page entitled "Leading Foreign Territory Motion Picture Theatrical Grosses" reveals that (1) there are an average of six U.S. pictures of the top ten grossing pictures in these six dominant global territories, and (2) that U.S. pictures earned 60 percent of the theatrical gross revenues in these territories in 1997. Though final scores are not all in, 1998 earnings in these territories exceeded 70 percent from U.S. pictures, as they also did in 1996. U.S. produced motion pictures dominate foreign-territory motion picture releases and earnings.

Figure 3.1
Leading Foreign Territory Motion Picture Theatrical Grosses
1997

Territory	Picture	($) or Admissions	% US
Australia	MEN IN BLACK	$15.4	
In US Dollars, In Millions	LIAR LIAR	$14.4	
	THE LOST WORLD	$13.7	
	BEAN (UK)	$13.1	
	THE FULL MONTY (UK)	$13.0	
	MY BEST FRIENDS WDDNG	$11.7	
	JERRY MAGUIRE	$9.5	
	BATMAN & ROBIN	$9.2	
	ROMEO + JULIET	$8.8	
	STAR WARS SPCL EDTN	$7.7	
Total Gross		$116.5	
	8 US Pictures	$90.4	78%
Italy	TITANIC	$45.7	
In US Dollars, In Millions	FIREWORKS (ITALY)	$29.4	
	LIFE IS BEAUTIFUL (ITALY)	$25.7	
	THREE MEN & A LEG (ITLY)	$18.0	
	BEAN (UK)	$13.7	
	MY BEST FRIENCDS WDNG	$13.5	
	HERCULES	$11.0	
	SEVEN YEARS IN TIBET	$11.0	
	THE FIFTH ELEMENT (FR)	$10.0	
	THE DEVIL'S ADVOCATE	$10.0	
Total Gross		$188.0	
	5 US Pictures	$91.2	49%

Figure 3.1 *continued*
Leading Foreign Territory Motion Picture Theatrical Grosses

Territory	Picture	($) or Admissions	% US
France	THE FIFTH ELEMENT (FR)	7.5	
Admissions, In Millions	MEN IN BLACK	5.6	
	LA VERITE SI JE MENS (FR)	4.8	
	THE LOST WORLD	4.7	
	101 DALMATIANS	4.0	
	HERCULES	3.6	
	LE PARI (FRANCE)	3.6	
	BEAN (UK)	3.0	
	DIDIER (FRANCE)	2.9	
	ALIEN RESURRECTION	2.5	
Total Admissions		42.2	
	5 US Pictures	20.4	48%
Japan	PRINCESS MONONOKE (J)	$76.0	
In US Dollars, In Millions	INDEPENDENCE DAY	$61.4	
	THE LOST WORLD	$41.1	
	LOST PARADISE	$16.3	
	DORAEMON (JAPAN)	$14.2	
	SPEED 2	$14.2	
	STAR WARS TRILOGY	$13.5	
	THE FIFTH ELEMENT (FRN)	$12.1	
	SLEEPERS	$10.6	
	THE END OF EVGLN (JPN)	$10.3	
Total Gross		$269.7	
	6 US Pictures	$157.1	58%
Germany	MEN IN BLACK	7.3	
Admissions, In Millions	BEAN (UK)	5.8	
	THE LOST WORLD	5.5	
	KNOCKIN' ON HVNS DR (G)	3.5	
	ROSSINI (GERMANY)	3.3	
	THE FIFTH ELEMENT (FRN)	3.2	
	THE ENGLISH PATIENT	3.1	
	THE LITTLE ARSEHOLE (G)	3.1	
	RANSOM	2.6	
	CON AIR	2.6	
Total Admissions		40.0	
	5 US Pictures	21.1	53%
United Kingdom	THE FULL MONTY (UK)	$65.3	
In US Dollars, In Millions	MEN IN BLACK	$57.3	
	THE LOST WORLD	$41.3	
	101 DALMATIONS	$32.6	
	BEAN (UK)	$28.1	
	STAR WARS SPECIAL ED	$21.8	
	BATMAN & ROBIN	$23.5	
	EVITA	$22.7	
	RANSOM	$20.5	
	THE ENGLISH PATIENT	$20.2	
Total Gross		$333.3	
	8 US Pictures	$239.9	72%

Average Number of US Pictures and US Gross in the Major Foreign Territories:
6 pictures and 60% of gross bring these together

Statistics from the International Film Guide
Worksheet for "The Producer's Business Handbook."

A broader view of American films in the global market is revealed in the second chart, entitled "Leading 30 Motion Pictures in Foreign Territories." These statistics clearly indicate the broad spectrum of motion pictures that capture audiences globally, the picture preference similarities between U.S. and foreign audiences, and the earnings dominance of U.S. films in foreign territories.

Figure 3.2

Leading 30 Motion Pictures in Foreign Territories
and the Foreign Share of Global Box Office

All amounts in US Dollars and in millions

Foreign Earnings Rank	Motion Picture	Released	Gross Box Office		Foreign Share
			Foreign Territories	Global	
1	TITANIC	97	$1,206	$1,807	67%
2	JURASSIC PARK	93	563	920	61%
3	INDEPENDENCE DAY	96	505	810	62%
4	LION KING	94	454	767	59%
5	LOST WORLD:JURASSIC PARK	97	385	614	63%
6	FORREST GUMP	94	350	680	52%
7	MEN IN BLACK	97	336	586	57%
8	STAR WARS	77	319	780	41%
9	TERMINATOR 2	91	312	517	60%
10	E.T. THE EXTRATERRESTRIAL	82	305	705	43%
11	GHOST	90	300	518	58%
12	INDIANA JONES/LAST CRUSADE	89	298	495	60%
13	THE BODYGUARD	92	289	411	70%
14	PRETTY WOMAN	90	285	463	62%
15	MISSION IMPOSSIBLE	96	272	453	60%
16	ALADDIN	92	262	479	55%
17	DIE HARD: WITH A VENGEANCE	95	254	354	72%
18	TWISTER	96	253	493	51%
19	HOME ALONE	90	248	534	46%
20	GOLDENEYE	95	244	351	70%
21	THE EMPIRE STRIKES BACK	80	244	534	46%
22	RAIN MAN	88	240	413	58%
23	DANCES WITH WOLVES	90	240	424	57%
24	BASIC INSTINCT	92	235	353	67%
25	SE7EN	95	230	330	70%
26	THE FLINTSTONES	94	228	358	64%
27	ROBIN HOOD: PRINCE OF THIEVES	91	225	390	58%
28	THE HUNCHBACK OF NOTRE DAME	96	222	322	69%
29	SCHINDLER'S LIST	93	221	317	70%
30	TRUE LIES	94	219	365	60%
	Totals		$9,744	$16,544	60%

This analysis is for "The Producer's Business Handbook."
This information is used courtesy of Internet Movie Database

The top 30 pictures earned $16.5 billion in global box office receipts, with $9.7 billion of this income earned from foreign audiences. It should be remembered that the single largest earnings territory for U.S. pictures is the U.S. However, it is crucial for U.S. producers to understand that (1) approximately 60 percent (and growing) of their pictures' income is earned from foreign audiences, and (2) that well over half the foreign audience income comes from the six territories shown in the

"Leading Foreign Territory" chart, which are the United Kingdom, Japan, Australia, Germany, France, and Italy. Producers should include the leading studios and distributors within these territories in their motion picture development and production

Current global consumption of American motion pictures contrasts sharply with that of foreign territory audiences of twenty years ago. Foreign income of U.S. pictures has more than doubled in the last ten years, and steady growth is projected for many more years.

Producer Relationships with Foreign Distributors

Producers should attend the three major motion picture foreign markets: (1) MIFED, held in Milan, Italy, usually in late October or early November, for one very focused week of picture rights sales; (2) the Cannes Film Festival, held in Cannes, France, in May, the most relaxed of all the festivals, focusing more on production packaging than rights sales; and (3) the American Film Market, held in Santa Monica, California, in late February and early March, which focuses on sales, yet accommodates the full spectrum of foreign studio relationship activities.

Producers should begin their major foreign territory relationships for each of their pictures as they develop them. License relationships in these major territories naturally occur as part of development activities. Consequently, these three events are highly productive sales markets that expedite foreign territory relationships, but they are not the beginning or heart of these alliances.

Balanced producers most often use these markets:

1. To centralize their meetings with major foreign territory distributors, studio heads, and other studio chiefs. The distribution top executives may attend meetings in London before the Cannes and MIFED events, and/or may stay in Cannes or MIFED for a few days, attending meetings, and leave actual market attendance to their staffs. This is also true of the American Film Market (AFM). Foreign studio heads often travel to Los Angeles just prior to AFM's opening and stay perhaps into its first week or longer. But they may exclusively conduct their business outside the market.

2. To pursue and consummate all non-major foreign territory sales. The major territories should be sold in the manner introduced in the preceding chapters, which is reviewed in Chapter 12.

For pictures to flourish in foreign territories, producers should do the following:

1. Manage relationships with foreign studios and distributors much as they manage and value their U.S. studio relationships, applying the relationship principles presented in Chapter 2.

2. Recognize that the best foreign studios are distribution centered, and as such, focus on target audiences and the power of each picture's campaign.

3. Recognize that foreign distributors have their various marketing strengths, just as U.S. studios do. One studio may have greater capacities and successful experiences distributing romantic comedies; another may be stronger in releasing action-adventure pictures. It is important that producers develop an understanding of, and eventually relationships with, all the leading

studios in every market, so that each picture will have the benefit of the greatest earnings power, matched with its particular audience dynamics.

4. Though each of the largest territories has the four major distribution windows, the window timings vary in each territory, and all of them are different from those in the U.S.

   Territories entering license agreements prior to a picture's production completion commonly license all that picture's distribution rights within their territory. Territories that license after a picture's completion, however, may license theatrical, video, premium cable/satellite television, free television and the other rights separately or in combination with other rights.

5. Each major territory distributor allied with a picture should participate in the production of that picture from its earliest development. The producer's mantra to foreign studios is the same as it is to those in the U.S.: "We will not develop, and we will not produce, a motion picture that you are not committed to distribute." This commitment and performance, on a global basis, allows producers to evaluate clearly the whole global dynamic of each picture before financially significant development begins, and to sustain global marketplace integrity throughout production.

   When a producer is on fire for a picture, there is a natural reluctance to accept negative comments about it. However, with over half the audience and income coming from outside the U.S., American producers clearly need to listen to global audiences through their distributors. Producers must at least understand each major territory's response to every picture's creative, audience, and earnings performance profile. Only when producers approach and receive responses from these major territory distributors can they make accurate and informed judgments on "go" or "pass," talent, and other creative decisions for their pictures.

6. Each foreign territory has language and cultural peculiarities. It's a little frightening to see how pervasive American culture has become and is advancing within global cultures. Entertainment is the dominant source of this impact. Its influence escalates not only as governments relax import and programming restrictions, allowing people to decide what they will watch, but also through satellite and other new technologies, which deliver a more direct entertainment link between the provider and the audience. Producers demonstrate integrity and receive significant business benefits when they are sensitive to the major cultures and peoples who are their largest combined audiences. The American entertainment community substantially feeds the hearts, minds, and civilizations of the world. U.S. producers should review the numbers on the charts and accept the responsibility for affecting more people in foreign nations than do these nations' own producers.

   At a recent Los Angeles industry event, motion picture line producer James Dennett said to an attentive audience, "Television is the church and religion of our day." I wrote it down. It is a scary notion. We may not openly acknowledge that motion pictures and television have such an influence on who we are, but regardless of our position, its effect remains. We certainly have a responsibility to consider the social impact of our productions in the lives of U.S. audiences. This sensitivity should be even greater for those societies in which we are guests.

7. Through dubbing or subtitling, producers and distributors substantially mold and shape each picture to better mesh with foreign audience cultures. In addition, creative suggestions should also be sought from each territory's distributor, and if they do not compromise the creative integrity of the picture, these suggestions ought to be used to prepare cover-shots, captured during principal photography, that will be used in the pictures released in these markets. The intent is to be empathic to each culture and magnify each picture's creative, audience, and revenue performance.

Establishing New Foreign Distribution Relationships

Engaging new relationships with each of the major foreign distributors is a natural part of the balanced producer's operations. Chapter 12 discusses in detail a producer's earliest development plan, which most often precedes even the literary property acquisition and includes meetings with at least one studio in each of the leading foreign territories. This may be a producer's first meeting with these distributors, but usually the producer and distributor have already met during film industry events. Meetings with foreign distributors should be set four to six weeks in advance, as these executives are important people with tight schedules.

In the first meeting, distributors expect the customary producer presentation. This presentation is creative focused, leaving the distributor to perform most of the picture's research and analysis work. Knowing this, producers should not be offended by distributors' first-contact skepticism or lack of enthusiasm.

Be prepared and confident by doing the work discussed in Chapters 1, 2, and 12. In almost every situation, as soon as the executives you are meeting with realize how you do business, they will be grateful and receptive to the presentation.

As distributors realize you understand and value their position, they will become earnest meeting participants. You should present them with three to five pictures comparable to yours, including these pictures' earnings from the major distribution windows in their market, with the income adjusted for inflation to show today's value. You should disclose your picture's target audiences, campaign elements, and projected grosses in the distributor's territory.

The distributor's reaction to this presentation determines if the pitch continues. If they respond positively to their review and your discussion, then present the story and the perceived audience satisfaction with the picture.

If the foreign distributor is enthusiastic about the picture, you should (1) summarize the information already presented, (2) demonstrate that you are fully funded to proceed with the development of the picture, (3) and, if they are preliminarily committed to distributing this picture in their territory, you will immediately begin the picture's development, following a schedule that will allow you to deliver it to them during a specific predisclosed release time, for instance, spring 2001 or fall 2002.

The objective of this meeting is not to have the distributor sign an agreement or even provide an unbinding letter of intent. You are simply establishing the parameters of the relationship. These basic parameters are:

1. We (the producer) are convinced that you (the foreign distributor) are the ultimate distributor to release our picture in your territory.

2. We are going to perform as your fully funded development and production unit for this picture.

3. If you are not interested in distributing this picture, we are not inclined to proceed with its development. (In fact, if this studio is not interested in releasing the picture because they have a similar one already scheduled during that period, or for any other reason, you might approach a competing studio in that territory. However, this studio is your first choice.)

4. We are proposing a best efforts, good faith, no obligation relationship.

5. We will include you, and you will assist us, in validating our continuing audience research for this picture in your territory.

6. We will continue to request your creative consultation throughout the major steps of this film's development and production.

7. We will exclusively communicate with you for all matters relating to this picture in your territory.

8. We will exclusively coordinate with you the press and advertising for this picture in your territory.

9. We will provide you copies of all this picture's promotion and advertising material for your use in promoting this picture during the various trade events in your territory.

These parameters may seem simple and undynamic, but they are impressively strong compared with the more common approach of saying, "This is our script, this is our budget, these are the creative elements we have attached so far, and we would like a production investment." Sometimes such offers make sense, but after the producer leaves, the distributor is still left having to research similar pictures, identify and evaluate the target audiences, break down the script for the strongest campaign elements, and so forth. Following this analysis, if the distributor is still interested in the picture, he or she is faced with the formidable relationship deterrent of *premature deal engagement*. From the distributor's perspective, this is the difficult phenomenon of their beginning to invest in a picture both (1) before development and preproduction are complete, and (2) before the producer has demonstrated that he or she will closely correlate the picture's creative and marketing aspects with the distributor as the producer prepares for production. Considering the most common prior-to-production relationship offered to distributors, producers should expect distributors to be wary when they approach them for the first time.

Nurturing the Relationship

This process is wonderfully straightforward, though to the uninitiated, it may seem sophisticated. Each time producers meet with their foreign distribution partners, they fulfill a mutual objective and begin a mutual next-step target. These objectives and targets weave integrity into the deepening relationship.

The objective following the first meeting is to successfully negotiate the rights to the motion picture's literary property. The next target is to assemble the proposed list of the picture's directors.

If the producer successfully acquires rights to the literary property, each of the participating foreign territory distributors and the U.S. distributor are immediately and confidentially notified of this progress, and of the dates and methods for the producer's trade press release and advertising. Within a week, the press announcement, and soon thereafter, the first trade ad with the picture's initial look, appear in the entertainment trade papers.

In the next meeting with each distributor, the producer reviews the list of proposed directors. Again, the producer leads this meeting with an overview of how the proposed directors' pictures have performed in the distributor's particular territory. A producer rarely chooses a director who is the unanimous first choice of all the territories. The producer's target after the second meeting is to successfully negotiate the director. The next objective is to prepare with the director, the ultimate leading cast.

After the producer successfully attaches the director, each of the distributors is immediately and confidentially notified and given promotion and advertising plans. Within a week the promotion and advertising appear in global trade papers.

As this process continues throughout development and initial preproduction, the distributor becomes increasingly confident in the producer's competence and delivery. In addition to development and production meetings, and other communication, the producer is meeting with this picture's distributors during the three annual foreign markets.

Foreign Territory License Timing

License timing is categorized in two ways: (1) licenses that are part of the producer's presale plan and (2) licenses that are outside the producer's presale plan.

Producers should principally use bank financing to fund the production of their pictures. Presale licenses are the primary collateral for these bank loans.

As part of the final preproduction process, the producer performs a final participating distributor analysis, and prepares a presale plan that by this time is obvious. This plan lists the fewest possible participants, including foreign territories and possibly premium cable or network television. Presale participants are in a separate category because they receive motivations unique to their presale participation.

Presale participants are typically approached about six months before the picture is delivered. They have been closely associated with the picture for several months and are comfortable with the distributor and their own territory's advance response to the picture. These participants are given two substantial incentives to participate: First, the picture becomes officially theirs and is no longer subject to competitive bidding. Second, the advance is discounted by an average of 20 percent. The producer usually knows, before approaching the proposed pre-buy licensees, if the financial and inventory incentive will be sufficient to engage participation in this licensee category.

The licensees in this category typically advance the producer 10 percent of the license fee and guarantee the balance with a bank letter of credit, due after the completed picture's elements are received by the licensee.

The remaining licensees are approached much differently. Though the producer exclusively matures specific distributors in each territory, the final license negotiation is affected by the natural existence of competition for the picture within each respective territory. This competition often prompts the distributors remaining after the presale to seek to license the picture before it is ready for delivery. Though predelivery licensing may occur, the discounts associated with presale participants are not available.

License Documentation

The American Film Marketing Association, or AFMA, operates the American Film Market. AFMA has developed and continues to refine effective and high-demand foreign license resources for global producers and distributors. They have standardized foreign rights sales *deal memos and licensing agreements.*

AFMA is a singularly responsible resource for independent producers. Most of the forms and instructions essential for carrying out the operational aspects of documenting and fulfilling foreign territory rights sales and delivery relationships are available through this universally recognized organization.

Licenses' terms are most often agreed to during a meeting of the parties and confirmed in the form of a *deal memo* soon thereafter. Deal memos are generally letters that set forth the basic agreed terms and typically provide for the other party's confirming signature.

Though there are license relationships that are bound without additional documentation, most sales are further documented by an actual *license agreement* that fully addresses all the terms and conditions relative to the license relationship.

Figure 3-3 offers a copy of the "AFMA International Multiple Rights Deal Memo, Basic License, and Financial Terms," provided courtesy of AFMA. The complete package of foreign license materials that producers will eventually need is available through AFMA at 9000 Sunset Boulevard, Suite 420, Los Angeles, CA, 90069, USA; by phone at 310-446-1000; or through their Web site at www.afma.com.

The review of this deal memo begins at its upper left and continues down to its lower right. Areas that are explained in the document itself or that are self-explanatory are not addressed in this text.

Picture(s). In this area the producer identifies the licensed pictures. For original releases, this is typically only the new picture. For re-released pictures, most often for television syndication, either several are listed or a package title is included with a picture list attached.

Territories. Though we have only spoken of territories individually, multiple territories are often licensed together. This occurs by nature of (1) a distributor's marketing dominance in multiple territories, which often happens in Europe, (2) a distributor servicing similar language markets, for instance "France, French-speaking Switzerland and the following French-speaking African AFMA License Colonies," (3) a distributor servicing geographically linked territories, for instance, "the Pacific Rim, including . . . ," or (4) a single distributor serving several small territories, for instance, "the fourteen islands known as . . ."

Figure 3.3
AFMA International Multiple Rights Deal Memo

AFMA® INTERNATIONAL MULTIPLE RIGHTS DEAL MEMO©
BASIC LICENSE AND FINANCIAL TERMS

DATE: _____

This Deal Memo, consisting of these Basic Terms, and incorporating the Deal Terms and Standard Terms and Definitions of the AFMA Model International Licensing Agreement ("MILA") (unless expressly revised below), and any attached pages, constitutes the agreement of the parties as follows:

Licensor:	Distributor:
Address:	Address:
Phone:_____ Fax:_____	Phone:_____ Fax:_____
E-Mail:	E-mail:
	State/Country of Incorporation:
Picture:	Agreement Term starts on execution and ends on _____.
	License period starts on _____ and ends on _____.
Territory:	Authorized Language(s):
	[ ] Dubbed [ ] Subtitled

Authorized Video Use(s):			Authorized Telecasts:		
[ ] PAL	[ ] SECAM	[ ] NTSC	Pay TV: ____ Playdates ____ Runs		
[ ] Cassette	[ ] Disc	[ ] Other:	Free TV: ____ Playdates ____ Runs		

RIGHTS LICENSED AND RESERVED (TR = Theatrical Release, VR = Video Release)

RIGHTS LICENSED			HOLDBACKS UNTIL	RIGHTS LICENSED			HOLDBACKS UNTIL
Cinematic				**Pay-Per-View** ("PPV")			
Theatrical	[ ] Yes	[ ] No	_____	Residential	[ ] Yes [ ] No	____months from [ ] TR [ ] VR in Territory	
Non-Theatrical	[ ] Yes	[ ] No	____months from TR in Territory	Non-Residential	[ ] Yes [ ] No	____months from [ ] TR [ ] VR in Territory	
Public Video	[ ] Yes	[ ] No	____months from TR in Territory	Demand View	[ ] Yes [ ] No	____months from [ ] TR [ ] VR in Territory	
Video				**Pay TV**			
Home Rental	[ ] Yes	[ ] No	____months from TR in Territory	Terrestrial	[ ] Yes [ ] No	____months from [ ] TR [ ] VR in Territory	
Home SellThru	[ ] Yes	[ ] No	____months from TR in Territory	Cable	[ ] Yes [ ] No	____months from [ ] TR [ ] VR in Territory	
Commercial	[ ] Yes	[ ] No	____months from TR in Territory	Satellite	[ ] Yes [ ] No	____months from [ ] TR [ ] VR in Territory	
Ancillary				**Free TV**			
Airline	[ ] Yes	[ ] No	____months from TR in Territory	Terrestrial	[ ] Yes [ ] No	____months from [ ] TR [ ] VR in Territory	
Ship	[ ] Yes	[ ] No	____months from TR in Territory	Cable	[ ] Yes [ ] No	____months from [ ] TR [ ] VR in Territory	
Hotel	[ ] Yes	[ ] No	____months from TR in Territory	Satellite	[ ] Yes [ ] No	____months from [ ] TR [ ] VR in Territory	

Initial Theatrical or Video Release of the Picture in the Territory must occur within ____ months after Licensor's Notice of Initial Delivery. All rights not specifically licensed or invented or known at the time of signing are reserved to Licensor. Any right not checked is reserved to Licensor.

PAYMENT AND ALLOCATION OF GUARANTEE

Guarantee: US $_____

Percentage or Amount:	When Payable:	Method of Payment:
% ____ US $ _____	On execution of this Agreement _____	__ W/T __ L/C Other ____
% ____ US $ _____	On start of Principal Photography _____	__ W/T __ L/C Other ____
% ____ US $ _____	On Licensor's Notice of Initial Delivery _____	__ W/T __ L/C Other ____
% ____ US $ _____	On _____	__ W/T __ L/C Other ____
% ____ US $ _____	On _____	__ W/T __ L/C Other ____

Note: Method of Payment: W/T = Wire Transfer, L/C = Letter of Credit

ALLOCATION

% ___ US $ _____ to Cinematic Licensed Rights	% ___ US $ _____ to Video Licensed Rights	% ___ US $ _____ to Pay TV Licensed Rights
% ___ US $ _____ to Ancillary Licensed Rights	% ___ US $ _____ to PPV Licensed Rights	% ___ US $ _____ to Free TV Licensed Rights

Note: If no allocation is indicated, the entire Guarantee is allocated to Theatrical Rights, if granted.

DISPOSITION OF GROSS RECEIPTS ("GR")

Costs-Off Deal:	Distribution Deal:	Distribution Deal:
Applicable to the following licensed rights	Applicable to the following licensed rights	Applicable to the following licensed rights
[ ] Cinematic [ ] Video [ ] Pay TV	[ ] Cinematic [ ] Video [ ] Pay TV	[ ] Cinematic [ ] Video [ ] Pay TV
[ ] Ancillary [ ] Pay-Per-View [ ] Free TV	[ ] Ancillary [ ] Pay-Per-View [ ] Free TV	[ ] Ancillary [ ] Pay-Per-View [ ] Free TV
GR will be shared separately for each licensed right in the following order:	GR will be shared separately for each licensed right in the following order:	GR will be shared separately for each licensed right in the following order:
	____% First GR to Licensor	____% First GR to Licensor
____% Distribution Costs recouped from first GR	____% Next GR to Distributor	____% Next GR to Distributor
____% / ____% Sharing of GR until Recoupment	____% Distribution Costs next recouped from GR, if app.	____% Distribution Costs next recouped from GR, if app
____% / ____% Sharing of GR after Recoupment	____% / ____% Sharing of GR until Recoupment	____% / ____% Sharing of GR until Recoupment
	____% / ____% Sharing of GR after Recoupment	____% / ____% Sharing of GR after Recoupment

Cross-Collateralization:	Publicity/Advertising Commitment:	Print Commitment:
	Minimum: Maximum:	Minimum: Maximum:

Additional Terms:

This Deal Memo is a binding Agreement upon execution by both parties. The parties intend to prepare and sign a more formal agreement incorporating the terms of this Deal Memo and additional terms contained in the AFMA MILA applicable to the Licensed Rights, version V:22294, or the most current other version available. Unless and until such an agreement is signed, this Deal Memo, incorporating the Standard Terms and Conditions contained in the MILA, is a binding contract between the parties. **ANY DISPUTE ARISING OUT OF THIS DEAL MEMO WILL BE RESOLVED BY BINDING ARBITRATION UNDER THE AFMA RULES FOR INTERNATIONAL ARBITRATION IN EFFECT AT THE TIME THE NOTICE OF ARBITRATION IS FILED.** Unless otherwise specified, the Forum for any dispute under this Deal Memo shall be Los Angeles County, California, using California and U.S. law.

LICENSOR	DISTRIBUTOR
BY: _____	BY: _____
(Its) _____	(Its) _____
(As Agent For) _____	(As Agent For) _____

My first foreign sales event was the 1976 MIFED. I was stunned by the number of foreign territories represented and how extensive global distribution was even then. Hundreds of small villages and hamlets without utilities have paying audiences. Some of these local audiences are served by exhibitors that travel to their locals with their film reels and sometimes just a single projector, often mounted on a truck bed. The picture is either shown against a wall, or on a screen drawn between poles. Weather permitting, after the sun goes down, the generator is fired up, and the picture is screened-one reel at a time, if there is only one projector. These remote areas are often licensed for a flat fee, using one or more previously used prints, rarely in their audience's language.

Rights licensed and reserved. This section of the deal memo sets forth the particular rights covered by this license and the window length for each.

Under "Cinematic Rights," the "Public Video" rights refer to territories that have public video exhibition.

License income. Earnings may come to the licensor from two sources: an advance/guarantee or profit participation. One direct distribution expense difference unique to foreign territories is the often substantial post-production expenses related to talent and dubbing or subtitling. One unique income category from foreign territories is that of payments from the distributor for elements provided by the producer. These elements include mechanicals or color separations for printed promotion and advertising materials along with tangible film and video elements of the picture and its related video and film advertising, promotion, and publicity products.

Guarantee. The guarantee amount initially performs as payment "binder" to the agreement. The guarantee amount may be paid in installments as indicated on the deal memo.

A payment is most often triggered by delivery of the picture, or by access to specific elements of the picture by the licensee. To delay payment, the licensee may not accept immediate delivery of the elements, though they have been delivered to a freight forwarder within the territory, on the licensee's behalf. This is the reason for the language in this section stating that the licensee will take delivery within two months of notification that the materials have been received.

Letters of Credit are reviewed in Chapter 5. An example of a new release picture payment configuration is "10 percent on agreement execution, via wire transfer, 90 percent within fourteen calendar days from agreement execution, by letter of credit."

The guarantee is advanced against specific licensed rights. The percentage of the advance applied to each right is specified in the next section of the deal memo. This amount may be deducted from the licensor's share before the licensor participates in the profits of the picture earned from that specific right.

Disposition of gross receipts. In a "costs-off deal," income accounting with foreign distributors is very similar to the accounting with U.S. distributors. Distribution fees are paid on first receipts, direct distribution expenses are recouped, the guarantee is recouped, and then, typically, the producer participates in the picture's remaining profits. "Distribution deal" accounting is most commonly used in licenses with little or no advance guarantee.

Cross-collateralization may bind the terms of this deal memo, including the distributor's advance recoupment, with the specific license rights to other pictures.

The AFMA Deal Memo has many advantages. Because it is widely used, it is widely understood, accepted and litigation interpreted. Further, its menu form allows easy selection, and it compels the parties to consider all the major points of the license.

However, the deal memo is a form, and as such, has wasted spaces and limitations. It is too rigid to accommodate sophisticated license terms that may end up scribbled in the margins. This being so, many companies use the letter form of deal memo. Regardless of what you use, the AFMA deal memo remains an excellent guide for those less accustomed to the foreign licensing process.

Territory Differences

Each territory's earnings value is not defined so much by its size and population as by the territory's media sophistication, which is principally gauged by the presence and availability of all four major distribution windows, as well as by concentration of television households among its total population. This value is also defined by the strength of the economy, measured substantially by the audience sizes per capita, for each media, and by ticket cost, video rental cost, and premium cable service subscription cost, along with average consumer discretionary spending and currency exchange value.

Strengths vary greatly between territories. For instance, Mexico has a land mass about five times that of Japan, but only a fraction of Japan's population. Further, Mexico has comparatively underdeveloped media and, though a high percentage of the population attend theaters, the admission price in Mexico is several times lower than in Japan. The most effective territory financial comparisons are drawn by examining each territory's box office and four major media category earnings records.

Managing Global Relationships

Though the producer will engage and sustain first-person relationships with the leading territories, this will not be possible for most other foreign territories. These other valuable relationships are typically managed by a small, very busy, in-house foreign sales staff. This is a powerful and increasingly important area, worthy of each producer's focus, accountability, and generous investment. With the same picture inventory, the only difference being the dynamics of the foreign department operating team, revenues can shift in either direction by one-third. The foreign sales department deserves the placement of a highly skilled, focused, wired, and genial team.

Though a producer may not pitch the major territory distributors on pictures they have yet to place in earnest development, distributors hope their independent producers will become regular suppliers of significant films. It is important for these distributors to understand their producers' five-year plans and the scope of pictures they intend to produce. Whether it is three pictures a year or two every three years, distributors need to know. Knowledge of production plans significantly affects the value distributors attribute to each production company relationship.

As a producer's inventory of motion pictures increases, so does the power to trade all pictures, both new and library releases. It is good business for producers to consider the library they are building, not just picture by picture, but by the effect each new film has on those in their libraries.

Foreign Trends

Foreign territories are a continually changing landscape that producers ought to keep their eyes on. Consider these two trends:

Foreign Production of American Style Pictures

In 1997, Gaumont, a studio based in France with multiple European media business interests, produced a very American motion picture, *The Fifth Element*. This creatively and financially bold experiment was extremely successful, with U.S. and foreign audiences responding equally to the American motion pictures after which it was styled. This picture was both an indication of the aggressive and culturally wired status of foreign studios for U.S. coproduction relationships, and a precursor of what may be expected from this and other major foreign studios.

Global Leading Territory Day and Date Theatrical Releases

The very savvy distribution team at Dreamworks released *The Prince of Egypt* on December 18, 1998. This was the first time in motion picture history that a film was released in all major global markets on the same day. Global theatrical day and date releasing requires massive creative (especially dubbing and subtitling) and distribution coordination. The success of *The Prince of Egypt's* global release should lead the way to satisfying the demands of foreign audiences who resent having to wait for pictures until after their U.S. openings.

Summary

As a group, U.S. consumers outspend every other global audience in every distribution window. However, the global growth area for American motion pictures is the foreign territories.

With over half of the average American motion picture's earnings coming from foreign territories, and an average ratio of 8 to 1 foreign to U.S. audiences viewing these pictures, producing for foreign audiences should carry for American producers a weight of focus almost equal to that of U.S. audiences.

Producers who understand the play and earnings dynamics of their pictures develop and produce their pictures to maximize performance in at least the leading foreign territories. Motion pictures created by these producers are better received by foreign audiences and consistently turn in substantially higher earnings.

Chapter 4

Ancillary Markets and Rights

This chapter presents the ancillary markets and rights for theatrically released motion pictures; reviews their audiences, income, and license relationships; and details how producers should manage them.

The Effect of Theatrically Released Motion Pictures on Other Windows

For a motion picture to warrant beginning its distribution in theaters, it must meet the theatrical audience's expectations. This audience expects these pictures to be substantive entertainment. Theatrical feature films should create an emotional fire in their audiences. This quality ought to be the "event" in event motion pictures. Special-effects driven films may generate a respectable gross in the first or second film in which a new effect is used, but effects quickly lose an audience's respect if they are a picture's centerpiece.

One of the finest expressions of this was made by motion picture industry living legend Peter Guber, as he addressed independent producers during a 1996 session of the American Film Market:

"So is there a specific ingredient that's essential for [a picture's] success? My instinct, my curiosity and my experience tell me that the key component is emotion. The story must have resonance and emotion. It must reside in the story. . . Watch your audience come out of a movie and see their state. Ask them to tell you about the film. . . When they tell you, or better yet show you, the impact it has on them, the emotion generated, then you better buckle your seat belt because you have a hit, even if the reviews aren't good. That doesn't mean a film can't be thoughtful, it means the emotion must carry the infor-

mation, not the other way around. What you have to move are not boxes of popcorn, or subs on a cable system, but people's hearts and spirits."

Audience reactions are the ultimate measure of a picture's entertainment power. Audiences look to theatrically released pictures to entertain and move them more than any other pictures made.

Theatrically released motion picture campaigns create an event aura that continues with these pictures through all distribution windows. If they deliver the emotion-packed entertainment they promise, audiences will view them again as these pictures pass through subsequent windows.

Audience Sizes In Major Windows

In Chapter 2, I discuss how difficult it is for pictures to become profitable in their theatrical distribution alone. But for most pictures, the larger their theatrical audience and earnings, the greater will be their ancillary audiences and earnings.

Though the following audience statistics are for the U.S., the leading foreign territories perform similarly, and they are consistently moving closer to matching the U.S. ratios. In the United States there are approximately 100 million television households and a potential audience of 1.8 per household (anyone between the ages of 5 and 80 is considered a potential audience). This creates a total potential audience of 180 million people for each picture's several distribution windows. Each picture's audience varies depending on the number of target audiences the picture appeals to and the dynamics of the film's campaign.

According to the National Association of Theater Owners (NATO), the average picture's U.S. theatrical gross box office revenues among all pictures released in 1997 was $13.2 million; the average gross box office per picture for major studio releases alone is closer to $26 million. Most pictures are considered successful if they attain a U.S. box office gross of $50 million. At the NATO-reported average ticket price of $4.59, a picture with a gross as high as $50 million will have played to a theatrical audience of approximately 11 million people. Picture titles attaining such success become household names to most consumers, but will have been seen by approximately 6 percent of their potential audiences during their theatrical play. These statistics can be very helpful when evaluating the massive potential audiences for pictures in their ancillary markets.

During its video release this $50 million picture may earn another $75 million. With an estimated rental rate of $2.20 and an estimated audience of 2.1 people per rental, this picture may reach a video audience of about 71 million viewers. This increases the total audience that has viewed the picture to about 45 percent of the total potential U.S. audience.

One year after its theatrical premiere, the picture is released on premium cable, and this household-name picture still has not been seen by over half of its potential audience. Premium cable audience penetration is difficult to track accurately. An ample premium cable allowance assumes 27 percent of the total U.S. audience: another 49 million viewers that increase the total U.S. audience reach to 72 percent. This leaves 28 percent of a picture's potential audience (over 50 million viewers) for the network television premiere, which traditionally occurs about 30 months after the theatrical release. Though theatrical release motion pictures often win the dominant network audience share, the networks typically only broadcast a picture once, leaving a substantial audience for television syndication.

In every distribution window there are repeat viewers, which are not represented in the figures above. These are especially important revenue-building audiences for network and syndicated television.

Many theatrically released motion pictures become important social references that are a must-see-early for their target audiences and a free television curiosity tune-in for their distant fringe audiences. Whether it is *Regarding Henry, Ghost, You've Got Mail, Die Hard,* or *Toy Story,* most of the 180 million potential U.S. audience will eventually experience theatrically released motion pictures, even if it is at home on their surround-sound, big-screen television where they must sit through ads or channel-surf during a few commercials. Theatrically released motion pictures are often powerful, culture-shifting audience attractions that uniquely sustain their value, substantially because of their entertainment power and their position as a major theatrical event.

Ancillary Audience Characteristics

Each of the major four ancillary windows (video, premium cable, network television, and syndicated television) has unique audience characteristics, which are defined more by their audiences' lifestyles than by their economics. While audiences spend more of their entertainment time in their particular favorite distribution window, most consumers have purchased the equipment, are prepared, and want to experience each motion picture in the distribution windows they determine the motion picture warrants.

Consumers are passionate about making merchandise decisions, and motion pictures carry unique social importance. Pictures are exotic merchandise, universally known and talked about, and our opinions about them make them one of the most requested consumer product categories.

Consuming motion pictures is all about emotions, and most people make up their minds about how they will view a picture by the time they have seen a picture's third commercial. Typically, emotions rule over financial considerations. Choosing among an $8 theater ticket, a $3 video rental, a $5 monthly premium cable subscription, or free network television, is rarely as important as wanting to see it now, or with a friend, or on a theater screen, or in its full length.

Some pictures are so compelling that our media preferences have little effect on our viewing preferences and habits. Many people who never see a movie at a theater, or never rent a video, or who never see a movie twice, do so with certain pictures. This is demonstrated by especially audience-motivating entertainment like *Titanic, Forest Gump, Independence Day,* and *E.T.,* all of which draw uncommonly high audiences in all distribution windows.

In addition to our emotional connections with pictures, capriciousness often sways a person's viewing choice. Consumers may just *feel* like seeing a picture at a theater or renting one from the video outlet, and so go to the local multiplex or video store and seek a title. If there isn't one they have made a previous theatrical or video rental decision about, they most often buy a ticket or rent a picture anyway. It may even be a picture that they have already relegated to a later ancillary window; they take a chance.

Because of this phenomenon, producers and distributors often stage their release windows during the summer or the Christmas and New Year holidays. These are the dominant seasons during which consumers seek more movie experiences, often making their picture selection while they are in the marketplace. This tendency is largely the motivation behind the industries' six-month window structure; the holidays and summer are six months apart. Many of the strongest pictures are released in their two most critical distribution windows (theatrical and video) during the seasons when audiences are most aggressively seeking entertainment.

U.S. audiences consume more entertainment than any other territory's audiences; Western European and Japanese audiences are close behind. According to Nielsen Media Research, more than 99 percent of all U.S. households own at least one television and receive one or more major network television signals. 85 percent of these television households have at least one VCR, and according to the Motion Picture Association of America (MPAA), annually purchase more than 673 million copies of prerecorded video cassettes. 68 percent of these television households have basic cable, and according to the MPAA, 59 percent are pay-cable subscribers.

Despite the increasing availability and audience acquisition of sophisticated home entertainment equipment, theater audiences have steadily increased over the past ten years. The MPAA reported a 1998 total U.S. box office of $6.95 billion, exceeding the prior year by 9.2 percent.

The entertainment consumption rate has also increased in the ancillary windows, with VCR household penetration up 3 percent in 1998 to 85 percent of all television households, basic cable up 3.1 percent to 68 percent of all television households, and pay cable up almost 8 percent to 59 percent of all television households.

The following theater audience statistics closely mirror each of the major ancillary (video, premium cable, network, and syndication) audience profiles.

Total Admissions by Audience Category

Age	12–17	18+	18–29	30–39	40–49	50–59	60+
Percentage of Yearly Admissions	14%	88%	35%	20%	16%	7%	10%

Frequency of Audience Attendance by Age

	12–17	18+	All audiences 12 and over
At least 1x/month	42%	27%	28%
2x/year	44%	34%	35%
1x/year	7%	9%	9%
Never	5%	30%	27%

As these NATO-prepared statistics indicate, eighteen to twenty-nine year old adults are the most important single demographically categorized audience, buying 35 percent of the all tickets purchased. However, for sheer entertainment consumption aggressiveness, by each participant in a demographic category, 12- to 17-year-olds are way out front, with 42 percent buying a ticket at least once a month, demonstrating that youth are both easier to please and will accommodate a greater quantity of pictures than any other category.

Youth are the greatest consumers of motion pictures in *all* media. As a group, they attend the theater more often, rent more videos, and watch more premium cable, network, and syndicated television. They are also easier to sell to because they view and listen to more advertisements and have less discretion than older audiences as to what they will buy and watch.

Another interesting analysis of audience preferences is shown in the chart below; couples with children at home attend the theater more often than couples without children at home. Not surprisingly, single adults attend the theater more than married adults.

Frequency of Audience Attendance by Family Status

	Married	Single	Children	No Children
1x/month	23%	35%	27%	30%
1x/6 months	33%	31%	39%	28%
1x/year	11%	8%	11%	9%
Never	32%	24%	22%	32%

Although ten years ago there was a margin worthy of interpretation between men and women motion picture attendees, MPAA statistics reveal it is now less than 5%.

Statistics are important indicators that are worthy of analysis by those who produce, distribute, and license motion pictures. However, statistics are easily misinterpreted. For instance, has the gap between men and women motion picture viewers closed because women are more independent, or because there are more pictures being produced and distributed that interest them? The consensus of the best industry analyzers supports the latter conclusion. Responding to the eagerness of women to view theatrically released motion pictures in all media, producers and studios are beginning to cater more to this powerful audience.

Regarding family movie viewing, there is a fairly even split among industry mavens, between those who believe families don't attend theaters more regularly because they spend less discretionary money than other audience categories and those who believe that there are simply fewer motion pictures that are targeted to couples with children at home.

Motion pictures such as *Nightmare On Elm Street* and *Dirty Rotten Scoundrels* have almost exclusive single audience skews, while films like *Sleepless In Seattle, Dead Poets Society* and *The Fugitive* are made for multiple target audiences. All of the above pictures were successful, and targeting for a specific audience often ensures a solid response; however, pictures with a strong appeal to more than one target audience have a higher potential income in all distribution windows and rights sales.

Producers Rely on Ancillary Earnings

For U.S. and all major foreign territories, the theatrical release is unquestionably the most important distribution window through which each motion picture passes. This is almost exclusively so, because this is where audience perception of each picture's entertainment value is established. As discussed in previous chapters, producers should not project any producer profits from the theatrical distribution of their pictures; however, producers should be keenly aware that, though their largest audiences and substantially all of their income will come from their pictures' ancillary windows, the size of these audiences and earnings will be determined by the pictures' performance during the theatrical release.

It is important that producers take into account the whole performance and earnings dynamics of each motion picture. A picture may have a projected $10 million gross box office, offset by a theatrical television campaign of almost that amount. If it performs to its projection, this picture may conclude its theatrical run with a distributor's net loss of approximately $8.75 million, without any offset to its negative (production) cost. Examine the numbers below:

Theatrical Release Earnings Analysis

Source	Amount (in millions)	Balance (in millions)
Gross box office earnings	$10	$10
Film rental	$5	$5
Distribution fee	$1.75	$3.25
Direct distribution	$12 million	($8.75)
Expenses (advertising $9 million; 1,200 Prints @ $1,500 each; other expenses $1.2 million)		
Distribution Net Loss	($8.75 million)	($8.75 Million)

If the theatrical window is analyzed alone, neither the producer nor the distributor would release the picture. But when the ancillary windows are also considered, pictures often become sound business. For instance, if the $9 million in advertising and additional associated promotion and publicity for the picture sufficiently motivates the picture's audiences, then its first ancillary audience—the video audience—may even be larger than traditional ratios by drawing in theatrical audiences who did not get a chance to see the picture during its unusually short theatrical run. As the example below indicates, even at the traditional "three times film rental" performance, the picture is almost at a "break-even" status ($800,000 loss), as it moves into its video ancillary window.

Video Release Earnings

Source	Amount (in millions)	Balance (in millions)
Video gross	$15	$15
Distribution fee	$5.25	$9.75
Direct distribution expenses	$1.8	$7.95
Distributor's net	$7.95	$7.95
Theatrical loss forward	($ 8.75)	($.80)

After analyzing these earnings, one might wonder why more movies don't begin distribution with video, spending the $9 million in advertising there. This would be the logical choice, save for the "theatrical luster" it would never be able to gain, no matter how much video release advertising is done. If the project is made for the small screen first, it will never shake its small-screen stigma. The only motion picture exceptions are children's audience animation sequels, which perform in a uniquely "toy-like" manner for this particular audience.

The First Ancillary Window: Video Distribution

This window traditionally opens six months following a picture's theatrical premiere. When these pictures open in video, they still carry their theatrical marketing power and sometimes are still playing off in theatrical situations (usually dollar theaters). As indicated previously, most of the potential audience (93 percent for an average picture) still have not seen this picture; having missed seeing the picture while it was in theaters, they are either waiting for its release on video or for a later ancillary window.

Using the customary video gross revenue projection formula of three times a picture's theatrical film rental is sufficient for a distant analysis of the film's success, but hardly touches on understanding how to manage this window.

Traditionally, a picture is released into its video life as a "rental product," converting to a "sell-through product" after its first year of video release.

As a rental product, a picture is released at a wholesale price of about $65, paid by the video outlet. The substantial margin between this wholesale cost and an actual video production cost of about $3 leaves the studio and the producer with a share of the rental revenues.

Following the primary video "rental" life of the picture (about one year), many of these pictures are released again at a wholesale sell- through price of between $10 and $15. This second release motivates consumer purchases; the highest purchase volumes usually come from mass merchandise retailers.

There are pictures that are exceptions to this tradition. If a picture's gross box office revenues exceed $100 million *and* it has a dominant target audience other than men, 18 to 35 (who typically don't purchase many videos), it will usually begin its video window at a sell-through price of $10 to $15. To justify beginning the picture's video life at this price, the picture should project unit sales at least five times greater than the traditional rental volume unit sales.

The premise of a high wholesale price during the rental release of a motion picture is an awkward deal-making device. High wholesale prices deliver neither the studios nor the video outlets their fair profit share. There are several experimental deals now in use that may evolve into a more equitable relationship. The studios want to sell the greatest volume of video units possible, and video outlets want sufficient copies for rental demand without any excess. To encourage higher volume, studios are offering some outlet chains several variations of a scale that allows them to buy greater video copies at lower costs after they have purchased an initial supply at the normal rental price. Studios are also trying rental-sharing relationships with the larger video chains, including the largest of these, Blockbuster Video, earning about 25 percent of the total U.S. video rental income. From these experiments, a studio/video outlet deal structure that more fairly distributes profits to all participants will likely evolve.

Since video earnings represent the highest single income category for most pictures, every studio's video distribution department configures a separate release strategy, including price variance for each picture, which keeps the studios, as well as video outlets and mass merchandisers, on their toes. The only change that may be apparent to consumers is that now more pictures are offered initially at sell-through, and there is a better chance to find the movie they want at their local video outlet.

Each of the major studios have excellent video distribution units, and they video release most motion pictures that they theatrically distribute. They are also the primary marketing source for both video-rental and sell-through. Video outlets advertise in their stores, some of them by direct mail, while larger chains advertise on television. The studios provide video retailers co-op advertising support (paying for a portion of their advertising media costs) to encourage their campaigns. Each video outlet's co-op amount is usually based on a percentage of its purchases.

The producer's video distribution agreement with the studio is typically associated with the theatrical distribution agreement. Terms vary, but the traditional relationship pays the studio a 35 percent distribution fee, recoups the studio's direct distribution expenses, then the studio's loss-carry-forward from theatrical distribution if there is any. An operating reserve is then deducted to continue the video sales process, and finally, the balance goes to the producer.

The Second Ancillary Distribution Window: Premium Cable Television

Consumers eagerly embraced this release window, and it experienced aggressive growth during the early 1980s. The premium cable window provides solid consumer motion picture delivery, and subscriber growth continues in mostly single-digit annual percentages.

Premium cable networks provide an important audience and earnings window, delivering a far less complicated arena for producers to work in. There is a short list of potential licensees, which includes HBO and its sister channel, Cinemax; Showtime and its sister, The Movie Channel; Starz and its sister Encore channels; and the Disney Channel.

These networks are very competitive for pictures because of the stability and growth of their subscriber bases, which are determined by the popularity and quantity of the pictures they broadcast. These networks gain subscribers almost exclusively by delivering major theatrically released motion pictures. There is no revenue sharing on this playing field. The license fees paid are the total income from this release category.

In this window, the exclusive premiere license is the greatest single income tier. The premiere license provides for a limited number of airings for a limited period of time. The fee normally ranges from $2.5 million to $6 million, but, if the license is engaged prior to a picture's theatrical release, it will probably carry an escalator clause. This clause calls for the license fee to increase if the picture's gross box office earnings exceed a certain minimum (for instance, $40 million) and then increases it again for every additional gross box office increment attained (for instance, each $10 million), but not to exceed a total license amount (for instance, $20 million).

The nonexclusive premium cable license tier allows for a greater number of airings for a substantially reduced license fee, and is most often included in the premiere license agreement. This tier continues until the network premiere occurs. Following the network premiere, the picture may still be licensed by premium cable networks, but for lesser amounts.

Consumer marketing in this window is accomplished by the licensee network, primarily through network promotional spots, crossover network advertising through cable systems, and print ads.

Producers are capable of managing these licenses directly. The producer must know each picture's value to the network. Producers discover this as they research each picture during the preparation of the picture's first draft liquidation breakdown. This was discussed in Chapter 1 and will be reviewed in Chapter 12. Basically, this is the process of identifying recently released pictures with very similar target audiences, campaign elements, and entertainment delivery. Then producers identify these pictures' audience and financial performance in the U.S. and leading foreign territories. This information allows the producer to confidently prepare and negotiate these rights.

To assist them in securing and managing these licenses, producers often use an independent producer sales representative, hire an employee experienced in ancillary sales management, or use their industry attorney.

The Third Ancillary Window: Network Television _____

Licensing network television is similar in most respects to licensing premium cable networks, although the marketplace is quite different. The economy, the networks' broadcast time allotment and content constraints, and their average 30-month window from theatrical premiere to network premiere make for very different chemistry.

The network premiere of motion pictures is one of the most important distribution windows for two reasons: The network premiere is the first opportunity for audiences to view the picture without cost, and more importantly, it is the first opportunity for almost every person in the U.S. to watch the picture at the same time.

At a time when network executives are challenged more than ever to capture high audience shares for their respective network, motion pictures consistently deliver dominant audience shares. In some respects, the time from a picture's theatrical release to its network premiere works to build its audience. Many viewers who have seen the picture before and enjoyed it will tune in again. Pictures that have been aired so heavily through the three prior windows (such as *Rain Man*, *Schindler's List*, and many others), pull massive audiences, both new and repeat, to their network premiere.

As with premium cable, there are just a few potential licensees in the television market. These include NBC, ABC, CBS, Fox, and TNT. Unlike premium cable, the common license calls for a single broadcast and a window length of 12 to 24 months.

Since audience share determines the value of each picture to the network, the difference in license fees paid may be much greater than the premium cable license. Typical fees range from $2.2 million to as high as $40 million, averaging $4 million to $7 million.

As with premium cable, producers should license network television directly. The preparation for this license is a natural part of the whole development and production process. Prior to earnest development, producers should have identified the most likely network license candidate and the value of the picture to this network. By preparing thoroughly, producers can explore entering pretheatrical release licenses with the network that can accommodate a tie-in "film-about-the-film," which could provide programming to the network and additional marketing heat for the picture during its theatrical release. Dreamworks crafted such relationships with NBC for its release of both *Antz* and *Prince of Egypt*.

The network provides promotion and advertising for the picture principally via promotional spots over its own network. Again, the participation of the producer's attorney is essential in this process. Most producers either use in-house ancillary sales talent or a producer's representative to fulfill and maintain these relationships.

Occasionally producers license directly to network television, collapsing the premium cable window altogether, which substantially washes out premium cable premiere earnings. Producers electing to do this are motivated by aggressive networks willing to pay license fees equal to the combined traditional premium and free television premiere fees.

The Fourth Ancillary Window: Free Television Syndication _____

Television syndication is the evergreen audience and earnings window.

Syndication opens 12 to 24 months following the network premiere and continues to license-renew as long as people care to be entertained.

This window is sophisticated, because it deals with many television station groups and independent stations. It requires continual sales, license management, and physical delivery maintenance. This window is usually managed by a television syndication organization, which is compensated through distribution fees and expense recoupment.

License fees vary widely in this window, depending substantially on the number of airings allowed, the audience reach, the number of stations, and the length of license.

Other Ancillary Rights

Every rights area has value, and the producer should be able to manage each of them. Some of the following are worth seven- and even eight-figure amounts and can also substantially increase income from the primary release windows.

Novelization

There are profits for producers from novelizing a screenplay or re-releasing an existing novel the picture is based upon. Typically, the greatest advantages are realized through motion picture promotion, by having a novel released a month prior to a picture's theatrical premiere, with the picture's "one-sheet" (poster) on the front cover. Producers are best served if they negotiate first with publishers for the quantity of the run and retail placement, then for profit participation. Having the novel at most mass merchandise, supermarket, drugstore, bookstore and airport checkout lines just prior to a picture's theatrical premiere is very valuable advertising.

The management of novelization rights begins before the literary rights are negotiated. Some producers manage the whole universe of their pictures, including novelization rights, as part of their negotiations for their picture's story. No matter how strong the novel has been previously, the motion picture will likely become a household name and drive novel sales as no other influence can.

If producers fail to acquire their picture's novelization rights, then they should at least participate in the novelization (or re-release) publishing profits and should receive publisher participation in the novel's distribution tie-in to the picture's theatrical marketing.

Each picture's novelization should be scheduled with the publisher before principal photography commences, allowing at least five months for the publishing process.

Product Placements

An effective UPM (unit production manager) will make notes of proprietary items needed for principal photography. These are critical, and depending on a picture's target audiences and how the products or locations may appear in the picture to the audiences, they may be provided to the production company at no cost.

Motion pictures are the most powerful merchandise vehicles with which other branded merchandise can be associated. More than the typical reach and frequency methods used by advertising agencies to gauge audience exposure, motion pictures can elevate a brand by putting it in the highest sphere of consumer consideration. Even negative use of a product in a motion picture may have substantial positive marketing effects. Because of this, sophisticated brands increasingly participate in and out of motion pictures, which helps propel their products with greater power than they can achieve from alternative promotion and advertising processes.

There is no income amount that should motivate producers to infringe on the integrity of their pictures; however, the best brand relationships have deepened pictures' creativity, increased their profits, and pumped up their marketing campaigns. There are well over a hundred excellent examples of this, such as *Wall Street*. Motorola was one of the only players in the then-sluggish cell phone business. It just was not launching at dynamic proportions. When audiences around the world watched Michael Douglas using his cellular phone as an indispensable lifestyle device, an entire industry was dramatically launched.

Producers should carefully review their pictures, even period productions, for opportunities to engage brand relationships that have mutual benefits. Product placement companies will make these arrangements for a modest fee.

Most brands, from private aircraft to bottled water, are very eager to establish these relationships. A call to most corporate headquarters will put a staffer in touch with the company's executive directing product placement.

With a little research on prior pictures, the producer can use comparable brand relationships to assist in negotiations for his or her picture.

All of these relationships must be documented, and all documents should be reviewed by the producer's attorney. Items included might be: Who is the insurer in the event of loss or damage to the designer luggage? Is the contract language "a minimum of 5 seconds of brand name recognition" reasonable, and if the picture delivers 3 seconds, how does this affect the relationship? Is the payment reduced, and if so, by how much and who determines the amount? Working out these details up front seems like a bother at the time and like a dream when problems happen.

Premium Tie-ins

Like product placement, premium tie-ins are related to consumer brands becoming more dominant through their association with a motion picture.

A fast food restaurant chain gives away or sells products related to the motion picture. The public can only receive them through these outlets. They include character figures, special cups, hats, T-shirts, and toy tractors or spaceships. Whatever they are, they must mobilize the picture's target audience to come to a brand outlet primarily through television advertising. As they do this, they sell the picture.

How much does the producer get paid to participate in such a promotion? Usually not anything directly. He does, though, indirectly—$5 million or $10 million or more—when a television ad campaign is engaged that simultaneously markets the picture. Some of these relationships have more than doubled the amount of advertising that would have been spent launching their motion pictures. In 1998 the strongest opening picture of the year was *Godzilla*. With an amazing number of promotional tie-in partners, the picture grossed over $44 million its opening weekend. Promotional partners with kids, youth, and family target audiences received reciprocal benefits from the producers, whose picture grossed $136 million in the U.S. and over $210 million in foreign territories.

Soundtracks and Music Publishing

The soundtrack for almost every motion picture will become a substantive income-producing product. Knowing this will affect how producers (1) select the composer and needle drops (use of already released music in the picture); (2) create a separate soundtrack production and distribution plan; (3) set the soundtrack duplication and release schedule; (4) handle contract deal points with the composer and other related music contributors; and (5) negotiate the soundtrack distribution and music publishing license(s).

Soundtracks are especially powerful earning and marketing elements of a motion picture when one of the picture's primary target audiences is youth.

Again, the most reliable approach to managing these rights is researching recently released pictures with similar target audiences which have well-managed soundtrack marketing and licensing. Producers should study the successful deals that have been made, with whom they made them, and how these relationships were managed. From this information the producer should create the model he is confident best serves the picture and will be served by it. After consulting with an attorney, the producer should then move forward with the marketing and licensing plan.

Soundtrack and music publishing is normally licensed to one or two highly skilled and experienced companies. The producer's task is to understand the earnings and promotion power of this license area, evaluate the license, negotiate and manage the license relationship, and set a schedule allowing these rights to be exploited to the maximum earnings and promotion benefit for the picture.

Toys and Merchandising

Even motion pictures that appear unlikely candidates for toys and merchandising should be carefully considered. Often, there are toys or other merchandise items for adult, youth, or children's audiences that seem like an amazing stretch. As producers become more involved in this licensing area, the wide appeal of movie merchandise for extensive global audiences becomes more apparent.

Each picture should be examined exclusively from the perspective of this license category. After a potential product list is made, research ought to be performed using films with comparable target audiences. After the producer prepares a basic merchandise plan, approaches should be made by, through, or after consulting with a producer's representative, who specializes in this licensing area. These licensing companies typically need at least one year prior to the motion picture's theatrical release to prepare.

Retail Game Sales and Arcade Games

Companies specializing in the game industry understand the power motion pictures have in launching games of all kinds. This category includes board games, electronic hand-held games and computer games—all sold at retail—as well as arcade games.

Producer's representatives specializing in this licensing area should analyze a picture's game licensing prospects for the opportunity of representing the picture to this industry. It is best to have each picture reviewed by at least two competing representatives and have an attorney review the representative agreement as well as the licenses.

In-Flight

During preproduction, every picture should be separately reviewed for cover shots needed by its ancillary markets. These add expenses during principal photography but save much more money later. They also increase the picture's ancillary value and allow the producer to deliver a seamless version of the picture to each participating licensee. Cover shots may be needed for foreign versions, airline audiences (the in-flight version), and the network version that must comply to time and network standards.

There are a handful of excellent and very competitive in-flight distribution companies. Each studio also has an exceptional in-flight department. Producers should meet with competing companies and, with the support of their attorney, enter a distribution relationship.

Planning for this version in development and preproduction allows the producer to budget for cover shots and post production time, and to deliver a print at the opening of this market, which is during each picture's theatrical release.

Hotels and Motels, Military, Schools, Indian Reservations, Ships at Sea, Prison Systems

It is common for independent producers to use the studio that is theatrically distributing their picture to distribute these rights. Each of these rights areas is a small, five- and six-figure income category, but together they can earn seven-figure income.

Understanding that these ancillary earnings niches exist allows producers to plan for them, enter relationships with studio or ancillary rights distributors, to exploit these rights, and expand the audience and earnings for their pictures.

Summary

The most powerful producers are very involved in planning and managing the ancillary rights of their pictures. They understand that these are the rights that deliver the largest audiences and profits.

Producers are the parents and ultimate stewards of each picture. They must understand the audience and earnings dynamics of each picture. They must also measure them, plan them, and enter into relationships with others to dynamically exploit, manage and ensure the prosperity of these relationships.

To succeed in each rights area, the producer must plan early, value each rights area separately, do the research to discover each picture's potential value for each right, use industry specialists, and always include his or her attorney in negotiations and documentation.

Entertainment Banking

This chapter is a review of the entire process of production funding, including how producers prepare for, borrow, and strengthen their banking relationships for initial and continuing production funding.

Beginning with the end in mind is a life practice of many successful people. Production bank financing is the end of the development process and should be part of the development plan from its beginning. Assurance of production financing affects the producer's perception of and ability to develop each motion picture. Development financing is most often raised from private sources. This process is reviewed in Chapters 9 and 10.

With the exception of public offerings, producers should receive their production financing from banks. Knowing a picture's production financing source is a bank both assures the picture will have solid, leading global territory distribution and that there will be no financing participant at risk without complete collateral offset.

The Banking Business

Banks are often referred to as institutions. They are certainly governed by more agencies than most other businesses, but banking is a business. Banking decisions are profit motivated and predicated on business principles.

Every time the trade papers carry a story naming a specific bank supplying production funding to an independent producer, that bank's entertainment department receives calls from naive producers. They set up appointments and arrive, armed with a script and budget, ready to pitch the bank as if it were a studio. But banks make their decisions with different criteria than studios do.

Knowing someone at a bank, like knowing someone at a studio, is helpful, but it has little effect on the bank's lending decisions. The similarity between banks and studios is that to obtain their support, it is critical to understand their criteria for making decisions and the way in which they operate.

Every bank's inventory is its money. Banks earn profits by lending this money at interest. Like most businesses, banks sometimes have shortages or excesses of inventory. Though lending decisions have limited elasticity, when a bank's lending reserves are low, its lending decisions become more restrictive. When lending reserves are high, its lending decisions are more relaxed. It is an important question, and proper form, to ask your loan officer the status of the bank's current lending reserves.

Banks with strong entertainment divisions will always have the capacity to lend, even if they aren't primarily lending bank funds generated from deposits. If the division is making "good" loans, then the loss ratio is low, the loans serviced according to terms are high, and overall profits are high. With a strong loan portfolio, these divisions can perform as the lead bank with other participating banks, as well as engage other outside lending-capital scenarios. When choosing the lead bank that will manage your production borrowing, dealing with one that has a sound, experienced entertainment banking team is very important.

Each bank has loan amount preferences. There are small banks seeking loans in the six- to low seven-figure amounts, mid-range banks seeking loans in the seven- to low eight-figure amounts, and more sophisticated banks seeking loans in the mid-eight to low-nine- figure amounts. It is important to know a bank's loan size criteria.

Basis of Lending Decisions

The ultimate assurance of payment is the borrower's pledged collateral. If the business plan, for whatever reason, is insufficient to pay the borrowed amount according to the terms of the loan, there must be assets pledged to the bank that will repay the remaining balance.

Collateral alone, however, is not sufficient for loan approval. Banks do not want to lend if there is even a modest probability that they will be forced to move on collateral to recover a remaining amount due. The borrower must demonstrate the capacity to service the loan based on existing business operations, or a business plan. Motion picture licenses provide an ideal collateral as they are also the natural means of loan repayment.

Producers typically create motion pictures that are made available to foreign distributors and global licensees, who enter license agreements that provide for an advance payment against the producer's future earnings participation. These payments are due when the pictures become available to the licensees.

The pledged license agreements typically have only one condition before the advance payment is released. This condition is the licensee's receipt of an access letter, making the picture available to the licensee before a specific date. The risk of this delivery, as well as the completion of the picture within its proposed budget, is assumed by the completion guarantee company.

Banks make their lending decisions based on a combination of elements that must be represented clearly and completely in the loan package. For loan approval, this material (the loan package) must demonstrate that the bank (1) has collateral assurance for its return of principal and interest, and (2) that the loan can be reasonably debt-serviced through the production company's regular course of doing business. For most production loans, the collateral is made up of license agreements for the yet-to-be-produced motion picture, whose pledged payments repay the loan's entire principal and interest.

Each loan memorandum submitted to a bank should include, and its approval is substantially determined by, the following:

1. Cover letter. This letter presents what the loan proceeds will be used for, the requested amount, the expected interest rate, the production timing, and the plan and timing for loan processing. The payment plan, collateral, participating distributors, and a brief description of the motion picture should also be presented.

2. Table of contents. The pages of the bank memorandum should be numbered and there should be a table of contents, following the cover letter, which will assist the bank in reviewing the completeness of the package and in locating specific information in the memorandum.

3. Application. The bank's loan application should be completely filled out, signed, and made a part of the memorandum. Some parts of the application may be referenced by "see page number," if the information is completely set forth in another section of the package.

4. Activity and cash flow projections. Each of these projections should be month-to-month for the first year and cover at least six months beyond the anticipated active loan period. Each of these projections should have narrative "Notes To Projections," which describe important characteristics about the projections that are not self-evident. The cash flow projection must include the loan proceeds and debt servicing, calculated at the rate represented in the cover letter.

5. Distribution windows and liquidation breakdown summary. This reveals the picture's planned distribution windows and a conservative version of the liquidation breakdown estimate, including the producer's gross receipts.

6. Collateral. In the initial loan memorandum, this is a descriptive list of the license agreements as they are expected to be provided to the bank. This list should indicate each specific licensee and each estimated license amount.

7. Conditional documents. The bank will not take any substantial risk. If the license agreements used as collateral specify any conditions in addition to picture delivery, which is satisfied with the completion bond, these further conditions must also be satisfied. The most common additional condition in these license agreements is that the picture must be released in the U.S. by one of the ten major studios. If this is a condition, a copy of the U.S. distribution agreement or a binding commitment letter acceptable to the bank must be included in the loan package.

8. Completion bond commitment. In the initial loan memorandum, this may be in the form of a conditional commitment letter that will become an unconditional guarantee in the final loan documentation.

9. Loan calculation. To simplify your understanding, a sample calculation is part of this chapter. To further assist producers in preparing these forms, a worksheet is included on the CD-ROM provided with this book. This indicates, in accounting form, the collateral list with individual amounts, the collateral total, the form of the collateral by total and in separate sections (for instance, letters of credit have a different loan value than bankable contracts), the respective discounts for each form of collateral (letters of credit may be discounted in their loan value by 10 percent and bankable contracts discounted by 20 percent), the new subtotal, the total loan interest amount, the adjusted new subtotal, the motion picture budget (including a detailed list of the actual production amount, promotion, publicity, sales events, travel and any other expenses related to the picture, including production company operating expenses), and the remaining amount, shown as a collateral contingency.

10. The picture's creative information. This section should include the picture's title, a brief story synopsis, a list of the picture's primary talent and their referenced credits, the picture's production dates and locations, and the projected U.S. theatrical release date.

11. Business history. The production company may be new, a resurrection of a prior company, a merger of other companies, or something else. The bank needs to know about the company's genesis and progress; the roots tell of the branches and the fruit. This section is usually in narrative form.

12. Organization chart. This is a simple chart that reveals the members of the production company team by their responsibilities and relationships to one another. There is a production company chart in Chapter 9 and a worksheet on the book's CD-ROM.

13. Principals' biographies and balance sheets. The operators of the business are a key factor in a bank's loan review. The bank looks at the experience of those who manage the business and the experience and balance sheets of those who substantially own the business. The bank may not ask for owners to guarantee the loan, but the owners' financial profiles demonstrate their combined experience and success in asset management. This information is typically presented to the bank through brief, but specific, biographical summaries and recent balance sheets of each individual.

14. Company financials. These are the production company's current balance sheet and, if applicable, a recent profit-and-loss statement. These should be signed by either an in-house bookkeeper or preferably, reviewed and signed by the company's certified public accountant.

15. References. This is an important list of references who importantly point to the way in which the producer does business and with whom. This list typically includes the completion guarantor (the firm and the producer's contact); the producer's law firm and primary attorney; the producer's current bank and officer; the producer's accounting firm and primary accountant; substantial trade references and contacts; and clients, studios, distributors,

and licensees with whom the producer has dealt, along with each of their contacts.

The Loan Approval Process

Producers usually work with a bank loan officer. This officer helps the producer to:

1. Complete the loan package. The package must be complete before it can be reviewed.

2. Perform a preliminary review. If the loan package underperforms in the loan officer's evaluation, it is rejected. Common reasons for underperformance include insufficient or unstable collateral, an unstable management team, or an unpredictable repayment plan.

3. Present the package to the bank's loan committee. The bank loan committee then reviews the package and approves or declines the loan.

4. Deliver the decision to the producer.

5. Prepare and process the loan documentation.

6. Open the funding facility to the producer.

Production Financing Worksheet

The producer prepares a production financing worksheet that is the basis for the presale plan and the bank financing package.

Throughout the motion picture's development process, relationships intensify with distributors in the leading foreign markets, as well as with prospective U.S. premium cable and network television licensees. It becomes increasingly apparent which of these licensees will enter preproduction licenses.

Except for needing the bank loan collateral, producers would not presell their pictures, as licensees must be motivated with special license considerations to pre-purchase rights. These motivations include (1) acquiring the picture for a lesser license advance than they will negotiate after the picture is completed (typically this discount is approximately 20 percent), and (2) taking the picture off the market and away from competing licensees.

Before the producer ever approaches the major foreign territories for their initial greenlight (see Chapters 1, 3, and 12) the producer has prepared the first liquidation breakdown for the picture, evaluated the picture in consideration as compared to at least five pictures with similar target audiences and campaign elements, and has selected the foreign distributors with the greatest propensity to garner the highest gross for this picture in their particular territories. These prospective licensees become the representative correspondent distributors for this picture in their particular territories. If these foreign distributors had refused the picture's initial greenlight, it would not have commenced earnest development. Though there is no license agreement during this time, all the participating distributors have been involved in the development and preproduction of the picture, have represented the picture to the press and the theatrical and ancillary media in their particular territories, and have scheduled its release in theatrical and other distribution windows. The producer has corresponded exclusively with and given press, promotion, and advertising materials to these distributors. However, the picture has not yet been licensed to these distributors.

At the very first distributor contact, when perhaps the producer has not even acquired the picture's literary rights, these distributors have little motivation to tie up the picture's rights. But as the picture becomes more substantive, with a shooting script, director, cast, locations, production design, film and printed promotion materials, representation at the major markets, firm release dates, and novelization and other rights mature, each of these distributors becomes increasingly motivated to secure the picture's license for their territory.

The production financing worksheet becomes an extension of the liquidation breakdown and places on paper the various presale scenarios, allowing the producer to select the most advantageous course. This becomes the basis for the presale plan.

Examine the bank financing worksheet that follows. This worksheet is for a picture with a production budget of $40 million.

Figure 5.1
Bank Financing Worksheet

Description	Amount	Reference
Foreign Presales	$60,000,000	$75 million discounted 20%
License Advance	$6,000,000	10% of the License Amount
Letter of Credit Amount	$54,000,000	
Bank Discount Amount	$5,400,000	10% of Collateral Amount
Loan Value	$48,600,000	Before Interest Reserve
Network Sale	$3,200,000	$4 million Discounted 20%
License Advance	$320,000	10% of the License Amount
Bank Discount Amount	$576,000	20% of Collateral Amount
Loan Value	$2,304,000	Before Interest Reserve
Total Loan Value	$50,904,000	
Interest Reserve	$4,500,000	Projected Loan Interest
Collateral Loan Value	$46,404,000	
Loan Amount	$45,000,000	
Collateral Margin	$1,404,000	

Worksheet for "The Producer's Business Handbook."

The first step determines how much collateral will be needed to release loan funds sufficient for the production budget, plus an additional 10 percent production contingency and a $1 million operating reserve, bringing the total loan proceeds to $45 million.

The foreign presale amount for this plan is $60 million. This is actually $75 million in license value, discounted by 20 percent, yielding $60 million. Foreign presale license terms with the licensee typically call for a 10 percent advance amount to be paid at the time the license is entered into, with the balance guaranteed by a bank letter of credit. The conventional bank discount for letters of credit is 10 percent, reducing the license loan value to $48.6 million.

The network presale amount for this plan is $3.2 million. This is actually a $4 million license value, discounted 20 percent to $3.2 million. Following a 10 percent advance and a customary contract discount of 20 percent, this leaves a loan value of $2.304 million.

The total loan value of these two sources is $50.904 million. This amount is subject to a final reduction for loan interest reserve. If this is a one-year loan (projected delivery of the picture in nine months, allowing a time reserve of three months), and carries an interest rate of 10 percent, the interest reserve is $4.5 million.

After the interest reserve is deducted, this leaves a collateral value of $46.404 million, allowing a collateral margin of $1.404 million in addition to the loan amount.

Types of Loans

If the production loan is in the form of a line of credit, the producer has access to the entire loan amount but is only charged interest on the loan amount actually drawn. Though the interest reserve remains the same, the actual interest charged will be less, and usually substantially so. With $4.5 million in potential interest, even a 10 percent savings (which is very possible with prudent cash management) will save $450,000. Draws for a loan of this size may be in minimum seven-figure increments.

Gap Financing

The more sophisticated bank entertainment divisions accommodate gap financing. This financing is based on licenses that are not yet entered, and on values established by territories that have already licensed the picture being financed.

The producer's advantages to gap financing are primarily that (1) fewer presales are made, allowing higher after-film-completion licenses to be earned from these licensees, and (2) the producer does not have to do the pre-sale work for these territories. Banks participating in gap financing increase their margin of risk. To offset this risk, all remaining foreign rights to the picture being financed are pledged to the bank as collateral for the loan.

The bank uses two sources to evaluate the unlicensed collateral. The first criterion is at least one (and preferably two or more) presale(s) of the picture from among the six leading territories. The other is a foreign sales matrix, often created by each bank using their history of clients' foreign sales. This matrix allows a bank to apply the picture's actual presales to the matrix and then calculate the picture's estimated remaining foreign license value.

For instance, if the presales totaled $20 million and represented one-third of the presale value for the six leading territories, the bank could lend against an additional $40 million in collateral value, as $20 million is one-third of $60 million. This additional $40 million is the gap financing.

When to Approach the Bank

Using bank production funding strengthens many aspects of producer operations. The bank relationship and its other related benefits should become very integrated into and affect many aspects of the producer's business.

New producers should meet with their bank of choice even before financing their first development company. Producers should be comfortable with their banks before there is a need for production borrowing. Initial meetings will introduce the bank to the producer's business plan, establish when the producer intends to develop and produce the first pictures, and clearly show the bank's essential participation in the process. As a producer, you should rehearse your commitment to mature participation in the borrowing process, maximizing the ease of loan application and servicing. Unfortunately, this is uncommon, but it is consequently very well received.

Producers should ask the loan officer for permission to use the bank and the officer as a reference to others relative to the producer's intention to use the bank as the production funding source for pictures. Most bank entertainment divisions are willing to allow producers to do this, as long as their representations are in keeping with the relationship. Using the bank as a reference to potential licensees and other sources in connection with the producer's presale plan lends substantial stability, especially for new producers in new relationships.

Producers should meet with their bank officer about once a month. The bank officer should have the most recent copy of the production company's activity projection (this projection is traditionally for five years, month to month for the first year and annually thereafter).

In addition to production financing and later operating capital funding, bank officers can be well used as business consultants and mentors, contributing excellent business expertise to the production company and opening the way for expanded business relationships.

Summary

Banks are vital businesses, eager to expand their customer bases and lending portfolios. Understanding how they operate prepares producers to approach them with confidence and wonderful predictability.

Banks are producers' powerful allies. In addition to production financing and operating capital, they can provide very helpful foreign and domestic data (useful in many areas, including liquidation breakdowns, foreign evaluations, foreign currency, and global industry trends), as well as other information. Producers should engage their bank relationships early and keep them well exercised; they are vital commercial operating team participants.

Chapter 6

Completion Guarantors

This chapter presents the essential associations producers should have with completion guarantors, and reviews the application process and benefits of an expanded relationship.

A completion guarantee is sometimes referred to as a completion bond and is an essential requirement for bank production financing. As is reviewed in Chapter 12, completion guarantors participate fully when engaged by producers during each picture's development and soon after the first studio greenlights have been obtained, and the picture's literary rights have been acquired.

What Completion Guarantees Do

A picture's completion guarantee ensures the provider bank that the bonded picture will be completed on time and within budget constraints. If it isn't, it assures that the guarantor will pay for the related losses. Consequently, the bank does not evaluate the producer's production schedule and budget but relies on the completion guarantor to assure the credibility of these elements.

Completion guarantors are insurers, and the major bonding companies are owned by large insurance organizations. One of the oldest and most well-known insurers is Film Finance. This company is owned by Lloyd's of London, headquartered in London, but its most active office is in Los Angeles. The major guarantors also have sister production insurance organizations owned by their parent insurance company. The largest production insurer is Entertainment Coalition, a subsidiary of CNA Insurance, which is also headquartered in Los Angeles. Its very professional completion bond company is Cinema Completions International (CCI), which operates from its Los Angeles headquarters.

Motion picture completion guarantors are highly specialized. To assume the risk of production overruns and completion delays, these companies are classically conservative. They insure a picture whose budget is achievable, incorporate margins for the exceptions that will likely occur, and provide an additional overall contingency.

Producers' Perceived and Real Value of Completion Guarantors

The motion picture industry has a uniquely demanding production process. Producers create new products, one at a time. A producer cannot learn about producing a particular movie (even franchise pictures), and then use this experience to produce the same picture again. Every picture is unique in its production chemistry. Production techniques are sometimes similar from picture to picture, but the above-the-line talent (even if they are the same people), combined with the below-the-line crew and production demands, perform in a substantially different manner each time.

Unit Production Managers (UPMs) are responsible for planning and quantifying the physical production process in time and costs.

Balanced producers sustain an often painful balance between each of their picture's creative options and its cost. Producers seek production managers who will plan and budget these pictures in a manner that will fulfill the producer's vision. Consequently, the producers also seek and value UPMs who understand and employ economies that allow more production substance to be delivered at less cost. This is a challenging balance to maintain, with many offsets negotiated and often renegotiated for exceptions throughout development and production.

Because of this tightly woven give-and-take planning, negotiating, and budgeting process, some producers resent their relationships with completion guarantors. It isn't that these producers aren't confident in their work. They take meticulous care to achieve a delicate balance between a picture's production quality and its schedule and budget. It is that the producer's sophisticated work is then independently reviewed by the completion guarantor, whose bonding criteria often upset the picture's fragile economy.

Although tradition has it that the only reason a completion guarantor participates in the production process is to facilitate bank financing—and that is the central purpose—guarantors often are and should be invited to contribute more. Each picture's guarantor can be the second set of careful eyes, confirming that the production team, plan, schedule, and budget are sound and achievable. More often than not, the guarantor's observations and suggestions substantially contribute to their picture's overall success.

The guarantor has a fresh evaluation advantage. Guarantors have no political relationships influencing them, so they evaluate from a new, rather than an evolutionary position. Since they often have substantially deeper production review experience than even their most prolific producer clients, they are more current in their references of primary production and performing talent, as well as global costs.

Guarantors should be included in the producer's determination of each picture's director, principal cast, and even department heads. They must keep current on the personal stability and relative performance capacity of all substantial talent. For those about whom they do not possess internal information, they can obtain it from other reliable sources. There is no cost for this assistance, and it is exceptionally helpful throughout the planning process. The guarantors will eventually evaluate the bondability of primary talent anyway. It is better to take full advantage of their information when the producer is performing this evaluation—information that can save time and money, and often render these decisions substantially more obvious.

Completion Insurance Relationships

For a business focused on numbers and details, completion guarantors are substantially affected by their producer client attitudes, application approach, and relationship care. It is important for producers to sustain a clear understanding of the operational intent of the completion bond participants.

There are three participating parties: the insurer, the bank, and the producer. These parties participate with a common understanding that, for most pictures—no matter what happens—*the picture will not go into default.* This understanding is the single most influential characteristic of the relationship.

When a picture defaults, the guarantor incurs additional expenses and unwanted production stewardship, the bank is open not only to potential loan payoff from sources other than pledged licenses, but also to possible litigation and collection activities. Additionally, the producer must allow the guarantor to assume the governing position in deciding how the picture will be completed and delivered.

Because each participant is substantially motivated to avoid this radical upheaval, completion insurance defaults are rare.

When a picture's schedule or budget or both are threatened, the producers stabilize the problem, if necessary, by revising the collateralized license agreements with new delivery dates, entering and pledging additional presales, if needed, and adjusting the bank loan and completion bond to conform to these changes. This involves sophisticated maneuvering and is made possible by the confidence of all parties in the producer, the picture, and the fairness of their particular participation.

Schedules and budgets that may have appeared to contain egregiously conservative elements prior to production are often embraced as very welcome safety nets during production.

The Completion Bond Package

In qualifying for a bond, the guarantor must become as familiar with the picture and its production as the producer is. The application for a guarantee should reflect the producer's understanding and empathy for this process. The completion bond package should include the following elements:

1. An introductory letter setting forth the picture's title, its total below- and above-the-line budget, its production schedule, the expected guarantee cost, the anticipated U.S. and leading foreign territory distributors, the production financing bank and the loan officer's name, and the approximate date the guarantee is needed.
2. A copy of the shooting script (hard copy and disk).

3. A copy of the budget (hard copy and disk).

4. A copy of the script breakdown (hard copy and disk).

5. A copy of the production boards (hard copy and disk).

6. Copies of the major talent deal memos with attachments.

7. References. (These are the same as in the bank package discussed in Chapter 5.)

To sustain the highest validation integrity, guarantors traditionally prepare their initial planning and budgeting materials exclusively using the shooting script. If their schedules and below-the-line budgets are close to those submitted by the producer, then the producer's budget documentation is reviewed.

If the plans are close, but there are questions, an intermediary meeting with the producer may be set up, or, if it is in keeping with the relationship, with the UPM.

After the review is completed, there is typically a meeting with the producer. At this meeting, the guarantor presents the producer with a provisional acceptance letter. Within or accompanying this letter is a list of items to be resolved to the guarantor's satisfaction before the picture's budget and delivery will be insured. The picture and these provisional items are discussed during this meeting. An acceptance letter is sometimes presented following the guarantor's initial review, but producers should not expect this unless the guarantor has been included in reviewing and responding to questionable issues during the planning and budgeting process.

Some common reasons for provisional letters are:

1. Key talent (director or primary cast) are not bondable. Guarantors are necessarily very sensitive to this production aspect. Key talent can cripple a picture. If they are unstable for any reason, they may not be bondable until they restabilize.

2. Unstable weather conditions. Most often locations are scouted during a different season than the season of principal photography. In fact, when they are lensed out of natural season, producers can turn the leaves green or amber and crimson, but this problem must be listed in the schedule and budget. Then there are the big items that may occur, like the need to shoot in tropical summer when the picture is scheduled during typhoon season. It is difficult to overcome major weather problems.

3. Unstable political or social conditions (insurrection, war, currency problems, and so forth.).

4. Insufficient time or budget contingencies. Always include a full 10 percent budget contingency.

5. Unstable critical talent deal memos or contracts (ability for talent to abandon their commitment for ambiguous reasons, such as benefits or accommodations too sophisticated for the producer's predictable delivery, etc.)

Completion Insurance Cost

Producers typically allow three percent for completion bond expense in their budgets, but usually negotiate less. Producers can suggest bond structures that reduce the insurers risk and increase their volume, which result in some producers paying close to half of what is commonly budgeted.

Completion insurance is competitive, and although new companies regularly enter the game, just as many bow out. The result is few participants, and they must be acceptable to the lending bank.

Like banks, these insurers specialize in pictures with differing budget ranges. Some insure pictures with six- to mid-seven-figure budgets; others with mid-seven to low-eight figures, and the largest companies insure mid-eight- to low-nine-figure budgeted pictures.

Summary

Completion guarantors are essential participants for producers in the production of their pictures. They are sophisticated organizations that reaffirm and often refine a producer's production plan. These organizations are best utilized if invited to participate early, thus facilitating many development and preproduction processes, including talent evaluation, bondability, and banking. When understood and used effectively, completion insurers are welcome production allies who contribute consistently and positively to each picture's production.

Chapter 7

Attorneys, Negotiations, and Entertainment Law

This is an introduction to the relationship producers ought to have with their attorneys and associated firms, how producers should participate in negotiating and documenting, the processes that can limit and protect against litigation, and the very valuable extended benefits available to producers from their attorneys and firms.

Attorneys and Their Firms

There are several excellent entertainment law firms, most of which are head-quartered in New York and Los Angeles. Some of these are large, multi-location, multi-floored firms; some are full-service, one-location firms; and others are specialized, boutique firms. Large firms are not better than small firms or vice versa. The critical factor is the right attorney, in the right firm, who is well matched to the producer's needs.

A producer's attorney should be, and typically is, involved in a producer's creative, business, and legal activities. In other words, the attorney is substantially involved in most aspects of a producer's work.

Seasoned entertainment attorneys bill in the mid-three figures per hour, junior attorneys in the low-three figures. This is not a relationship to be penurious with. A producer's new-contact credibility, capacity to reach every talent and global distributor, and ability to negotiate fair terms and to protect himself are all largely affected by the attorney's industry standing.

It is always best to engage in a relationship with an attorney who has become a well-known presence in the entertainment industry. For the most part, these are the attorneys who have the experience and understanding that renders them valuable as counselors and advisors in all significant business and legal activities. They may also provide exceptional creative counsel. Producers deliver all appropriate matters to their attorney. In turn, their attorney may assign less sophisticated matters to junior attorneys and staff.

Attorneys and the firms they are associated with should be evaluated separately. Simply being represented by a lead entertainment law firm such as Loeb & Loeb (the largest entertainment law firm) has a substantial value. It may not be that the senior level attorney within this firm is the producer's designated attorney, but even a junior attorney will have access to the firm's impressive team of powerful legal icons. Attorneys have access to the full service capacities of their firms, including securities, contract, litigation, and business, as well as creative packaging talent. Additionally, many of these larger firms have offices in global business centers where producers may most need them. Further, producers have an instant sociability (and consequently more direct access) with their firms' substantive clients.

Producers should settle into a relationship with a law firm and an attorney who functions at optimum for their particular needs. There is a balance of benefits that should be obtained. The smaller the firm, the more important the producer's relationship with it. There are several boutique firms with high-profile partners who are powerhouse attorneys to their producer clients. It is not even essential for a producer's firm to be full-service. For instance, if a particular firm does not provide securities work, it may supervise another firm to accomplish this work and fulfill its client's needs in a manner not much different from using another department within a full-service firm.

The following are a producer's most important considerations in evaluating and selecting entertainment law relationships:

1. Does the attorney have a recognizable, positive reputation in the entertainment industry? Does the attorney communicate pleasantly and clearly with the producer? Does the attorney understand the producer's objectives? Is this person committed to supporting the producer in accomplishing these goals?

2. Does the law firm have a recognizable and positive reputation in the entertainment industry? Is it a full-service firm, or are the firm's services able to address the primary needs of the production company?

3. Do the firm's clients have a business sociability that is complementary to the producer's business?

Producers Performing as Attorneys

Producers should never perform the legal aspects of their business without the experience and counsel of their attorney. Having said this, producers should understand that they will be pressed, almost continually, into activities that will demand their knowledge of entertainment law. Further, it is not practical or affordable for producers to have their attorney with them all the time. Consequently, they must obtain a basic understanding of entertainment law to prevent compromising their production company's negotiating power and legal protection. Contract law is the dominant area of law with which producers are most involved. It is no accident that many very powerful producers have either obtained law degrees in preparation for their careers or have hired in-house counsel.

A producer's best legal preparation is a law degree, but even this is not a satisfactory substitute for experience. A producer's first five years should be spent under the tutelage and coaching of his or her attorney. This is expensive only until it is compared with the damages that may occur without the benefit of very involved counsel throughout this time.

Almost everything a producer does has substantial legal consequences. Does this sound paranoid? It isn't. The industry is riddled with stories of overconfident, easygoing producers who were either tossed up like tennis balls and whacked out of the industry, or were severely bludgeoned, both financially and emotionally, before they learned this important lesson: Producers are almost *always* involved in conversations and correspondence about potential relationships. These are contract-related experiences for which producers are particularly held legally accountable. Suits are levied against producers that, to them, may appear to be ridiculous nuisance suits. These suits eventually come to trial through very congested court systems (especially in New York and Los Angeles), one or two years later. Depositions of verbal conversations overheard by people whom the producer may not even recall were present, along with notes on napkins and casual letters the producer didn't consider or intend to be binding, may be used as evidence.

Producers should ask for and keep copies of everything. When asked if they would like a copy, producers should always answer affirmatively, and then file it.

As with most other responsibilities in life, *experience* in legal affairs increases our power to manage them. However, prior to this experience, if an attorney is not deeply involved in the producer's early-career legal affairs, the producer may make multiple, very expensive, wrong moves.

Contract law is especially slippery and powerful until the language is understood. Verbal representations can be binding, and contract law language definitions do not necessarily correspond with dictionary definitions. What a producer says and writes, hears and receives—whether the producer intends for an item to be binding or not—may be used as contract evidence. Further, it may even mean something quite different from what the producer meant to communicate. Producers must become aware of those communications they engage in that are contract relative.

Producers should (1) study all phases of entertainment law, particularly contract law (there are several excellent books on entertainment law), (2) have their attorney present during key negotiations, (3) review with and be coached by their attorney for meetings they may attend without their attorney, (4) immediately report everything potentially litigious to their attorney, (5) have their attorney prepare most deal documentation, and (6) send all other in-house prepared documentation to their attorney for review before it is used.

Negotiating

The only good agreement is one that is fair to all parties. Getting excited about acquiring something for less than its value is a sure sign of impoverished ethics. Everyone is best served when the deal is balanced to the contributions of all participants.

The all-too-common negotiating scenario is played out by participants who often indelicately demand more for their respective position than is fair. These negotiations are fiery, confrontational, and most often end with all parties feeling short-changed and, unhappily, distanced from one another.

Fortunately, this does not always occur. There are producers who refuse to engage in negotiations in this fashion, and they find talent, agents, and attorneys willing participants, though they may initially be understandably suspicious.

It is in the best interests of the producer determined to set the pace toward a gentler path to take hold of this alternative negotiating style and use it. In the final analysis, after production and primary distribution of a picture are concluded, this approach consistently ends up being more financially advantageous than the "me first, you whatever" approach to deal making.

There are three vital principles that should be applied to every negotiation and deal-making relationship that a producer enters into. These principles may be thought of as (1) the universal approach to deal making, (2) the negotiations that are on the same side of the desk, and (3) the decision to weigh a deal in proportion to the scope of the picture.

The "universal approach" requires simply looking at the deal without preference to a single party, aggressively considering what is fair from all parties' points of view and then negotiating to secure the best position for each participant. This approach is often easily derailed by one or more party taking the common car-buying position which starts at a higher position than is fair with a mind to ending the negotiation still above what they should reasonably receive. The relationship poison associated with the car technique is that even if this party ends up with a greater than fair portion, they still may be discontented that they did not get even more.

"Getting on the same side of the desk" is waiting to negotiate until all parties are working for the good of the picture. Putting the picture first naturally allies the participants, all working together for a common objective. This helps motivate the "universal approach," in which all parties clearly see that from the picture's perspective, the producer is not more important than screenwriter, or the screenwriter than the director, etc. This puts the negotiators in position to consider the deal elements in light of what is fair and most beneficial for the particular picture.

The process of "weighing the deal to the picture" can only be accomplished by balanced producers. This is especially helpful when negotiating deals with potential profit participants. The producer uses the picture's liquidation breakdown and budget to reassess a lucrative cash-only deal as a percentage of the producer's gross profit less the picture's budget. This process is typically only done for the most substantial contributors to the picture, namely, the writer, director, and principal acting talent. This analysis tends to cast a very constructive deal-making light on the negotiations. It renders an exceptional deal orientation when participants confidentially review and thoroughly understand these numbers and relate them to their own position. For instance, if a picture has a projected, after negative recoupment, a producer's gross of $30 million, and the cash-only directors fee is $3 million, this percentage "weight" is 10 percent. The participating point application should not be proportional to the fee amount, as there are risks and time-related-to-point income. With this ratio as a reference, this example could yield the director a $2 million fee plus five points. If the picture achieves its projections, this agreement will provide the director with another $500,000, compared with the fee-only relationship—that along with long-term earnings from the picture's continuing rights sales. The plus-points terms also deepen the director's relationship with the picture, naturally motivating the director to make the greatest contribution possible in creating the film.

Using this approach to deal making strengthens each individual relationship and establishes a universal integrity among all participants. No one believes another talent cut a better deal because they negotiated more shrewdly. Rather, there is a spirit of fair play and common good. Perhaps the audience won't recognize the source, and this is never the sole reason for a picture's success, but this has a substantial resonant effect on all participants, the work they do, the level of sanity sustained, and consequently, on the picture itself.

How is this achieved? The producer is largely responsible for setting the tone of every relationship. When producers focus first on the picture along with the universal application of the fairness of the deal to all parties, they always influence all other parties associated with the deal. If they haven't dealt with the producer before, agents, attorneys, and business managers may initially be suspicious of this approach. However, it is my experience that engaging these principles has an exceptionally positive effect on establishing solid relationship foundations and arriving at deal parameters that are of high integrity and as close as possible to being unshakable.

Vital Legal Aspects Relating to the Story

A producer's first and continuing stewardship is to discover stories worth telling in the motion picture media; then to evaluate, acquire, develop, produce, and liquidate them. Literary rights searches, property reviews, negotiations, acquisitions, and rewrites are a roiling pot of potential litigation!

Literary Releases

Writing is the genius art. Skilled writers may complete five finished screenplay pages a day. For them, a screenplay may represent several weeks of research and five to eight weeks of writing. If this is a "spec" script, it may represent three to six months of work. Such a literary property is potentially worth six or seven figures. The screenplay is the writer's most valuable asset and must be protected.

The protection issues relating to stories appear much different from a producer's perspective. A producer's literary department may review an average of thirty property submissions per week. These come in a variety of forms and typically from a variety of sources. A story department may have two very similar stories come through on the same day, from completely unrelated sources. Topical stories may even have several similar submissions during the same month.

Unfortunately, most stories fall into one of the following three categories, from most to least prevalent: (1) stories that are poorly written and not worth being told, (2) stories that are well written but not worth being told, and (3) stories worth being told that are not well written. The third category are the stories most often optioned and put into story development.

There are substantial treasuries set apart for the acquisition of the sort of literary properties that most production companies are looking for. Stories that are worth being told, are well written, appeal to at least one major target audience, and that contain driving campaign elements are those most valued.

Studios and successful production companies are excellent negotiators for literary rights. They are well funded and often prepared to spend more than a fair amount to purchase the all-too-rare great properties. They have every motivation to acquire material from writers—yes, especially first time writers—employing ethical and respectful business practices. They do not and will not steal stories. In the unfortunate and rare instances when individuals working for these companies are found abusing the creative trust and operating policies of these organizations, they are immediately released.

Most writers find it difficult to empathize with the producer's liability position associated with reviewing such a sea of properties. Indeed, many of these scripts are not read past the fourth or fifth page.

Before submitting their material, writers protect themselves by a variety of means, only to be presented with a literary release letter before studios and producers will accept their material or pitch. These letters substantially limit the writer's legal recourse against the producer and, in their various versions, the writer releases the reviewing producer from legal liability, under certain conditions, and from using "material containing features similar to or identical with those contained in" the material submitted by the writer.

Some writers complain that this gives producers license to steal their material. In fact these letters substantially limit the legal recourse of the writer. But without literary release letters, producers would be subject to relentless litigation.

A copy of a sample literary release letter is at the end of this chapter, as well as on the CD accompanying this book. After a review, it should be abundantly clear why writers may be reluctant to sign. However, considering the high volume of story material reviewed by producers, the similarity between many of these stories and the predominance of rejections, it becomes clear that producers must adhere to this fundamental legal process for their own protection.

The Step Deal

Writing is a very delicate craft. Consider this scenario. Writer "A" recently won the Best Screenplay Academy Award for a romantic comedy script. A producer has had a promising meeting with this writer to creatively perform a major rewrite of a romantic comedy script optioned by the producer. A relationship is negotiated satisfactory to all parties, is documented, and the writer commences. The producer is enthusiastic to see the script. The writing proceeds on schedule. Two months pass, and the producer receives the first draft. The producer rated the writer's previous Academy Award winning script a 9 out of 10. The producer rates this first draft as a 4 out of 10. The producer and writer have a tense but seemingly productive story meeting. The producer is convinced that the writer now embraces the fire of the story the producer wants to tell. Three weeks later the new property has been substantially rewritten, but it is no closer than the original draft to what the producer envisions. Two more increasingly tense meetings take place, each without an improved draft. The drafts are different but not any better in the producer's eyes. After three drafts, everyone is testy and uneasy. The writer has worked diligently, probably employing the maximum craft possible on this story. The producer realizes that this writer will never write the story needed. Sadly for the producer, next year, this same writer will author another romantic comedy script that, in the producer's evaluation, will be a 10 out of 10.

I have seen this happen many times. With some stories, exceptional writers may not be able to exercise their considerable craft to the producer's satisfaction. This rarely has to do with the writer's effort and diligence; rather, it is often simply that the writer and story do not connect. Although this may not happen even half the time, it happens enough for producers to approach relationships with writers in a fashion that facilitates the best experience possible.

In the preceding example, the writer and producer entered into their relationship with good intentions, but now a new writer must be engaged, and fees, writing credits, and other deal points must be renegotiated to accommodate the new relationship. This forces the restructuring of the development schedule. Because of the additional development time and writing fees, development and production budgets increase. Further, the original writer renegotiation is typically uncomfortable, and because the writing budget was not configured to accommodate two writers, the new writer negotiation is often entered with less advance cash than the original development plan.

Because of this common phenomenon, producers protect themselves from these time and legal exigencies through entering "step relationships" with writers. Step relationships compartmentalize the writing processes into progressive steps. Each step has a fixed fee value and provides for evaluation and complete pre-agreed-upon exit remedies which allow the producer to be able to terminate the relationship following the review of each initial step.

Following positive creative meetings, perhaps three writers will enter individual step relationships and independently begin writing. It is essential to the integrity of the relationship that the writers know that multiple writers are being used.

The agreement's first "step" typically calls for the writers to author a synopsis of the story. Whether or not their synopsis is acceptable to the producer, the writers are all paid for their work. If a synopsis is not accepted from one writer, that writer does not proceed. Depending on the terms of the step deal, that writer may not receive any writing credit.

The writers whose synopses are accepted then author a comprehensive treatment of the story. It is possible that all the writers will proceed with this step. Again, the writers are paid for their treatments, regardless of their acceptance. If particular drafts are not acceptable, a writer may not proceed and may not receive any writing credits in the film.

Typically, following the treatment, there is a single writer selected to continue with the final relationship step and write the screenplay. If there are characters, a subordinate story line, dialogue, or other elements the producer wants continued to be developed by one of the other writers for eventual use in the screenplay, there may be a good-faith negotiation with that originating writer to become a co-writer along with the primary writer of the screenplay.

Producers should always do their best to enter step writing deals, even if it is with a single author. This relationship allows for reevaluation at each step and prevents costly renegotiations. This does not imply lack of confidence in the author. It clearly indicates the producer's seasoned understanding of the delicate fundamentals of the writing craft and the preparations necessary to manage this relationship propitiously.

Multiple-author step writing deals are always initially more expensive than single-author relationships. But they may actually cost less in the long run, especially if the original single-author relationship does not succeed.

If there is one place a producer should risk overspending, it is on the story. Producers are best served by a multiple-writer step agreement approach to screenplay development. This prevents the high probability of being pushed off schedule and over budget, and assures that the writers will have crafted the ultimate story.

Literary Greenlight Review

After producers discover literary properties they are interested in, they proceed through a development phase before they are prepared to option or acquire it. This period is called the producer's "internal greenlight" of each project. (See Chapters 1 and 12.)

Prior to outside participation in the analysis of the story of a proposed picture, producers should receive written permission from the story's author before they refer to the story in any way to anyone outside the producer's organization.

A simple deal memo should be prepared. This letter should express the producer's interest in the property and willingness to invest in a creative and marketing review to discover the viability of the producer's eventual acquisition of the story. The letter should state that the producer is prepared to proceed with this investment pending the writer's approval. In this memo, the producer warrants that the approach to creating a motion picture from the writer's story and its title may be confidentially discussed with a limited number of commercial partners relative to their interest in the eventual distribution of the proposed picture. The producer further warrants that representations will be clearly made that the story rights have not yet been optioned or acquired by the producer, that this is exclusively an evaluation inquiry, and that these meetings will not at all be related to the financing of the picture or the acquisition of the property. The producer acknowledges that this nonexclusive evaluation will not continue longer than a set time (for instance, five months) and may be terminated within 24 hours of the writer's written request to the producer, for any reason.

This deal memo protects the writer and producer from misunderstandings and clearly sets forth the speculative, arm's-length nature of the relationship. It serves as well to warm the writer and agent to the producer's serious interest in the property.

Literary Rights Option/Acquisition

After a picture has obtained the critical in-house greenlight, the first development move is to acquire the rights to the literary property.

If a literary review memo is in force, an initial rapport will already have been established among the producer, the writer, the agent, and/or the attorney.

Mature production companies have internal development funds, allowing them to negotiate and acquire or option properties in a more unregulated fashion than new producers, who may be using development funds from investors for a fixed number of pictures. Whichever is the case, the producer's best approach to deal-making is to reveal the production company's position to the writer and/or the agent.

The picture will already have a summarized budget, prepared during the internal greenlight. This budget's story allocation should represent the producer's estimation of a fair acquisition price for the property. This should be affected by how closely the property being acquired resembles the actual shooting script of the picture. The majority of scripts purchased represent little more than a compelling story concept. Many writers are excellent imagineers but not very skilled screenwriters. A separate, detailed story budget, which reflects a conservative and predictable activity and expense schedule for taking the acquired story to a shooting script, should be prepared. These projections should be the centerpiece of the acquisition agreement.

There are two budgets typically at play in this process. The development budget has a fixed elasticity for the option advance. The production budget has a more flexible capacity for the actual acquisition payment(s).

The genesis writer may participate in a step writing arrangement with other writers—the difference being that the genesis writer will have continuing benefits which will not be offered to the other step-deal writers.

Each writer will need payment allocations relative to his or her option/development payments and balance/production payments. The producer has development funding sufficient to pay for option advances and will have substantially more funding through production financing to pay the balance.

The originating writer, together with all other participants, benefits the most upon the picture's successful development. This results, in everyone's principal photography payday, in the picture's successful production and in everyone's creative satisfaction, fame, and increased value of their craft.

Achieving a successful greenlight is no small feat. Producers should move into the literary rights negotiation with a clear understanding of the creative and global earnings potential of the pictures. They should be further motivated by the fact that their distributors are looking for positive reassurance that their pictures are in active development. Producers want, of course, to realize benefits from the initial development time and money invested. However, first time producers are subject to the check and balance realities of fixed development budgets.

The success of most negotiations are dependent upon these crucial elements:

1. The strength of the story. The stronger the story, the more easily the negotiations go;
2. The flexibility of development and production budgets. If development funds are exceptionally tight, production payouts should more than proportionally increase to offset the front-end shortfall;

3. The strength of the producer and other creative players. Everyone wants to play on a winning team. A strong story, along with a powerful director and/or producer, will have a drawing effect on all other elements;

4. The initial global enthusiasm for the picture. The findings of the in-house greenlight should be shared with all primary participants. The stronger this evidence, the greater will be each player's enthusiasm;

5. The willingness of the negotiating parties to be flexible between the deal points. Everything should equal out. Deal points, for any number of reasons, are rigid. If this creates an unfair position for a participant, then other deal points should be added or increased. If all parties are determined to move the pieces until they are fair and acceptable to each participant, then the deal gets made.

The option agreement includes all the acquisition deal points and all the specifics pertaining to reoptioning the property. This allows the relationship for future good-faith negotiations to proceed without hesitation.

Typically, producers deal with literary agents in the negotiation and acquisition of properties. First-sale screenwriters who are not represented by an agent are especially vulnerable during the deal-making process. Therefore, such relationships are always best served if the producer acts as a protector and tutor and even overcompensates to offset the writer's susceptible position. First-sale screenwriters may have a script similar in creative value to that of a more experienced writer, but since they are new to the bargaining table, they may be paid less for their property. Nevertheless, they should receive a full measure of all the benefits they are due.

Deal Memos, Letter Agreements, and Long Form Contracts _____

Of the three forms of deal documentation, deal memos are by far the most prevalent form used for most of the producer's relationships. In fact, many relationships never require documentation beyond the original deal memo. Often longer, more formal documents are in the process of being negotiated, but negotiations become protracted, pictures get completed, and finally, it is the deal memo that remains the only document defining the relationship. The notable exceptions are most U.S. distribution and license agreements, which are typically done in the long form.

Deal Memos

Deal memos are the workhorse deal documents of the entertainment industry. These typically come in letter form, originating on the producer's letterhead and containing the following information:

1. Identification of the parties involved in the deal.
2. What each party is specifically contributing to the relationship.
3. What they get for their contributions.
4. Anything else relating to the basic understanding of the parties.
5. Any specific representations from the parties, examples being "I am the sole, original author," or "There are no liens or encumbrances."
6. The county and state of legal jurisdiction.
7. How disputes will be settled.

8. When the deal will be in force.

9. A place for the parties to acknowledge by signature that the deal is acceptable to them, along with a signature date.

Although deal memos often contain some casual letter language, they are very enforceable contracts and are contract-language structured.

Letter Agreements

These agreements are more formalized than deal memos. They are also prepared on the producer's letterhead and are in letter form, but they use more formal contract language, though in a more relaxed format than long-form contracts. These agreements typically use contract titles (Bruce Joel Rubin, herein "Writer"), and contain limited casual letter remarks. The nine contract elements referenced in the above deal memo are included in the letter agreement, but in more formal contract language.

Long Form Agreements

These agreements are printed on neutral-party blank white paper. They use an agreement title at the beginning and are written to equally express the position of all participants. These documents are in full agreement dress and use formal contract language. They are long, often impressive by their sheer weight, and, frankly, many times the girth is extremely helpful when troubles arise.

The Benefits Associated with the Producer Preparing Deal Documentation

Among deal-making parties, the producer is usually best served by volunteering to prepare the deal documentation. Whether the producer actually prepares it or the producer's attorney does is not the point. The point is that this allows the producer the opportunity to establish the deal-making integrity between the parties, to understand the universe of the deal's architecture by being its originator, and to sustain continuity between as much of each picture's documentation as possible.

Producers should never succumb to the temptation of allowing someone else to prepare the documentation on the basis that it would be one less thing they need to do, or that it may save their legal fees. The document origination benefits far outweigh any other considerations.

Deal Reviews

One of the best ways for producers to learn contract language and to interpret all forms of deal documentation is for them to review the documentation before they meet with their attorneys.

One of the most efficient review techniques is called "line-outs." This may seem tedious, but the producer should take three sheets of paper and the contract, then head one paper "us," another sheet "them" (if there are more parties, use more sheets), and the final sheet "questions."

Starting with the first line of the agreement, the producer should check to see if the production company name appears first and is correct. If so, he should draw a line through it. If it says, "herein producer," he should write "producer" at the top of the "us" sheet and then cross the "us" phrase out. If the other party's name is next and it is the same as what he thought it was, he should cross it out and proceed to their "herein" reference. The producer then writes it at the top of their page and then crosses it out on the agreement.

The producer should continue with the entire agreement, writing down each deal point on the sheet that applies to him and likewise on their sheet when it applies to them. Language that has a unique "contract" sense about it (for instance, "not unreasonably withheld," "best efforts," or "favored nations") should, if it is unfamiliar to him, be put down on his "questions" page, circled in the agreement and put on a page with a paragraph reference next to where he wrote it.

When the producer has completed the entire agreement, he should review each page. If there are elements expressed for his part or the other parties' part that appear out of harmony with the agreement as he understands it, he then should make notes of these. It is at this point that the producer is ready to meet with his attorney, ask his questions, review his concerns, and listen to his counselor's instruction and advice.

This process of line-outs usually goes very quickly and will reveal everything important to know about the deals in process. Remember, there are no unimportant phrases or words. Producers should find out what they mean. They may be benefits or pitfalls important to the deal.

The Attorney as Counsel

Some time ago I had a preliminary relationship closed between a producer client and a distributor for an animated feature. The deal was warmly received by both parties, and a pre-contract closing meeting was arranged. The attorneys substantially took over the meeting, and, within a half day, had all but ruined the good feelings between the parties. At that point, documenting the deal appeared improbable.

One of the attending producers was an amazingly creative writer and animator. He slipped me a sketch. It was a picture of a cow. We were pulling its horns, the distributors pulling at its tail, and the two attorneys were underneath the cow, milking.

This is a bit unfair, as the attorneys for both sides were doing their aggressive best to achieve the finest deal and the greatest protection for their respective clients. However, the picture serves as an excellent reminder that although it is important for the actual parties of agreements to allow their attorneys to make their contributions, those parties should continue to sustain control and responsibility for their relationships and transactions.

Attorneys are often the voice of their producer clients. Consequently, it is always appropriate for producers to apologize to other deal participants if their attorneys say something damaging to those with whom they are dealing. Producers should be careful to treat their attorneys with respect, especially in front of others. If producers want to redirect a meeting, it is most appropriate for producers to stop the meeting, take a break with their counsel, and then reconvene, moving in the direction they have decided, in light of their attorney's advice.

Dispute Resolutions

Every form of documentation should declare how disputes should be resolved, if they arise. The primary choices are either mediation, arbitration, or litigation.

If the document simply states that it will be governed according to the laws of a certain state, then disputes will be settled by traditional litigation. In major metropolitan areas, because these matters will not be heard for months, this could be very expensive to resolve and the outcome determined by judgments of fact, legal points and case precedents that may be substantially disassociated with what is a fair resolution by either party's evaluation.

Either of the other two options, arbitration or mediation, referred to by the court systems as ADR (Alternative Dispute Resolution) are preferred by most producers.

The more formalistic of the two ADR methods is arbitration. This process calls for a mutually agreed upon or appointed arbiter (or arbiters) to hear the case, much like a judge who makes a determination that the parties have agreed in advance they will adhere to.

Perhaps the most effective and exercised entertainment industry arbitration organization is The American Film Marketing Association's Arbitration Tribunal, which serves the entire film industry and is mostly serviced by attorneys or retired judges.

For many disputes, the best resolution is mediation. A mediator is like an arbiter, except a mediator explores the issues. There is only a resolution if both sides agree to a suggested proposal. Mediated cases differ most substantially from litigation and arbitration in that there are no winners or losers. Both sides participate in the solution. Both must agree, and the solution often improves the relationship between the parties or at least provides for a future one. Though some become protracted, most mediated issues are settled in one day.

Summary

The development, production, and liquidation of motion pictures engages the producer continually in the process of representations, negotiations, and documentation. The producer's attorney should be thoroughly involved in the producer's business. Consequently the selection and use of an attorney and law firm are critical factors in the producer's success and protection. Further, the producer should be deeply involved and increasingly experienced in all manner of legal matters.

Date:_____   Proposed Title (if any) of Material
                                  Submitted:_____
                                  _____

Your Production Company Name
Your Address
Address

RE: Literary Release

Gentlepersons:

I am on this date submitting for possible use by you, my enclosed material (hereafter called the "Material"), with the understanding, and subject to the conditions, set forth in this letter. I acknowledge that the Material was created and written by me without any suggestion or request from you that I write or create the Material. I have enclosed a copy of the Material, a synopsis thereof, or a complete description of such Material, if in film or tape form. I am executing and submitting this letter in consideration of your agreement to review the Material with the express understanding that I limit my claim of rights to the features of the Material as specifically synopsized or as enclosed.

1. Except as otherwise specifically stated in this letter, I represent that:

   a. the Material is original with me;

   b. I have the exclusive right to grant all rights in the Material; and

   c. I have exclusive rights in the title, with regard to its use in any connection with the Material.

2. You agree that you will not use the Material as the basis for a motion picture or television program unless you first negotiate with me compensation for such use; but I understand and agree that your use of material containing features or elements similar to or identical with those contained in the Material shall not obligate you to negotiate with me or entitle me to any compensation, if you determine that you have an independent legal right to use such other material which is not derived from me (either because such features or elements were not new or novel, or were not originated by me, or because another person, including your employees, has submitted or may hereafter submit material containing similar or identical features or elements). Without limiting the foregoing, it is understood that any part of the Material which could be freely used by a member of the public may be used by you without liability to me.

3. I agree that I must give you written notice by certified or registered mail at your address set forth above of any claim arising in connection with any alleged use by you of said Material or arising in connection with this agreement, within the period of time prescribed by the applicable statute of limitations, but in no event more than ninety (90) calendar days after I acquire knowledge of such Claim, or if it be sooner, within ninety (90) calendar days after I acquire knowledge of facts sufficient to put me on

notice of any such Claim, as an express condition precedent to the initiation of any action hereunder. My failure to give you written notice will be deemed an irrevocable waiver of any rights I might otherwise have with respect to such Claim. I shall further withhold commencing any arbitration proceeding, as specified below, for a period of thirty (30) days after said written notice to allow you time to investigate any Claim. If you and I are unable to dispose of any Claim within such thirty (30) day period, the Claim shall be submitted to arbitration in LA, California before an arbiter mutually selected by us who is experienced in the field with respect to the use of materials similar to the Material; or, if we cannot mutually agree, then such arbiter shall be selected in accordance with the Commercial Arbitration Rules of the American Arbitration Association. The arbitration shall be controlled by the terms of this agreement, and any award favorable to me shall be limited to the fixing of compensation for your use of the Material, which shall bear a reasonable relation to compensation normally paid by you for similar material. Such award will provide for you and me, each respectively, to bear our own costs of arbitration and attorneys fees and the award will be final and binding on each of us and our successors and representatives.

4. I have retained a copy of said Material, and I release you from any liability for loss or other damage to the copy or copies submitted by me. Except as otherwise provided in this agreement, I hereby release you of and from any and all claims, demands and liabilities of every kind whatsoever, known or unknown, that may arise in relation to the Material or by reason of any claim now or hereafter made that you have used or appropriated the Material.

5. I hereby state that I have read and understand this agreement; that no oral representations of any kind have been made to me; that there are no prior or contemporaneous oral agreements in effect between us pertaining to said Material; that this agreement states our entire understanding; and that this agreement may be amended only by an instrument in writing signed by all parties. You may freely assign your rights under this agreement. Any provision of this agreement which is void or unenforceable shall be deemed omitted, and this agreement with such provision or part thereof omitted shall remain in full force and effect. This agreement shall at all times be construed so as to carry out the purposes stated herein.

Yours very truly,

Name: _____
      (Signature)

Name: _____

Address:_____

_____

Telephone: _____

Talent, Agents, and Agencies

This chapter reviews the delicate business aspects associated with producers' relationships with each picture's talent and their representatives.

Two effective metaphors for the relationship between a picture's producer and its talent are the relationships that exist between a general contractor of a construction project and the crafts-people, or a symphony's conductor and the orchestra.

Like a general contractor, the best producers are very familiar with, and consequently respectful of, the many talents necessary to create their pictures. The talent will have all, if not more, of the creative juice that these producers originally conceive. Writers, directors, cinematographers, actors, composers, set designers, UPMs, editors, ADs, costumers, make-up, casting directors, TRANSPORTATION (on my computer this always prints in capital letters), special effects, and many other critically important people contribute to their measure of brilliance to each picture.

Each of these talents is like a subcontractor in many respects. They maintain independent relationships with the producer—each responsible for performing according to the terms of the relationship—and contribute a crucial service that affects the rest of the picture.

Further, just as a building project would be hurt if the general contractor personally handled the plumbing, electrical, or some other building aspect, so would producers hurt their film project if they didn't delegate their producing responsibilities, such as directing, acting, or editing, to others.

The producer/talent relationship is also like an orchestra whose performers must be sensitive to each other in addition to the conductor. At certain moments, the brass section has to sound like one overwhelming instrument, not the trumpet section sounding distinct from the baritones or the French horns from the trombones. Brilliance, if it is out of harmony with other creative elements, fails miserably. A stunning set design that is incongruous with its story's action, costumes, and color, is counterproductive to the picture. The producer, like the conductor, must balance all the many elements of the picture in order to create the finest achievable product. Even during principal photography, though all eyes must be on the director, the director is also a talent who was brought into the picture by the holder of the ultimate baton, the independent producer. As with a symphonic performance, the producer must also have the attention, commitment, and loyalty of all the talent.

Great motion pictures are created by a team of artists who contribute their private interpretation, within the story universe and parameters provided by the producer and are harmonically tempered by all other immediate craft providers. For a producer to engage such a team of talent may seem improbable. Doing it well consistently, under the inevitable pressure that accompanies every picture's creation, is a clear indication of seasoned genius. Steady-handed veteran producers like Richard Donner, Sydney Pollack, and Ron Howard consistently select, inspire, and negotiate great talent teams for their pictures. These producers commence from a foundation of respecting their co-creators and treating them fairly, which naturally draws the best from them.

Creation in its most celebrated form is both intimate and delicate. Losing oneself in the work and celebrating in the personal and collective triumphs is largely possible because of the temper and tenor of the producer. The producer establishes the universe in which everyone works. When producers are committed, skillful, valiant, wise, grateful, patient, merciful, generous, and capable of being a good friend, then the wrenching, chaotic frenzy that seems to necessarily settle in on the creation of motion pictures can actually be sweet when it is thought back upon.

This chapter focuses on the business aspects of the fragile and crucial task producers undertake to engage talent relationships that stir their enthusiasm for the story, give them the creative freedom to perform, and motivate them both creatively and financially to give the ultimate expression of the story's entertainment fire.

The Relationship Evolution

Since writers were discussed in Chapter 7, this chapter will consider other talent relationships, especially those involving directors and principal actors.

Director and principal cast selection usually commences before the conclusion of the first story read. This search intensifies during the internal greenlight, becoming more informed as studio responses are discussed during the first picture meetings with them. After the literary rights have been acquired, it then becomes a keenly focused, studied experience. At this time, prior pictures of prospective talent are screened and studied in context of the picture in development, and discussions with the producers concerning these referenced pictures become important sources of information.

Directors, then actors, are listed in the order of the producer's preference. This is done prior to global distributor director meetings, and in the next round, distributor actor meetings. It is uncommon for these studios to unanimously agree on the producer's choices of directors or actors. The two primary purposes of these talent-studio meetings are to inform the producer relative to the marketing and relationship advantages that each person being considered could bring to each major territory, and to advance each distributor's commitment through each one's participation in the selection process. During these meetings, the producer's discoveries are presented to the studios—sometimes with video clips—demonstrating the craft and various advantages of each talent.

Following these meetings, the producer reevaluates the talent in the light of the distributors' responses and configures the final producer talent list. This list is confidentially presented to them, detailing the factors that moved the producer to this configuration. Producers should have five or more selections on their acting and directing lists. More often than not, the producer's first choices end up being the top three selections of each of the participating distributors.

Meetings with Talent and Agents

Agents deliver many essential benefits to their talent clients. Among them are negotiating and documenting fair deals and assisting their clients in both the search and evaluation of pictures that will advance their careers.

Creative protectionist producers are classically undercapitalized. One of the consequences of this chronic condition is their aggressive attempts to attach talent to their pictures without the agents' participation, or to represent that talent are attached before the producer, in fact, has a documented relationship. These pre-deal attachments are most often used to assist these producers in their attempt to obtain production funding for their pictures.

There are many more creative protectionist producers than balanced producers. Consequently, many creative meetings are setups for clients who become entangled in a litany of abuses associated with stories that are usually never made into motion pictures. Agents have, therefore, become fierce guardians of their clients against the several easy abuses associated with this approach. As a consequence, agents save their clients from misrepresentation and having to defend associated legal actions.

Because balanced producers have both development funding and use bank production financing, they have no motivation to set up pre-deal talent representations. However, they are substantially motivated by other benefits to set up talent creative meetings before deal meetings.

Because each motion picture is a new story, a unique creation and a new business venture, its producers must assemble a new team of co-creators to deliver their independent and harmonic blend of craft and capacity. Therefore, producers need to test each major talent's creative affinity for the picture before negotiating the financial aspects of the relationship. Producers want to know, in strict confidence, whether a particular director or actor has both the vision and passion essential for a critically important creative contribution for the picture in question. So it is during this process that the producer and talent must "fall in love" around a picture. It's comparatively easy to agree on a convenient schedule and monetary amounts, but, if this is the primary basis for the relationship, it yields a thin, incomplete foundation among the picture, the talent, and the producer.

Most producer/talent creative meetings are delicate, especially if they are a first-time alliance. Fortunately these meetings are often accomplished with the cooperation and blessing of their respective agents. If not, producers should be prepared for a well deserved, testy agent response.

If, for any reason, there is a meeting with talent before an agent is called to participate, the producer should immediately assure the talent and agent in writing that: (1) no representation will be made to anyone outside the production company that the talent has been contacted regarding the picture, or that any relationship exists between the talent and the picture, the producer, or the production company; (2) the producer will not talk with the talent about money or other deal points without their agent's participation; and (3) should there be future discussions about the picture, these will be accomplished with the agent's participation.

If such a meeting takes place, most agents will not be placated by this letter or any form of repentance on the part of the producer. It is always best to take creative meetings prior to business meetings with the knowledge and participation of the talent's agent.

The purpose of the creative meeting is to obtain the most essential element in the producer's evaluation: how the talent feels about and envisions the story. Beyond reviewing their preceding pictures and discussions with prior producers, it is in these creative meetings that producers can receive a clear revelation of a picture's director and lead cast.

Once these creative meetings are finished, the producer then prepares to negotiate the deal.

Attorneys as Agents

Talent with brand-significant names may use their attorneys in negotiations along with their agents. Other major talent may only use their agents, and still others only their attorneys. Just as agents become very expert in the legal aspects of deal making, so do some attorneys develop an affinity for the creative aspects of these negotiations. And, for some talent, their attorney may be their agent.

Planning the Deal

When planning the proposed talent deal structure, it is best for producers to create the production deal first, then the development deal. The producer first discovers what may be a fair fee for the performer's services, keeping in mind the talent's current value, in context with the picture's projected gross, its budget, and the services demanded of the talent. The talent's fee, then, should be within the bounds of the production budget, or that talent should not have been considered in the first place.

Development Negotiation

It is essential that the production deal is agreed upon first, including (1) the schedule, (2) the payment amount (including points), (3) the talent's credits, and (4) all other associated benefits. Once the production deal is agreed upon, the stage is then set for development negotiations. The production relationship will not commence until after the motion picture has been completely developed.

The deal's development period typically will last somewhere between 6 and 12 months. Producers should add a contingency period to the actual development schedule to provide for unforeseen scheduling and other unexpected issues.

The development negotiation is really a deal within a deal, since the basis of this agreement rests on the production deal points. These deal points include: how long the development period will be; if there are to be renewals (and if there are, how long and how much these will be); if this is an exclusive or nonexclusive deal, which, if it is exclusive, actually will bind the talent to a specific performing schedule.

If the deal is nonexclusive and has an unspecified start date, then it will have a significantly lower development fee value, since it does not interfere with other talent relationships. Nonexclusive development deals are much easier to negotiate and have lower up-front fees; however, they can be very challenging in terms of schedule coordination as the development of the picture matures.

If the producer binds the talent to a set performance schedule, the producer should assume that during the picture's development, the talent will turn down other offers that conflict with the agreed-upon schedule. Consequently, the producer should include a fair "pay-or-play" payment guarantee, which ensures that the talent will be paid, regardless of whether or not the talent actually performs the production services.

Advance fees cover two general categories, the expenses incurred by the talent and representatives to investigate and negotiate the deal, and talent compensation for the value the producer receives in attaching the talent to the picture.

Development fees typically begin at 1 percent of the production performance fee and are often much higher than this. For example, if a director's production fee is $3 million, the corresponding development fee would be at least $30,000. Most directors and writers also provide services in a picture's continuing development and should be paid fees commensurate with their services.

Mature production companies typically have generous financial elasticity to match the demands of their deals. In contrast, newer production companies may be limited to rigid development budgets. In every case, though, talent should receive fair value for their participation. Even producers with budgetary restraints have the option to entice their talent with additional profit participation. The critical producer objective in these negotiations is not to end up with the maximum points or dollars, but to attach the ultimate team who feel appreciated, well treated, and confident in their relationships.

Points Participation

It is an advantage to the picture to have the director and principal cast participate in the profits of the picture. Nothing can take the place of the talent commitment and enthusiasm that comes with being a central participant in the telling of a great story. However, it always makes a difference, sometimes substantially so, when a producer adds the relationship-deepening qualities of profits participation in the form of points in a picture. This is no clever ploy, just good business.

Because points are most often represented by percentage, the producer should calculate the projected value of these points in dollars by applying the points percentage to the liquidation breakdown of the "producer's gross profit." This renders a critical point of reference for the producer, especially when evaluating a talent's offer. If this valuation is represented to others, it should always be given with the explanation that these are projected figures and cannot be guaranteed.

Definitions of long-form contract participation are typically several pages long. The sophisticated nature of these definitions renders some net participations greater than gross participations. The fairest point definition producers should make with their talent is for the talent to participate in the producer's actual gross profits. This is all the money that the producer earns from a particular picture before any of the producer's overhead is deducted. This is the amount that should be participated in by talent who have points in the picture.

Producers may finance in-house individuals or organizations who will directly license some of their pictures' rights. If they would have used a distributor to license these rights, that distributor would have deducted a distribution fee. It is therefore fair for the producer to apply such distribution fees and actual out-of-pocket direct distribution expenses before the talent profit participation. Regardless of the producer's sales ability, this fee should be the lowest commonly applied by industry independent distributors. The fairest deal is the one in which all the parties participate at the same level.

Preparation of a Fair Deal

Like Napoleon, prosperous producers owe much of their success in every area to studied tent work. Before talent and their representatives are approached, producers should become thoroughly familiar with all of the important aspects of each of the players under consideration. They should clearly measure the deal points and ensure they're in balance with the unique contributions of the talent, the demands of the picture, and its budget.

All the producers' research, analysis, and presentation preparation combine to assure them of the ultimate creative team attachment. In addition, it serves to reassure the talent and their representatives that they are appreciated, appropriately valued by the producer, are receiving a fair deal, and are beginning a relationship that is well planned and as unshakable as motion picture production and distribution can be. The beginning of this relationship should be reaffirmed in the producer's documentation and deal performance.

Agents as Creative Resources

For producers, agents and talent attorneys can be exceptional creative resources for talent, both inside and outside their agencies and firms. In seeking to make allies of these important resources, producers will find their studied approach will yield them easier negotiations, fairer deals and pictures with talent who are more content to deliver their maximum creative capacities. This approach will also avoid difficult negotiating deadlocks and development delays.

Talent Reserve

Producers should begin their first-choice talent negotiations having their secondary talent offers completely prepared and ready to go. Having done this, producers create at least two advantages for themselves: they won't be negatively influenced in the negotiations because they rely exclusively on a single talent; and if the need arises, the producers are prepared to segue into a secondary talent approach without loss of time. It often seems like the secondary choice would be a distant second. But this is not necessarily so, particularly when one looks at the long list of distant seconds—more than a half dozen of whom have been, in retrospect this past year, absolute genius selections—in comparison to the producer's first choice.

The Participation of the Producer's Attorney

Following the preparation of a talent proposal, producers should present a written summary of the deal proposal to their attorneys for review and comments. For even the most experienced producers, these reviews are often very beneficial.

Further, new or obscure producers often benefit by allowing their attorney to make the initial talent/agent contact. First impressions are important, and the substantive point-of-reference of the attorney and law firm is often more beneficial in the establishment of the relationship.

Summary

Although there are personal objectives involved, the strongest tie that binds producers and talent is the fact that great stories may become wonderfully entertaining motion pictures. The most effective beginning for the producer/talent relationship is in initial meetings in which each party is allowed to test the other's creative affinity for a particular picture, followed by deal-making meetings which have the blessing and participation of the talent's agent and/or attorney.

Research, planning, and preparation can help render talent attachment a predictable and pleasant experience.

Development, Production, and Producing Company Structures

This chapter presents the basic business structures of and the relationships between the companies used by producers to operate their motion picture development and production operations.

The Power of Company Structure

The purpose of each company's structure is (1) to provide the business entity with a legal identity recognized by governmental bodies (city, county, state, and federal governments), tax authorities, and other businesses and individuals, (2) to establish an independent, tangible, tradable business presence with the capacity to increase in value, and (3) to deliver company owners increased business/trading capacities, legal protection, and expanded taxation options.

An actor, owning three screenplays and functioning as an individual from a fully operational home office, is treated substantially different from this same actor, with the same assets, who forms an independent production company around these assets. However, that individual's capacity to communicate does not automatically increase, nor, unfortunately, do the screenplays become better, but the individual's deal-making power and the responsiveness from other businesses may be more immediate and serious than to the actor as an individual.

If a talent wants to coproduce a picture with a production company, a talent/company deal naturally transpires. If a production company wants to coproduce with another production company, a company-to-company coproduction deal transpires. The deal point array and relative benefits of the company-to-company transaction are much more extensive and potentially more beneficial to the talent than the talent/company transaction.

The Companies

Producers achieve maximum structure benefits through using three levels of companies. Each level has separate companies. The advantage of having multiple companies is that they deliver to the producer operating clarity, clear accounting separation for all profit participants, and critical picture-to-picture legal protection.

As represented in the chart on that follows, these three levels are the production company, the development companies, and the producing companies.

Figure 9.1
Business Structure and Revenue Flow

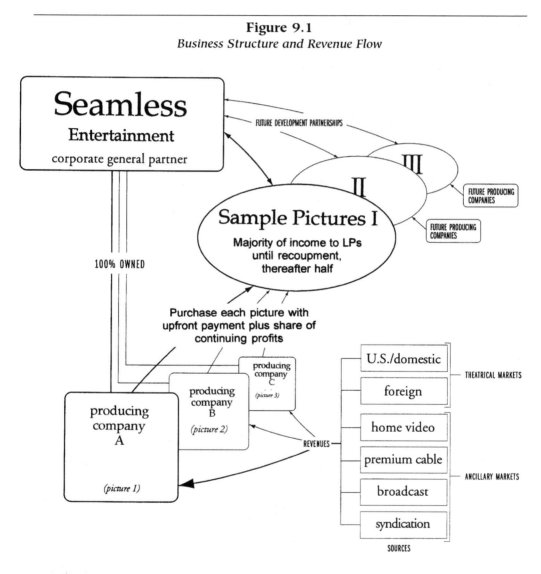

Production Company

The production company is a holding company for the producer's interests in all the development and producing entities. The production company is the producer's brand presence. Mandalay Entertainment, Caravan Pictures, and Castle Rock Entertainment are examples of these production companies.

The production company is the business entity for its owners, administrative team, permanent creative team, distribution group (unless operated as a separate entity), story department, producer's support team, and accounting operations. Producers develop and produce their motion pictures through their development and producing companies.

The production company is the producer's command central. Through this entity, the executive team defines, develops, and manages the producer's objectives. This company retains continuing relationships with all studios, talent, banks, completion guarantors, and other entertainment organizations. It also reviews all literary properties, receives all pitches, and receives all the advertising and public relations for the companies.

The production company is most often a corporation or limited liability company (LLC), which provides the producer with the most historically safe legal protection.

Development Companies

Development companies fulfill all the creative and business development of the pictures that are selected by the producers. The producers are typically the senior development directors of each development company, supported by other members of the production company's staff.

Each development company is established to develop a fixed number of pictures, usually at least three and less than ten. The development company referenced in the company diagram is organized to develop three pictures.

If the producer uses private investors, the development company is the entity in which these investors are invited to participate. If there are investors in the development companies, then these companies are normally a limited partnership or an LLC, both of which deliver the investors the greatest protection and the producer the greatest operating power.

Limiting the number of pictures developed by each of these companies yields specific earnings potential for these companies and further, segments liability.

Producing Companies

Because in many ways, each picture is substantially a separate business, it is highly beneficial for accounting and legal reasons to incorporate each picture as a separate business entity. This is the only picture this company will ever produce. The single company status isolates both the picture's accounting and its liability from the producers' other pictures. Each producing company is wholly owned by the production company and typically set up as a corporation or LLC.

Company Interrelationships

The permanent office location for each of the producers' companies is most often in the production company office.

As the producers' holding company, the production company usually owns all of each producing company and either all, or the producers' share, of each development company (if the development companies have investor partners).

Development Company Financing

Development is that creative gestation precursor essential to motion picture production. Each new development company is launched around a very specific plan, prepared by the producer, to develop and produce a specific number of pictures over several months. This plan is set forth in a month-by-month activity projection. The capital need for this company is discovered through the preparation of a cash flow projection that corresponds with the company's activity projection. These projections are presented in Chapter 10.

Seasoned production companies partially finance development from their own profits. Studios and co-production relationships are also common resources for development financing. If balanced producers use private financing for their pictures, it is allocated for the picture's development. There are financial advantages unique to motion picture development financing for both production companies and investors.

Investors evaluate investment offerings primarily by each offering's: (1) risk, (2) term until potential investment recoupment, (3) investment amount, and (4) earnings potential. Consider these qualities in the following risk evaluation comparing investing in motion picture development and motion picture production.

Motion Picture Development vs. Production Investment Risk Evaluation

Description	Development	Production
Risk	2 of 3 pictures, development only	1 picture, development, production, and distribution
Term until recoupment	18 months	36 months
Investment amount	$2 to $5 million	$25 to $50 million
Earnings Potential	For each: 300% gross over 5 years	

This analysis clearly exhibits where private investors should invest, and why production investments should reside with global distributors who have the capacity to protect their participation within their respective territories and markets.

Production companies seeking private investors for their development companies typically offer them: (1) 50/50 ownership in the partnership, (2) 80 percent to 100 percent of the first proceeds received paid to the investors until they have recouped 100 percent to 120 percent of their original investment, and (3) thereafter, an equal sharing (50 percent/50 percent) of the partnership's earnings.

Earnings flow into the development partnership from its sale of all right, title and interest from each fully developed picture to one of the production company's producing companies. The amount of each of these sales is preset as part of the development company offering. Typically this amount is equal to or greater than the amount necessary to return all of the investors' capital with the sale of the first two developed pictures if the company is configured for developing three pictures.

For example, if the development company's total capitalization is $2 million, and the investors receive 100 percent of all income until they recoup 120 percent of their investment, then the sale of each developed property could be $1.2 million, plus a partnership participation in the continuing profits of each picture. This relationship is structured to recoup the investors' investment, plus a 20 percent return, from the sale of the first two pictures ($2.4 million). This leaves the investors additional earnings from the sale of the third picture to another producing company owned by the production company. Additionally, the development company and its investors participate in the profits of the completed pictures.

Another highly appealing quality of this investment structure is that the investors' potential continuing earnings come from assets worth substantially more than the developed stories. The three pictures in this example have a combined developed value of about $2 million. With production budgets of $25 to $40 million each, the three pictures have a combined production value of $75 to $120 million. This is impressive leverage of approximately 37/1 to 60/1.

Securities

Investment offerings of all kinds must conform to state and federal securities laws. These laws and regulations are highly sophisticated, and producers should have the offerings prepared by their legal and accounting advisors. The planning and preparation of a development investment memorandum is discussed in Chapter 10.

Forms of Companies

There are several forms of company structures, each having several advantages. Producers are best served meeting with their legal counsel, who will lead them through a series of questions, the answers to which should reveal the best company structures for their use.

If there is just one person involved, a production company may be commenced as a sole proprietorship. Often, these organizations may commence their legal life as simply as filing a fictitious name with the county clerk in the county where the producer's office address is listed, and then publishing this name in a newspaper, according to the directions given by the county clerk. This gives the producer the documentation needed to open a bank account and officially use the name recorded in the county of residence. This is quick and inexpensive but does not give the producer legal protection that comes with more sophisticated company structures.

Once a production company is ready to commence earnest business, most attorneys will suggest they incorporate. This delivers the owners (shareholders) personal legal protection from actions that may be taken against their corporation. When the corporation is still limited in its shareholders and earnings, it can receive special tax status that will allow the tax liabilities to be passed through to the shareholders, so they are not burdened with an additional corporate tax.

Similar owner protection can be received from the more popular limited liability company (LLC) structure, which has single taxation rather than double. In most states, the cost of filing an LLC is the same as that for filing as a corporation.

Summary

There is a business entity pattern common among balanced producers that provides them with the greatest operating power, structural stability, flexibility, and personal and picture protection. Producers who model their operations after this pattern should receive these proven benefits.

Development Financing

This chapter discusses the purposes of development financing and the methods and resources from which to secure this financing.

The Essential Power of Funded Development

Producers generally share a common understanding about the schedule and resources it takes for the average motion picture to fulfill production; however, the schedule and resources for a motion picture to complete development often garner more questions than answers. Does a picture's development time include, and should related expenses be charged for, reading scripts and listening to pitches that lead to the discovery of that picture's story? And shouldn't most of a motion picture's final development activities and expenses also be part of its preproduction? The answer to these questions is certainly yes. Producers should understand, finance, and manage their pictures' entire development process to enable them to move through development at a steady, confident pace that will continue through production and distribution.

Every picture has its unique development and production schedule. The following is an example of a typical picture's schedule.

Motion Picture Development and Production Schedule

Description	Approximate months	Cumulative months
Development prestory acquisition (reading, researching, internal greenlight, first studio greenlights)	5	5
Story acquisition	1	6

Description	Approximate months	Cumulative months
Development preproduction (shooting script evolution, talent attachments, global liquidation prep, physical production prep, presale/completion, bond/production banking prep and fulfillment, commence trade/consumer PR, U.S. studio distribution agreement, publisher relationship establishment)	8	14
Preproduction	3	17
Principal photography	3	20
Postproduction	4	24

This model demonstrates that 14 (almost 60 percent) of the 24 months of a typical picture's complete production process is spent in development. As producers invest the majority of their time developing pictures, this should be, as is done in the best operated production organizations, a finely orchestrated process, performed according to schedules, budgets, and accountability in keeping with the integrity of the picture's production processes.

Most producers have multiple pictures in development and production at the same time. Multiple pictures sustain a continuous flow of projects and allow their production company to amortize (distribute) fixed development overhead costs over several pictures. Even with amortization, development overhead typically averages $400,000 per picture—not including story rights, writers' fees, and talent attachment expenses. In addition to these expenses, the accomplishment of the 19 development steps (as listed above) typically takes the development team 18 months, and often longer.

Producers should understand that development is the foundation of each picture. A strong foundation allows producers to produce their pictures with predictable confidence. A weak development foundation is the number one reason pictures don't get made, dissemble during production, or have lackluster earning power.

Understanding this, producers ought to ensure that each aspect of their picture's development is just as intricately organized, budgeted, and sufficiently funded as its principal photography.

Development Funding Sources

The most common sources of development funding are (1) from the production company, (2) from a studio, (3) from investors, or (4) from co-production relationships.

Production Company Financing

Most mature production companies fund at least some of their development expenses from cash flow or bank credit facilities. For many of these companies, this funding is only interim and is repaid to the production company when either a separately funded development company is set up or the picture is acquired by its producing company.

Studio Financing

In the main, studio development financing for independent production companies comes through the studios' production departments. Young production companies are most likely to take advantage of these accommodations, which often include offices on the studio lot and more traditional development financing that includes story acquisition and talent attachment. These expenses are accrued by the studio and charged against the producer's pictures that go into production.

Use of studio development financing usually relegates the producer to a close production and distribution relationship with the studio, referred to as the studio producer relationship discussed in Chapter 2. The primary studio motivation in these relationships is the ownership and distribution of significant pictures.

Investor Financing

Balanced producers often engage in relationships with a limited number of sophisticated private investors who provide development financing for their pictures.

Mature balanced production companies sustain cash flows from earnings and maintain bank credit facilities substantially greater than are needed to finance all their development expenses without engaging investment capital. Many of these companies still elect to use development private-investor partners. The primary motivation for this is that development investor partners (1) promote a more focused management for each picture's development progress, (2) provide tighter control of development expenses (which, for many production companies, may easily slip out of control), (3) balance the producer's risk, and (4) expand capital availability.

In Chapter 9, the terms and company structure that best accommodate development investors are presented. Producers should prepare such offerings with the assistance and under the direction of an experienced securities attorney.

The discovery of private investors who have the funds and inclination to invest is not sufficient reason for a producer to approach and engage in a development relationship with them. There are state and federal securities and exchange commissions (SECs) that have established regulations to which all investment offerings and relationships must conform. These regulations both protect investors and provide a structure that governs and identifies investment offerings.

Development offerings are most often prepared for the exclusive review and participation in an SEC investor category called *sophisticated investors*. This SEC category varies from state to state but basically refers to investors who are experienced in investments similar in amount and risk to the one being offered and possess a specific minimum net worth that demonstrates even greater sophistication and the investor's ability to risk the investment's failure.

The advantages of using this offering category are that first of all, the producer has an exclusive relationship with investors who are durable and experienced, thus allowing for less fear of investor impact if the development company, for any reason, fails to achieve its objectives. It also makes for smoother presentations to experienced, business-savvy potential participants. Another important advantage of sophisticated investor offerings is that they are simpler, less expensive, and less time-consuming to prepare than nonrestricted public offerings.

Sophisticated investor offerings are restricted in their content, presentation, and number of participants. Among other minimum requirements, sophisticated investor offerings must conform to SEC regulation language. This language gives investors and their representatives reference to each offering in relation to the laws governing it. It also includes complete and clear declarations of the risks related to the investment.

Sophisticated investor offerings are restricted in the number of potential investors to whom they may be offered and also by the number of investors who may participate. Consequently, the offerings are numbered, and a log is kept of each investor who has been presented an offering copy, those retrieved, and certainly, the number of investment interests actually purchased.

Depending on each state's SEC regulations, the number of participating investors may be limited to as few as ten. This restriction keeps the investor group to a manageable size, but it may result in a high per-investment amount (one-tenth), which may further restrict the number of potential investors.

For many sophisticated investors, managing their investment portfolio is their primary business. Most of these investors diversify their investments into a portfolio balanced with a mix of secure investments (treasury bills, municipal bonds, mortgages, etc.) and risk investments (stocks, business investments, etc.). As these investments mature, the returning funds must be reinvested to maximize earnings and restrict tax exposure. This return and reinvestment phenomenon sustains a continuing participation among potential investors in reviewing and investing in new projects.

A producer's first development offering is often the most challenging to prepare and fund. However, following the initial offering, subsequent offerings are simpler to author and fund. Typically, some of the original investors want to reinvest in one or more of the producer's future development entities, and new investors are now substantially easier to engage, using the first development company as a powerful point of reference. Recently, a Los Angeles-based independent producer, whose accountant keeps a list of investors who would like to participate in this producer's future development partnerships, reported that their current list exceeds 1,000 investors. This is unusual for several reasons, including the fact that most producers or their representatives will not add an investor's name to a list that exceeds more than 50 or one 100. However, this points to the availability of investors for development company investments.

To temper the previous statement, most producers will find it challenging to obtain their initial development financing. But sophisticated investors are just that. They are skilled investors, looking for exceptional investment opportunities. They wisely tend to shy away from untried management teams and industries in which they are inexperienced.

Coproduction Company Financing

Production companies can receive development financing for their projects from other production companies that have development funding and, consequently, are seeking the strongest stories.

The two most desperate development positions for producers to be in are (1) to have one or more sterling stories that have passed their internal greenlight but they do not have sufficient capital to develop them, and (2) to have development capital and either only weak stories to choose from or no story that has passed their greenlight.

Both of these conditions are common among producers, but the second is the most urgent and most common—common enough, in fact, to motivate the development and consequent production of too many motion pictures each year that are sufficiently strong for greenlight, but do not warm the producer's creative fire. These pictures are made, because if producers wait too long for a project, then they may run short of allocated development funds for the number of pictures for which the money was raised. If this is the case, then either new funding must be infused or fewer pictures developed. In either case, the eventual development expenses may become too high to be reasonably applied to the completed pictures.

Most producers have several pictures in their development pool. Because there are typically more development funds than there are truly great stories, producers are generally very receptive to story pitches from other producers seeking co-production relationships.

Codevelopment/production relationships are most often set up for a single picture. One production company provides the story and the development progress related to it; the other company provides the development capital. They both share in the development and production of the picture. Equity is typically divided according to the value of each party's contribution.

The Process of Securing Development Financing

There are seven basic steps to obtaining development financing:

1. Develop a plan. This is the cornerstone to success in obtaining the necessary funding. With a plan, there is order and hope. Producers should evaluate their resources (operating team, stories, cash flow) and recommit to or redefine their mission statement (why they are in business, the kind of pictures they want to make, the way they want to make them, style of doing business internally and with others, etc.) They should also make decisions about the basic development planning possibilities, including the number of pictures to be developed within the new development company, the stories (if any) that the producer has, and the most logical sources from which to receive development funding.

2. Prepare the activity projection. This is a list of the primary activities performed for the company's pictures during their development. These activities are presented in a month-by-month spreadsheet format, showing in a single projection each separate activity for all the pictures developed.

The activity projection shown on the next two pages has been set up for the development of three pictures. This basic form is currently being used by several production companies for planning and managing their development companies.

Figure 10.1
Sample Pictures, Ltd. Activity Projection

Page 1 of 2

ACTIVITY	1 Apr	2 May	3 Jun	4 Jul	5 Aug	6 Sep	7 Oct	8 Nov	9 Dec	10 Jan	11 Feb	12 Mar	13 Apr	14 May	15 Jun	16 Jul	17 Aug	18 Sep	19 Oct	20 Nov	21 Dec	22 Jan	23 Feb	24 Mar
Start - Up		Cannes					Mifed					AFM		Cannes					Mifed					AFM
UPM Retain	–																							
Entertainment Atty Retain	–																							
Publicist Retain	–																							
Write/Release Opening P.R.	–																							
Entertainment Bank Open	–																							
Prep & Release Distributor Anncmnt.	–																							
Development Creative																								
Read Screenplays & Lit Properties	–	–	–	–	–	–	–	–	–	–	–	–	–	–										
Internal Greenlight (Motion Picture Valuation, Budget Smry)			–	–	–	–	–	–	–	–	–	–	–	–										
First Distributors Greenlight			–	–	–	–	–	–	–	–	–	–	–	–										
Option Screenplay / Lit Rights						1				2					3									
Write Picture Definition						1				2					3									
Story scope and superobjective; Budget; Target audiences; Production schedule; Domestic theatrical and other major distribution street dates; Comparables; Earnings Projections.																								
Distributor Creative Correlation							1	1	1	1,2	1,2	1,2	1,2	1,2	1,2,3	1,2,3	1,2,3	1,2,3	1,2,3	1,2,3	1,2,3			2,3
List Director Considerations						1					2				3									
Meetings						1	1	1			2	2			3	3	3							
Select, Negotiate, Document								1				2					3							
List Primary Acting Talent						1				2					3									
Meet, Select, Negotiate, Document							1	1	1	1	2	2	2	2	3	3	3	3	3					
Story Meetings & Breakdown						1	1	1	1		2	2	2		3	3	3	3						
Additional Screenplay Drafts							1	1	1		2	2	2		3	3	3	3						
Shooting Script										1				2					3					
List Key Production Talent																								
Cinematographer									1					2				3						
UPM, Music, Art Dir, Costuming, Spcl FX											1	1	1	1	2	2		3	3	3	3			
Meet, Select, Negotiate, Document											1	1	1	1	2	2	3	3	3	3				
Spot Promotion																	3							
Prep Picture Logo and Printing						1print					2print							3print						
Story Board									1	1	1	1	1	1	2			3	3	3				

Figure 10.1 continued
Sample Pictures, Ltd. Activity Projection

ACTIVITY	1	2	3	4	5	6	7	8	9	10	11	12	13	14	15	16	17	18	19	20	21	22	23	24	As	As	As	As
(year)	00									01												02						
(month)	Apr	May	Jun	Jul	Aug	Sep	Oct	Nov	Dec	Jan	Feb	Mar	Apr	May	Jun	Jul	Aug	Sep	Oct	Nov	Dec	Jan	Feb	Mar	#'d	#'d	#'d	#'d
(markets)		Cannes					Mifed					AFM		Cannes					Mifed					AFM				
Development Production																												
1st Pass Production Budget										1									3									
Shooting Draft Breakdown and Production Boards											1			2						3								
Production Budget											1				2					3								
Production Schedule											1				2					3								
Completion Bond Set												1				2					3							
Picture Marketing, Prdctn Funding																												
Establish Presale Financing Plan						1				2				3														
Pre-Sale Negotiations						1					1,2	2	2	2,3	2,3	3	3	3	3	3	3							
Document Presales											1	1	1	1	2	2	2	2	3	3	3	3	3					
Create and Present Bank Memorandum											1			2														
Trade Releases						1	1	1	1	1,2	1,2	1,2	1,2	1,2	1,2,3	1,2,3	1,2,3	1,2,3	1,2,3	1,2,3	1,2,3	1,2,3	1,2,3	1,2,3				
Consumer PR									1	2	1	1	1	1,2	1,2	1,2	1,2	1,2	1,2,3	1,2,3	1,2,3	1,2,3	1,2,3	1,2,3				
Picture Introductory Meetings With Studio's						1			2						3													
Enter Domestic Theatrical Agrmnt												1				2		3			3							
Publisher Novelization Negotiations								1	1	1		2	2	2			3	3										
Engage Bank Production Funding												1	1			2		2		3								
Sell Picture To Producing Company																												
Pre - Production														1	1		2	2	2	2	2	3	3	3				
Principal Photography																1	1	1	1	1	1						2:Mar/02-Jun/02	3:Apr/02-Jul/02
Post Production																				1	1	1	1	2			2:May/02	3:Aug/02-Nov/02
Theatrical Trailer																						1						3:Oct/02
Release Dates and After Market																												
Sell Foreign Rights								1	1	1,2	1,2	1,2	1,2	1,2	1,2,3	1,2,3	1,2,3	1,2,3	1,2,3	1,2,3	1,2,3	1,2,3	1,2,3	1,2,3				
Paperback Release																								1			2:Jun/02	3:Nov/02
Domestic Theatrical Release																											2:Jul/02	3:Dec/02
Domestic Video Release																										1:Sep/02	2:Jan/03	3:Jun/03
Premium Cable TV Release																										1:Mar/03	2:Jul/03	3:Dec/03
Network Television																										1:Mar/04	2:Jul/04	3:Dec/04

This example is predicated on a particular producer's resources. The activities and format are universal. The layout may be very helpful to producers in planning their individual development entities. The timing represented is just an example—producers should not expect their plan to be timed like those in the example.

There are two activity projections on the CD-ROM supplied with this book. One is set up in the projection's format, but ready to be filled in. The other provides the projection with its live sample. This sample can assist users with points of reference until they become familiar with the planning process.

The far-left column is labeled *Activities*. Below this heading is a list of the major development activities, generally in the order of motion picture development progress. The rest of the columns to the right of the activity column list the succeeding months from 1 to 24, except for the last three columns, which presents dates beyond those months listed.

Various points about how the producer accomplishes the activities referenced in this projection have been presented in previous chapters, are presented below and are chronicled in Chapter 12.

The initial activities are labeled *start-up*. Some categories are for new producers who have not previously engaged an attorney, publicist, or entertainment bank, or who have had not started trade press releases for their production company.

UPM (Unit Production Manager) retention will be a new concept to some producers and many UPMs. If a producer does not have an in-house person who performs production budgeting work, it would be helpful to retain a *development UPM* who provides various aspects of this work during the development process for each picture. Retention increases both the consistency and integrity of the work. Just as breakdowns, boards, schedules, and budgets from a UPM are usually more thorough and better planned than if done by a UPM not attached to a picture, so is the work of a UPM who is retained to do all the UPM-related development work for a slate of pictures.

Development creative includes all the remaining categories listed on the Activity Projection's Page 1.

The initial portion of this section primarily charts the producer's story discovery plan. This plan includes developing stories that are already internally greenlit, as well as soliciting and reading scripts (as part of the search for new properties). Subsequently, the producer goes through the process of garnering the U.S. and foreign distributor greenlights.

In large measure, this process writes the picture's definition. It is each picture's as-detailed-as-possible creative and business definition. Substantially and naturally, it comes from preparing each picture's liquidation breakdown, audience research, and campaign development, as well as traditional creative preparation.

For most pictures, *attaching the director*, which includes researching, creative meetings, and negotiating, precedes attaching lead talent and most other development functions. A director is fundamental to each picture's creative life. It is essential that the director be brought in early and allowed to participate in all other facets of a picture's development and production.

The first five activities on the projection's second page are a continuation of *development creative* and are part of the picture's pre-production.

Picture marketing, production funding are just as they appear. These processes are substantially presented in Chapters 2 through 6.

Figure 10.2
Sample Pictures, Ltd. Cash Flow Projection

Prepared: January 4, 2000

Description	1 April '00	2 May	3 June	4 July	5 August	6 September	7 October	8 November	9 December	10 January '01	11 February	12 March	1st Year Totals	13 April	14 May
Events		Cannes				Scmply 1	Mifed	Director 1		Scmply 2		Director 2 AFM		Sell Pic 1	Cannes
US Theatrical Release															
Cash Receipts															
Investment Funds	5,000,000	0	0	0	0	0	0	0	0	0	0	0	5,000,000	0	0
Production Sale	0	0	0	0	0	0	0	0	0	0	0	0	0	3,000,000	0
Picture Participations	0	0	0	0	0	0	0	0	0	0	0	0	0	0	0
Total Cash Receipts	5,000,000	0	0	0	0	0	0	0	0	0	0	0	5,000,000	3,000,000	0
Expenses															
Brokerage Fees	500,000	0	0	0	0	0	0	0	0	0	0	0	500,000	0	0
Literary Rights Acquisition	0	0	0	0	0	200,000	0	0	0	200,000	0	0	400,000	0	0
Writers' Fees	0	0	0	0	0	0	50,000	50,000	50,000	50,000	50,000	0	250,000	50,000	0
Director Retainer	0	0	0	0	0	0	0	300,000	300,000	0	0	0	600,000	0	0
Talent Retainers	0	0	0	0	0	0	0	0	150,000	150,000	150,000	0	450,000	150,000	150,000
Unit Production Mngr	0	5,000	3,000	2,000	2,000	2,000	2,000	2,000	2,000	2,000	2,000	2,000	23,000	2,000	2,000
Publicist	3,000	7,000	3,000	3,000	3,000	5,000	7,000	3,000	3,000	5,000	3,000	7,000	52,000	420	420
Attorney, Entrtnmnt	0	12,000	0	0	0	7,000	1,000	7,000	1,000	7,000	5,000	7,000	47,000	5,000	0
Foreign Rep	0	0	3,000	3,000	3,000	3,000	3,000	3,000	3,000	3,000	3,000	3,000	33,000	3,000	3,000
Picture Artwork	0	7,000	0	0	0	10,000	3,000	7,000	7,000	10,000	0	0	47,000	0	7,000
Picture Promo Production	0	0	0	0	0	10,000	5,000	5,000	0	10,000	5,000	5,000	40,000	0	0
Rent	0	6,000	3,000	3,000	3,000	3,000	3,000	3,000	3,000	3,000	3,000	3,000	36,000	3,000	3,000
Telephone	3,500	2,000	2,000	2,000	2,000	2,000	2,000	2,000	2,000	2,000	2,000	2,000	25,500	2,000	2,000
Office Equipment	0	16,400	0	0	0	0	0	0	0	0	0	0	16,400	0	0
Printing	0	7,000	0	0	0	5,000	5,000	5,000	5,000	5,000	3,000	8,000	38,000	0	0
Supplies	800	800	160	160	160	160	160	160	160	160	160	160	2,400	160	160
Pstg / Dlvry Service	700	700	700	700	700	700	700	700	700	700	700	700	8,700	700	700
Eagle I, Variety, CelebSrvc	0	344	0	0	0	1,900	0	0	0	0	0	0	2,244	0	0
Exhibitor Relations	0	0	0	300	0	250	0	0	0	0	0	0	550	0	0
Motion Picture Sftwr	0	3,400	900	900	0	0	0	0	0	0	0	0	5,200	0	0
Advertising, Trade	0	10,000	2,000	2,000	2,000	7,500	7,500	2,000	2,000	7,500	2,000	10,000	54,500	2,000	10,000
Travel / Markets	0	10,000	3,000	3,000	3,000	3,000	17,500	3,000	3,000	3,000	3,000	12,000	63,500	3,000	10,000
Fees															
Dvlpmnt Directors, 2	6,000	12,000	12,000	12,000	12,000	12,000	12,000	12,000	12,000	12,000	12,000	12,000	138,000	12,000	12,000
Dvlpmnt Assistant	0	1,500	4,500	3,000	3,000	3,000	3,000	3,000	3,000	3,000	3,000	3,000	33,000	3,000	3,000
Operations Director	0	3,500	3,500	3,500	3,500	3,500	3,500	3,500	3,500	3,500	3,500	3,500	38,500	3,500	3,500
Payroll Taxes	780	2,210	2,600	2,405	2,405	2,405	2,405	2,405	2,405	2,405	2,405	2,405	27,235	2,405	2,405
Readers	0	500	500	500	500	500	500	500	500	500	500	500	5,500	500	500
Contingency	15,428	3,311	1,226	1,244	1,208	8,457	3,848	12,428	7,238	12,893	7,598	13,238	88,117	7,281	6,291
Total Expenses	529,708	113,665	42,086	42,709	41,473	290,372	132,113	426,693	248,503	442,658	260,863	454,503	3,025,346	249,966	215,976
Limited Partners Participation															
Total Limited Partner Participation	0	0	0	0	0	0	0	0	0	0	0	0	0	2,700,000	0
Monthly Balance (expense)	4,470,292	-113,665	-42,086	-42,709	-41,473	-290,372	-132,113	-426,693	-248,503	-442,658	-260,863	-454,503	1,974,654	50,034	-215,976
Cmltv Cash Flow	4,470,292	4,356,627	4,314,541	4,271,832	4,230,359	3,939,987	3,807,874	3,381,181	3,132,678	2,690,020	2,429,157	1,974,654	1,974,654	2,024,689	1,808,713

Figure 10.2 continued
Sample Pictures, Ltd. Cash Flow Projection

Years →	15 June	16 July	17 August	18 September	19 October	20 November	21 December	22 January '02	23 February	24 March	4/01-3/02 (2)	4/02-3/03 (3)	4/03-3/04 (4)	4/04-3/05 (5)
(events)	Scmply 3		Director 3							AFM				
(events)			Sell Pic 2		Mifed			Sell Pic 3			1:3/02	2:7/02, 3:12/02		
	0	0	0	0	0	0	0	0	0	0	0	0	0	0
	0	0	3,000,000	0	0	0	0	3,000,000	0	0	9,000,000	0	0	0
	0	0	349,852	0	0	0	151,860	0	0	0	501,712	3,539,590	3,678,976	0
	0	0	3,349,852	0	0	0	151,860	3,000,000	0	0	9,501,712	3,539,590	3,678,976	0
	0	0	0	0	0	0	0	0	0	0	0	0	0	0
	200,000	0	0	0	0	0	0	0	0	0	200,000	0	0	0
	0	50,000	50,000	50,000	0	0	0	0	0	0	200,000	0	0	0
	0	0	300,000	0	0	0	0	0	0	0	300,000	0	0	0
	150,000	0	0	150,000	150,000	150,000	0	0	0	0	900,000	0	0	0
	2,000	2,000	2,000	2,000	2,000	2,000	2,000	2,000	2,000	2,000	24,000	24,000	24,000	24,000
	2,420	420	420	420	420	420	420	420	420	420	7,040	5,040	5,040	5,040
	7,000	0	7,000	0	0	0	0	0	0	0	19,000	10,000	10,000	10,000
	3,000	3,000	3,000	3,000	3,000	3,000	3,000	3,000	3,000	3,000	18,000	9,000	9,000	9,000
	10,000	0	7,000	3,000	3,000	1,500	1,500	1,500	1,500	1,500	30,000	5,000	5,000	5,000
	3,000	5,000	5,000	3,000	3,000	1,000	1,000	1,000	1,000	1,000	20,000	5,000	5,000	5,000
	2,000	3,000	5,000	2,000	2,000	0	0	0	0	0	27,000	6,000	600	240
	0	2,000	2,000	0	0	0	0	0	0	3,000	18,000	2,000	2,000	2,000
	5,000	5,000	5,000	0	0	0	0	0	0	0	0	0	0	0
	160	160	160	160	0	0	0	0	0	0	15,000	1,000	1,000	1,000
	700	700	700	700	80	80	80	80	80	80	1,440	160	160	160
	0	0	0	0	350	350	350	350	350	350	6,300	300	300	300
	0	0	0	0	0	0	0	0	0	0	0	0	0	0
	0	0	0	0	0	0	0	0	0	0	0	0	0	0
	10,000	2,000	2,000	2,000	10,000	1,000	1,000	1,000	1,000	2,500	44,500	10,000	10,000	10,000
	3,000	3,000	3,000	3,000	17,500	3,000	3,000	3,000	3,000	12,000	66,500	0	0	0
	12,000	12,000	12,000	12,000	6,000	6,000	6,000	6,000	6,000	6,000	108,000	0	0	0
	3,000	3,000	3,000	3,000	1,500	1,500	1,500	1,500	1,500	1,500	27,000	0	0	0
	3,500	3,500	3,500	3,500	1,750	1,750	1,750	1,750	1,750	1,750	31,500	0	0	0
	2,405	2,405	2,405	2,405	1,202	1,202	1,202	1,202	1,202	1,202	21,645	0	0	0
	500	500	500	500	500	500	500	500	500	500	6,000	0	0	0
	12,891	2,931	12,351	7,131	5,904	5,109	609	609	609	1,014	62,728	2,325	2,163	2,152
	442,576	100,616	424,036	244,816	202,707	175,412	20,912	20,912	20,912	34,817	2,153,653	79,825	74,263	73,892
	0	0	3,014,867	0	0	0	136,674	148,460	0	1,379,203	7,379,203	1,729,882	1,802,356	0
	-442,576	-100,616	-89,050	-244,816	-202,707	-175,412	-5,726	2,830,629	-20,912	-1,414,019	-31,144	1,729,882	1,802,356	-73,892
	1,366,137	1,265,522	1,176,472	931,656	728,949	553,538	547,812	3,378,441	3,357,530	1,943,510	1,943,510	3,673,393	5,475,749	5,401,857

Sell the picture to producing company refers to the formal activity of selling all rights, title, and interest of each developed picture to a separate producer-owned producing company, as presented in Chapter 9.

Unless the producer has identified the picture to be developed, the Production and Distribution dates are estimates. Once the U.S. theatrical date is projected, the other distribution dates are laid in according to traditional distribution window timing, as presented in Chapter 1.

3. Prepare the cash flow projection. After the producer has projected specifically how development of a series of pictures will be accomplished, then a cash flow projection may be prepared. This projection applies expense amounts to the achievements chronicled in the activity projection, plus the related overhead, such as rent, phones, salaries, and taxes. Some of the production company's expenses are passed through to the development company. For instance, the producer is typically one of the development directors, so a portion of this salary, office space, and equipment will be paid by the development company during the picture's development.

A cash flow projection sample is presented on the following two pages. Like the activity projection, this is only a sample. Producers should prepare their projections with the assistance of their accountant and/or business manager and apply expense amounts appropriate for their organizations.

There are two cash flow projections on the CD-ROM supplied with this book. One is in the sample projection's format but without amounts, and ready to be filled in. The other has the sample projection's amounts filled in. This projection may assist users with points of reference until they become familiar with these expenses.

Extending for five years, this projection indicates expenses incurred monthly for the first 12 months and annually thereafter. Many production companies prepare internal cash flow projections monthly for the first 24 months, and annually thereafter for greater planning and analysis clarity.

The top of this projection lists the sales events attended by the producer, as well as the most significant activity benchmarks from the activity projection. These are not mandatory but are a very helpful reference.

Below the activity references are *cash receipts,* a listing of all the development company's income by projected receipt date. Each category should be referenced here, including, but not limited to, investments from the producer, private investors, and loans, as well as income generated from the sale of the developed pictures to the subsidiary-producing companies. If this sale includes a development company profits participation in the pictures, the income from this participation should also be shown. The investment amounts are usually left blank until the expenses are completed and totaled. Once the expenses are identified, the producer will know how much is needed to fund the picture's development.

Following cash receipts is a listing of the *development expenses.* The first items listed are options and retainers for literary rights and production/performing talent. Following these expenses are professional fees, then overhead items, followed by the investors' (in this example, Limited Partners) participation. (This is usually left blank until expenses are completed.) Payroll is listed, then a contingency, followed by the total expenses for that month.

The entry below *total expenses* is the *monthly balance,* which is the month's total income less the month's total expenses. On the next line is *cumulative cash flow,* which lists the monthly balance plus the cash remaining from the prior month.

After all expenses are filled in, the preparer can examine the total cumulative cash flow for the month following the first picture's theatrical release date and have a starting point in estimating the amount of development financing necessary to develop the proposed picture. Depending on development duration, it may be necessary to calculate the cash flow projection monthly for the first 24 months in order to determine how much the development company will need until it is self-sufficient.

Typically, development companies are set up for a fixed number of pictures, and the most expensive categories terminate after the pictures have sold to the producer's producing companies. After this time, the remaining expense categories substantially diminish.

Following the first expense pass, the producer often will reassess the basic elements of the plan. This includes looking at the number of pictures to be developed, the activity projection timing, and the major category expenses. There must be a balance between a sane development/production schedule, income and expenses, and producer/investor motivations. Several revisions are typically made to these two projections before a balance can be obtained with which the producer is content.

4. Select the development team and advisors. The development company will be operated by a team, including the development director(s), an operations person, and development assistants. There will also be outside professionals, including an attorney, banker, completion bond company, physical production specialist (retained UPM), and a publicist.

   The dynamics of the development team are projected into the pictures that they produce. Additionally, many investors look first to the development team when evaluating the development offering. The development team is reviewed in Chapter 11.

5. Formulate the investment. Even if the investment is completely internal, separate development entities should be formed and financed. As this occurs, terms of the investment or loan must be prepared between the companies. The pictures, production company, and investors should receive the greatest amount of protection, along with the most efficient tax consequences possible. If there are private investors, they will need reasonable incentives and protection also. This step is typically accomplished by the producer's accountant and attorney, who assist in the deal formulation, tax considerations, and securities issues. Many of the basic considerations relating to this step are reviewed in Chapter 9.

6. Prepare the investment's documentation. Even if the production company is the sole investment source, documentation must be prepared and entered into with legal, producer income, and tax consequences that facilitate the plan's formal engagement.

   The producer's attorney usually prepares this documentation. If funds are raised from private investors, a securities attorney should be involved. No securities documentation should be distributed until it has passed an attorney's review.

7. Make the presentations and fund the development company. Regardless of which of the four sources of development financing the producer receives, an

offering will be made, and, after acceptance, the documentation will be completed and the funding obtained.

If the funding is to come from private investors, and this is the producer's first private offering, it is often constructive to make a list of potential investors, another list of people of influence who may recommend sophisticated investors to consider the offering, and another list of brokers, investment counselors and securities dealers. The sources in each category should be prioritized and a plan prepared as to how to approach each source.

Raising private capital is especially challenging for the first development company owned by a new production entity. For these producers, (1) a strong team (presented in Chapter 11), (2) with exceptional stories under consideration, (3) making a professional presentation, and (4) offering a motivating investment, are critical to success in receiving the necessary development capital.

Summary

Like production, development should be financed to ensure a picture's success. Also, like production, development should be planned and carried out with a skilled team to ensure a smooth transition into funded production and into the hands of the various territories and media prepared to receive each picture.

The Team

This chapter reviews the internal and external players who are the operating and advisory teams of the production and development companies. It also presents the considerations related to planning the team, as well as evaluating, employing and/or retaining, and setting compensation and fees for all the players.

The Complete Team

No producer would attempt principal photography without a whole production team, yet some producers operate their businesses without a complete operating team.

Producers must have a person handling each of the stewardships demanded by their business. Most production companies begin with a sparse in-house team, supported with outside professionals that may include an attorney, accountant, producer's sales representative, foreign sales organization, PR firm, and/or an advertising agency. These may provide critical services at a more reasonable cost than comparable in-house executives. Regardless of the source, producers should be able to perform all the functions necessary to their business in a coordinated, seamless fashion.

The organization charts on the following two pages present the basic positions that are necessary to operate an independent production company and its development companies. Keep in mind that many development companies have a fixed creative life of two to five years, depending on the number of pictures they are designed to develop. The production company, on the other hand, has a continuing life and supplies most of the development company's operating and advisory team.

Corporate Structure

Production companies are usually corporations in order to provide legal protection for the principals and to facilitate growth, mergers, acquisitions, and so on. The producing companies will also probably be corporations, although they may be LLCs, because they rarely need the same elasticity as the production company.

Corporations are owned by their shareholders. The shareholders create a board of directors who are responsible not only for establishing the corporation's constitution, policies, and procedures, but also for appointing corporate officers, who are responsible for operating the organization.

Figure 11.1
The Production Company

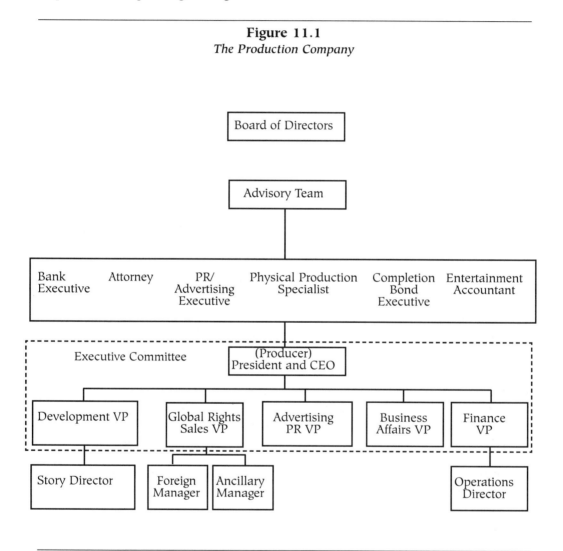

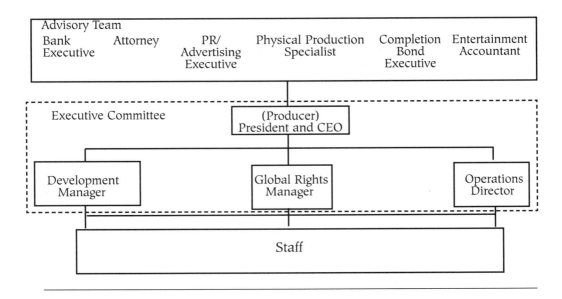

Figure 11.2
The Development Company

Advisory Team
Bank Executive · Attorney · PR/Advertising Executive · Physical Production Specialist · Completion Bond Executive · Entertainment Accountant

Executive Committee · (Producer) President and CEO · Development Manager · Global Rights Manager · Operations Director

Staff

In corporations, the shareholders wield the ultimate power. In their majority, shareholders can remove and replace members of the board of directors and override any other governing power within the organization.

On the production company chart on page 118, the board of directors is shown in a separate box, since it is rarely involved in the day-to-day operations of the corporation. Its members usually just meet annually, when they review annual reports and projections and participate in the review of matters related to mergers, acquisitions, substantial capital restructuring, or changes in corporate policy and procedures.

The Production Company's Team

The production company's chart shows three tiers of the team. The first tier is composed of a six-member advisory team, the second tier an operating team with six key players who are the production company's executive committee, and the final tier of the executive committee's staff.

The Advisory Team

Every production organization is substantially benefited by its advisory team. The members of this team are entertainment industry professionals who are rarely available or affordable for executive positions within a production company. They are seasoned industry icons, and their advice, counsel, the relationships they have with other powerful people, and their deal influence amplify the production company's industry position, broaden its reach, and sharpen its business and creative focus. This team is especially important for newer production entities.

The most common members of production company advisory teams are (1) an entertainment bank executive, (2) an entertainment attorney, (3) a brand-making professional who is most often an executive in a public relations firm or advertising agency, (4) a physical production specialist who is usually a line producer or UPM, (5) a completion bond executive, and (6) an entertainment accountant.

Some of the advisory team members may serve on the production company's board of directors, but their primary function is to serve the company individually as mentors in addition to providing more customary professional services.

Most potential advisory team members have no natural business motivation to serve as a member of a production company's advisory team except that they are mature in their professional duties in the industry and may be persuaded to guide organizations that need their help. The keys for newer production companies to win the support of these powerful people are the ethics and achievement commitment of the producer, the kind of pictures the producer is committed to create, and the approach the producer is taking to produce and distribute these pictures. Producers who are organized, focused, and determined to produce important, but not necessarily big or broadly commercial pictures are often the ones who are well received by these potential team members.

The production company may actually also retain the attorney, brand executive, physical production specialist, and accountant in an industry customary fashion. Typically, in these relationships, the team member is engaged in the company's exceptional situations, while someone else on their staff fulfills the more traditional needs. The remaining team members are the bank and completion bond executives, who are paid fees for the services that are extraordinary to their organizations which they provide the production company. For instance, a bank executive may assist the producer in obtaining a credit facility from a foreign bank, a competing domestic bank or a commercial organization.

The services provided by and the process of selecting and engaging a relationship with a bank are reviewed in Chapter 5, while completion bond executives are covered in Chapter 6, and entertainment attorneys in Chapter 7. Though certain loans may be too large or small for the bank with which the banking advisor is associated, usually legal and bonding services are provided through the organizations with which the producer's advisors are associated.

The services provided by a physical production specialist are presented in Chapter 10. This person is usually selected by research and reputation. Producers most often become familiar with line producers and UPMs by the pictures they have worked on. Like most industry talent, these professionals are very busy but quite approachable. Producers should meet with the three to five strongest candidates, present their company's purpose, and explain the relationship desired. Often the selection is obvious, but if not, producers should review their notes and discuss their options with their advisory and/or operating teams, and then make their decision. After the selection is made, producers should contact the other candidates in writing, thanking them for their time and consideration, as well as writing the selected person, reviewing immediate plans and expressing enthusiasm for their advisory team participation.

The Executive Committee

The executive committee consists of the producer and the department heads. These are the people responsible for ensuring that the company's objectives are fulfilled, its mission statement brought into continually finer focus, and its achievement-dynamic amplified. Responsible for all earnings and accountable for all operating expenses, this committee typically meets once a week, where it reviews company progress and revises projections.

The producer's corporate title is usually chief executive officer, president, or both, and the department heads are vice presidents. The producer is the team leader responsible for the ultimate creative and business bottom line of the company. The producer's duties are more fully presented in Chapter 12. The producer may have a subordinate officer who is primarily responsible for directing the department heads. This person may also serve as the chairman of the executive committee and have the corporate title of executive or senior vice president.

The primary stewardships of the development vice president are in soliciting and discovering stories. After they are greenlit, the vice president manages their development in the development company, under the direction of the producer, who is typically the development company's development director.

The *global rights sales vice president* is responsible for preparing the initial liquidation breakdown for each picture that comes under the scrutiny of an internal greenlight and the continuing revaluing, sales strategy, presales, and all initial and continuing rights liquidation of the company's pictures. This vice president may direct the activities of a staff, including a foreign sales manager and an ancillary sales manager, as well as the vice president's assistants.

The *advertising and public relations vice president* is responsible for establishing and sustaining the production company's brand to the entertainment global trade and global consumers and establishing each motion picture's initial brand with the global entertainment trade and global consumers. This person also manages the continuing brand in conjunction with the various global distributors, reviews and manages the producer's position relative to the media plans and media buys prior to and during the theatrical and videocassette releases, and audits media and public relations' expenses fulfilled by distributors on behalf of the producer. This vice president also may direct the activities of a staff of one or two assistants, plus the activities performed by promotions/public relations firms, advertising agencies, and other related vendors.

The *business affairs vice president* typically has a law degree and directs the deal documentation preparation for development and production-related issues, along with sophisticated rights sales and distribution. These vice presidents closely correlate their work with the company's attorney, direct an assistant, and usually participate in development and production negotiations.

The *finance vice president* manages the company's cash flow, accounting, tax management, government agency reporting, management reports, and the company's information systems. This VP also manages the relationship with the company's entertainment accountant and manages the efforts of the operations director and department assistants, if there are any.

The Development Company's Teams

The development company is a completely separate business entity from the production company. It has its own accounting records, government agency reporting, income and expenses. However, it is most commonly at least half-owned by the production company. The two entities have several common elements. Usually the development company physically resides in the production company office, uses the same receptionist and most of its team are also members of the production company team.

Like the production company, the development company's team has three tiers.

The development company's advisory team is exactly the same as that of the production company.

The development company's executive committee typically has four members. These are the development director (usually the producer), the development manager (commonly the development VP from the production company), the global rights manager (who is the production company's global rights sales VP), and the operations director (who is an employee unique to the development company).

A producer easily presses full-time attention into development director duties, after a development company's first picture has successfully completed its internal greenlight. The development company usually pays the producer for serving as its development director, while at the same time it is paid proportionally by the production company for fulfilling duties there. The same is true for every other member of the development company's advisory team, with the exception of the operations director. This person is usually exclusively fulfilling duties for the development company. The operations director serves under the direction of the production company's finance VP, and may continue in the production company's "family," moving to the production company's succeeding development companies.

The *development manager* is responsible for story search, evaluation, recommendation, and all aspects of each motion picture's creative development and preparation, in every respect, for physical production. This person uses the development VP's production company staff and physical production specialist on an expense-paid basis.

The *global rights manager* is responsible for establishing each picture-in-development's global value, by territory and right, and for preparing promotional, publicity, and marketing materials, meeting with global media and studios, negotiating and pre-selling some of these rights, and preparing all other rights for future sales. This person also manages all global film market activities. Some of the most critical liquidation relationships, for instance, those with U.S. studios, may be carried out by the producer. But even for these, the global rights manager is responsible for ensuring that they are accomplished.

The *operations director* is responsible for keeping the development company on task and holding the entire team accountable in order to sustain balance between the timing allocated for developing its motion pictures and the budget the team has to achieve this task. This person also fulfills all day-to-day accounting functions, through the delivery of trial balances to the finance VP for the purpose of adjusting entries and preparing interim, monthly, and quarterly reports.

Optimizing the Teams

There are as many production companies whose operating temperament is chaos separated by moments of sanity as there are companies whose operating temperament is steady, progressive achievement. The difference is rarely the amount of work being done, but rather the approach the teams take to accomplishing the work.

Operating temperament is set more by the producer than by all the rest of the combined team. It is crucial that each producer accept this responsibility. Producers set the pace. They establish the operating style. They determine the stability of the relationship government within the team and with all the others with which the producer's team relates.

Among the highest achieving and happiest production company teams there is one management principle observed more consistently than any other. This is the observance by the producer, and subsequently by the rest of the executive team, and so, the staff, of including these three phases in most things they do : (1) they plan through study and evaluation, (2) they do what is planned, and (3) they evaluate what was done. These phases are deeply interrelated, and employing all of them optimizes the producer's capacity to accomplish every desired task and sets the standard for the team to approach their stewardships in a similarly constructive style.

Planning our work creates the greatest assurance that the work we do will accomplish our short- and long-term objectives. *Working* moves us forward to the achievement of our objectives. *Evaluating* our work motivates, makes enlightened planning possible, and inspires more confident and focused work. Sacrifice any one of these three critical phases, and predictable achievement is crippled.

Applying this principle is especially helpful when selecting new teams or organizing or reshaping existing production and/or development teams.

Planning has been emphasized throughout this text. Just as discovering a picture we want to produce is only the beginning of planning how we are going to develop, produce, and distribute it, so is preparing a mission statement that sets forth why we are in business only the beginning of planning how we will achieve our objectives. Part of each producer's plan should be identifying the talents and capacities needed and desired in the individuals who will be their advisory, operating, and staff teams. The team members should embrace the production company's mission statement, contribute to its clarity, and share the producer's approach to doing business.

Discovering, Negotiating, and Compensating

Producers are best served by team members who are not just good at what they do, but also have the attributes, character, and operating styles complementary to the producer and the rest of the team.

Discovering

For existing teams that have vacancies, the best approach to filling them is to write a description of the person sought, their stewardship, and compensation. This description should be circulated among the executive and advisory teams. Additionally, industry personnel agencies and advertising in the trade papers should be used to allow fresh, vibrant talent to have the opportunity to join the team. Set a time for the decision. Include those in the decision making process who may share stewardships or parallel positions with the open post. Attempt to adhere to the time, but never select someone less than the stewardship demands. Team orientation and releasing someone are emotionally and financially expensive. It is always better to wait for someone who appears sure.

For new production teams, start with the advisory tier. These members are easy to spot, evaluate, and approach. Once they are in place, then use them as resources for the production executive committee. After the executive committee is set, use them and the advisory members to recommend staff.

Negotiating and Compensation

Before negotiating, research what the industry's fair compensation for a particular position's services is, then temper this amount according to the company's projected budget. Negotiate the best relationship possible with the person, and after the negotiation has concluded, agree to start them at a little more than they expect. Goodwill motivates a positive attitude and usually increases industry.

Production companies are naturally rigorous environments. Participating in a winning production team demands everyone's personal excellence. Driving successful pictures is emotionally—and should also be financially—rewarding. It is very good business for producers to set a percentage of pretax profits aside (perhaps ten percent) for all employees to annually participate in. Some producers require new team members to vest (mature) in their relationship for 6 to 12 months before they qualify to participate. Sharing profits builds team spirit and loyalty, which fosters a happier and more profitable environment.

Summary

New and existing producers are well compensated if they understand all the business and creative functions that must be accomplished to do the work required by their production and development companies. These functions should be defined in terms of the advisory, operating and staff tiers of the team. Producers should have complete teams to ensure their capacity to accomplish the company's goals.

The producer sets the operating style of the team. The producer should demonstrate a style that promotes the team's sure, successive achievement.

There is an abundance of very talented prospective team members. A good plan to discover them, patiently executed, using team resources, will draw them in. Both regular team evaluations and allowing team members to participate in the company's rewards promote solidarity and mutual success.

Chapter 12

Production Company Operation

This chapter presents the operations of production companies and their related development and producing organizations. The prior chapters have presented the independent fundamental operating principles of these companies. This chapter demonstrates both how they work together and the business elements that join them.

The operations of these companies in their complete forms are also revealed in this chapter. For those who have experience with the operating performance of the most successful production companies, the operations presented in this chapter may seem more cumbersome or thorough than necessary. Consider the performance of a new driver compared with the performance of an experienced one. Seasoned drivers may speed through yellow lights, may turn without using their signals if they don't see any oncoming traffic, and may consistently drive a few miles over the speed limit on the freeway. These are not recommended operating styles but may become entrenched habits of experienced drivers.

As dexterity increases, so does confidence. As this occurs, one has a natural tendency, especially under pressure (and producers operate under extreme conditions), to cut operating corners and to increase operating speed. Abbreviating, or especially missing any development or production steps risks the creative and earnings life of a picture. As with experienced drivers, accomplished producers often press pictures through the production process with amazing agility and success. However, like the best race car drivers, fine producers occasionally trash pictures that would otherwise have been successful and performed well in the marketplace, simply because those producers slighted certain steps or passed them altogether. Because this natural tendency exists, it is necessary to establish a development and production checking system through which each picture passes. This chapter presents this system.

It falls upon the development vice president to ensure that each picture accomplishes all the steps. No one likes to be told they are going too fast or don't have their seat belt on, especially the producer who is most often the company chief and who stands to lose the greatest amount from a picture's failure. But it must be done. By establishing this process, a production company can successfully maximize operating integrity, as well as each picture's creative and financial success. And to present the most comprehensive operating profile, the example in this chapter is of a new production company.

Defining and Establishing the Production Company

As presented in Chapter 10, producers should write a mission statement that sets forth their purpose for creating their company, along with the manner in which they intend to conduct their business. This statement is often several pages long in its expanded reference format for the executive committee and pared down to less than a page for use by others.

There are several advantages for two or more principals rather than one to create a production company. Multiple principals typically deliver a better system of checks and balances for the company—each principal reviews and, from a similar position of power, holds the other accountable for performance. If each principal shares the mission of the organization, but delivers different experience and capacities, the company's overall strength and operating ballast are increased. There are several excellent examples of this, including Ron Howard and Brian Grazer with their Imagine Entertainment empire, and Mel Gibson and Brian Davies in their Icon Pictures powerhouse. With each of these teams, both are producers, but one is more deeply creative and the other has a stronger business background, thus delivering an excellent balance to their respective organizations.

If the organization has more than one principal, these individuals should agree on the company's mission, their respective stewardships, contributions, equity, operating control, earnings, and profit participations. They should also enter a written agreement, and/or separate management contracts, reflecting these deal elements and others natural to such agreements. (They should be certain to include buy/sell terms and the method of dispute resolution.)

It is always best to have the producer's entertainment attorney or some other lawyer involved in both negotiating and preparing the principals' documentation. The attorney should also prepare and file the company's formation documents with the state and direct the initial organizing meeting.

The Story Search

Most mission statements share one critical common goal—that the production company find and acquire the kinds of stories it is formed to produce and distribute. The search for these stories will be a preeminent activity throughout the life of the production company. This should be the first focus of newly formed companies.

Although there is an abundance of scripts, only a few are worth producing. The search should start immediately and continue in an organized fashion. Chapter 7 provides information about the legal aspects of story review and the need for literary release forms.

In contrast to the stunning volume of stories presented to producers from traditional trade sources is the smaller but just as vital proportion of stories discovered from non-industry sources. Usually producers have their private treasure house of folks who may be willing to champion their story cause, including family, friends from childhood, teachers, and others. This group can become a pipeline of continuing story discovery. Most of these connections, when asked, will recommend stories they believe will make great motion pictures, thus, maximizing the benefits from this source.

Producers should make a list of everyone who may be willing to participate as story resources and compose a letter that can be easily customized for each person, telling them they now have their own motion picture production company and are looking for stories that may make great motion pictures. Specifically, they should enclose two self-addressed and stamped postcards, asking the group to take a moment right then to list at least one story from a book or other source that they could recommend, then ask them to keep the other card in a conspicuous place for the purpose of making future recommendations. Producers should include their fifth-grade teacher who was a story wizard, their Peace Corps companion who read a book a week, and so forth. They may be tough to track down, so the new producer should try the Internet or give the list to an assistant to do the detective work. This has proven to be a stunningly fine source of story discovery by some of the industry's most notable producers. Great stories from unpublished journals, out-of-print books and those that are known only to storytellers and have never been written down are also some of the most remarkable finds. It is essential that producers commence and continue the story search and review process throughout the predevelopment company preparation.

Stories of interest to the producer should be represented to investors only as such, unless they have been greenlit by a U.S. studio and distributors in the six major foreign territories. It should be emphasized to prospective partners that, in large measure, their confidence in the new production company stems from the fact that it will only develop and produce pictures that are closely coordinated with global distributors.

However, potential investors will ask if producers have stories they are interested in and will want to hear them pitched. This is dangerous, because tastes in stories differ widely, and in an even more critical consideration, although producers may be excellent in their craft, they may be weak in their capacity to pitch an investor on a particular story. Producers should expect story queries and be prepared by having multiple stories ready and their pitches well-rehearsed.

For investors, more important than story point of reference should be the producer's representation that they have several stories with development and production potential ready for the internal greenlight process.

Development Company Emphasis

As story discovery and development come before production and distribution, and these activities originate in the producer's development companies, the first order of business is the planning and financing of the first development company. The need for this process and its thorough analysis is presented in Chapter 10.

Many production companies are launched with only their development company financing and teams (these are presented in Chapter 11), because developing their first pictures is typically their entire initial business.

If this is their position, these producers begin by preparing the first activity projection of the development company. A sample of this projection and its review are presented in Chapter 10. Following the preparation of the activity projection is the preparation of the cash flow projection, also presented in Chapter 10, which expresses the costs of the development company's activities.

Most development companies will be financed privately, according to the methods referenced in Chapter 10. If this is the case, producers will analyze the cash flow projection in relation to the total operating cash needed and the potential income earned by the development company. The private investor's participation is then applied to the cash flow projection and reviewed for its impact on the producer and its appeal to the investor. This process determines the basic deal points offered to the private investor. Often several operating models are analyzed by passing their criteria through the projections until the producer settles on the ultimate balance among the number of pictures to be developed, the development pace, the total investment amount, and the appeal to potential investors.

Preparing the Investment Offering

With the activity and the cash flow projections prepared and the investment offering plan configured, the producer is ready to have the investment offer writing begin with the assistance of the producer's attorney and accountant.

The accountant prepares (1) the projections as they will appear in the offering, (2) the notes to these projections, (3) the source and use of funds analysis, and (4) the tax consequences.

The producer prepares the introductory letter, the partnership business section (a representation of the production company's mission statement as it applies to the development company, including the kinds of pictures and properties the development company is seeking), and the development team summary biographies.

The attorney authors the memorandum, including the final draft of the materials prepared by the accountant and the producer.

Assembling the Team

An important part of the offering memorandum includes information about the producer's team, insofar as it is assembled at the time the offering is published. Who will be managing the partnership's business is crucial to prospective investors. They learn early that a great plan is only as impressive as the team assembled to carry it out.

The producer should have most of the advisory team assembled and represented at the time of the offering, as this team represents much of the assurance that the producer will be able to accomplish the development company's plan.

As the attorney prepares the first draft of the development company's investment memorandum, the producer will be setting appointments, meeting, and selecting advisory team members. Chapter 11 comprehensively presents the producer's advisory team categories and how to approach them.

Producing the Investment Memorandum

After the team is selected, the producer completes the biographical summaries for the advisory team members and others who are identified in the proposal, the final draft of the introductory letter, and the business section of the memorandum.

The producer reviews the materials prepared by the accountant and delivers all these materials to the attorney, after which the attorney prepares a final draft of the memorandum for the producer's review. The attorney makes final content polishes, and hard and computer disk copies are given to the producer.

The attorney should have offering samples that the producer can review for ideas on the look of the published draft. Having prepared many of these over the years, my suggestion is to focus on the content. Keep it clean and simple in presentation. Investors may be impressed with the glitz of an ornate-looking offering for a moment, but their decision will be based on the deal, the plan, and the people. In the final analysis, glitz has little effect on a positive decision.

Some producers use designers to prepare the offering's look. However it is determined, the original is prepared and copies made and numbered for presentation to prospective investor-partners.

Raising the Development Financing

Though producers who are funding their first development partnership may make presentations to several people, and the offering is structured to accommodate ten or more investors, it is common for there to be fewer than five investors who actually participate. Typically, one investor will be enamored with the offering's merits and will influence one or more investor associates to join in the relationship.

As to the most effective approach, each investor should be considered individually. Some investors prefer to be in a group presentation, while others prefer a private meeting. Each investor should be approached with their most effective method and setting in mind.

It is well to remember that the person to meet with is the actual investor. Sophisticated investors often have assistants who afford professional courtesy to the myriad offers that barrage these sources. Producers should begin this process by amassing lists of investors, brokers, finders, and people of influence they know who might invest or open the direct doors to them of others who have the means to invest.

Most investors' knowledge of entertainment investments is limited to the deep well of dreadful stories associated with investing in the production of independent pictures. Most investors have never had the opportunity to invest in independent motion picture development.

The producer's best approach with most investors is to follow these suggestions:

1. Make the entire presentation brief (under an hour). Let them know before the meeting how long it will take.

2. At the beginning of the meeting, let them know that they will first receive an overview of how the most successful independent producers do business, then hear how the production company is poised to operate. Following that, there will be a review of this particular offering, allowing the investors to consider the relationship in whatever manner they may be interested in.

3. After this has been told to them, then proceed with the presentation of the three areas referenced above.

For most investors, this is a new and fascinating business playing field. They often have questions and comments.

Most investors place their confidence in the person, rather than the documentation. The offering is expensive, and the information it contains is critically important. Investors will want to be entirely convinced that the producer understands the industry, this particular plan, and that this venture has a high probability to succeed. A producer needs solid confidence that comes from (1) experience, (2) team integrity, (3) a deep understanding of the plan, and (4) a commitment to the plan's success. Many investors have an uncanny sense for this. If they believe the producer has these qualities, they are more likely to consider the offering seriously. If not, then they will pass. The presenters need to be prepared. They will have accumulated a substantial investment in this venture to this point. The professional production values of the memorandum and even the impressive deal points will not overcome a producer's weak profile. It is important to meet potential financial partners when the producer is at his peak potential in these four areas.

Prior to these meetings producers should meet with their attorney and banker. Their attorney will review with them the appropriate legal approach to these highly regulated relationships. Their banker will assist in opening an escrow account for the receipt of investment income from the sale of the development company's interests.

Investment the Partner Communications

Once a producer has received the investment capital, there is often no immediate motivation to communicate with the private investors, who, before this time, were sought after with the producer's passion, sincerity and rapt attention.

Though the partnership agreement may not require communication with partners more than annually, it is good form and builds relationship integrity to prepare and send a letter, at least quarterly, informing them of development, production, and distribution progress.

Producers build confidence in their investors through beginning this relationship with a letter of appreciation and encouragement to them. Then they should set triggers in their schedule for similar letters to continue. This will be challenging to do after development commences, but should be done, even if the letters are prepared by an assistant.

Working Development Plan

The development activity projection used in the investment offering is the producer's representation to the investors of what will be done and when it will be accomplished. The activities in this projection are the investors' benchmark expectations and should also be used by the operating team to gauge the company's progress.

Each activity in the projections should be accomplished as if it is crucial to the initial and continuing success of the production company and its pictures. Each item should be finely planned, collaborated upon as a team and accomplished at its zenith.

Below are the producer's activities in order of priority:

1. Story: Producers should work on story *every day*. This should be well-rounded work, including reading and reviewing fresh coverage and analysis reports. In addition, they should send more letter and postcard requests (referred to above), research story leads, and, where appropriate, write and direct writers.

2. Advisory member meetings: Producers should meet with each member of their advisory committee immediately after funding has occurred. Copies of the current development activity projection should be given to and reviewed with each member. Suggestions relative to the plan, story suggestions, and team candidate recommendations should be elicited. Meeting with the advisory members as a group is often most effective, but because of tight schedules, it's not often possible.

   The banker will transfer the entire invested funds from the escrow account to the development company's working and savings accounts. Retainers will be advanced to the attorney, the UPM, and possibly the publicist.

3. Finding and securing the team: The advisory team is an excellent resource for recommendations for executive team members. Stewardship definitions and remuneration parameters should be given to the advisory team members, and their help in finding excellent candidates should be requested.

   A clear advertisement should be placed in one or more of the daily entertainment trade papers with a request for faxed, e-mailed, or carrier-mailed resumes. One or more industry personnel agencies may be another excellent resource for candidates. Of these three resources, the executive team, followed by the agencies and finally the trade papers, is most likely to recommend the best people to the producer.

   From these responses, the producer will first interview, perhaps re-interview, and then consider the finalists with the counsel of the appropriate advisory committee members. Next, the producer negotiates with the lead candidates and then prepares and enters a management agreement with the finalist. Entering these agreements with each new member of the executive committee is essential.

   Once the executive team is assembled, the first meeting should be held. Each member should attend this meeting prepared with a written stewardship definition that includes the people for whom they have immediate higher and lesser accountability. These definitions should be reviewed, harmonized, and adopted by the entire committee. Doing this allows the team to begin with a clear mutual understanding of each person's responsibilities and accountabilities. This has a wonderful effect on the team's efficiency, peace, and stability.

Often the executive team members will make their own staff recommendations. If these are not sufficient to fill the entire staff, recommendations should be sought from other executive team members and the three sources referenced above. As each staff member is attached to the team, they should also prepare, submit, and have harmonized their stewardship definitions, as referenced above. These definitions should be available to every team member. Executive team meetings usually occur weekly at a regular time and place, as determined by the members.

4. U.S. and major foreign territory distributor announcements: The first creation of new production companies should be their at least printed introductory announcement to every major global distributor. Because there are so few balanced producers, the most important aspect of this announcement is the definition of the relationship the producer seeks to have with these distributors.

There are multiple distributors in each of the U.S. and major foreign territories, and every one of them should receive a personal letter with their announcement. As reviewed in Chapters 2 and 3, all distributors have their unique liquidation values and characteristics for specific pictures, and consequently, every distributor is important to the producer.

The quality of this announcement should demonstrate that the production company operates in the same manner as the finest production entities in the industry. In other words, it should look "major studio."

The announcement introduces the new motion picture production entity and its first fully funded development company. The announcement incorporates the spirit of the production company's mission statement, and, moreover, presents the company's operating profile as one that develops and produces those motion pictures that these distributors want to distribute.

The producer will introduce the company in a personal letter to the distribution chief of each studio and major foreign territory distributor. The number of pictures on the production company's first development slate should be listed, along with the producer's intent to make a picture-specific pitch to the distributor for their initial distribution interest consideration, in the future. Stated clearly in this letter is the producer's position that the production company will only develop and produce motion pictures that first receive distributor interest. The producer should assert that the company will continue a close relationship with the distributor throughout development and production to ensure each picture's strongest production values, to achieve its maximum audience performance in their territory, and to assure the distributor of the greatest support of marketing and public relations materials to help prepare each picture's audiences.

These letters, with their collateral materials, should be sent to these individuals and their organizations before press or trade ads, demonstrating how the production company will proceed with press announcements relating to each picture.

The producer should break trade press releases and publish trade paid advertising three to five days following the distributors receipt of their packages. The process, overall appearance, and quality of the ads and press releases should continue to appear as if they come from a studio or major independent producer.

Story Selection and Initial Green Lights

All submitted stories are reviewed by the development manager. Stories that the development manager recommends to the producer (who must approve them) are then passed on to the production company's executive committee for their approval for investment in the story's internal greenlight.

Stories that receive the committee's approval then pass through the internal greenlight process under the direction of the development manager. The development manager prepares a studio greenlight plan and budget that is carried out after it has been revised and approved by the production company's executive committee members.

When the producers have a picture that succeeds in this process and have rights owned by other parties, they approach the rights holders and/or their representatives and enter a non-exclusive relationship that allows the producers the right to continue production discovery related to the story.

Part of the internal greenlight information involves discovery of who would be its three strongest U.S. studios. A greenlight for this picture is sought from the first priority studio, as referenced in Chapters 1 and 2. If a greenlight is not received, then numbers two and three are approached. Should these studios not give the picture a development greenlight, the production company executive committee reviews the findings and determines if there are other U.S. studios to be approached. Then, if no U.S. studio development greenlight is obtained, the story is abandoned.

After the U.S. studio greenlight is obtained, the producer confirms in writing to the studio, the purpose of and the actions that will now be put forward, in consequence to this non-binding, commercial relationship.

As presented in Chapter 3, after receiving the U.S. greenlight the producer then prepares to meet with the picture's potentially strongest distributor in each of the six major foreign territories, as outlined in the plan prepared by the development manager. Usually most of the materials prepared for the U.S. studio are applicable to their foreign territory counterparts. If a major market is about to occur, the foreign territory meetings are usually set around the schedules for that event.

After greenlights have been achieved from the foreign territory distributors, confirmation letters are prepared and presented to each of these, with a new letter to the U.S. distributor, stating (if it is a property for purchase) that the producer will now commence negotiations for the story.

These negotiations proceed as presented in Chapters 7 and 8, and should include the agreement with the author for a joint press release announcing the right's purchase. The conditions of this release should allow the producer first to notify in writing each of the U.S. and foreign distributors of the successful purchase, then follow this notification with press releases and paid trade announcements regarding the picture's development commencement. As has been reviewed in Chapters 1, 2, and 3, this process of distributor participation and trade culture escalates each picture's value. It also raises the level of anticipation among the participating distributors.

Pre-director Picture Development

Once the story's rights are acquired, the picture's game is afoot and will not wane until almost a year following its theatrical release.

This process commences with a special executive committee meeting. In this meeting, the picture's basic development, production and marketing plans and schedules are set, and development and marketing assignments are accepted by all the team members. The story's pre-director development is reviewed and decided upon. Also, this is the time that director, acting talent, and production department heads are considered.

The picture's initial trade-brand presence is created at this time, including what will be shown and said in the immediate paid trade announcement, in the future sales conferences, and on the marketing materials sent to the participating distributors. Although the name may later change, as perhaps will the original look, this presence is crucial to the picture's initial and continuing marketplace positioning.

Work now begins on the story's pre-director development substantially under the direction of the producer and development manager.

Director Attachment

Once the director is attached, this person will substantially drive the physical development and production of the motion picture. The earlier the director is attached, the greater the creative cohesion and harmony of every aspect of the picture. Producers who are also directors by craft, but who will use another director for the picture, are especially well served by the earliest possible director attachment, so that every creative element is a collaboration.

Differences in producer/director creative vision have weakened many pictures and literally destroyed others. Early director attachment naturally establishes a strong producer/director collaborative creative foundation.

The producer presents a written list of director recommendations, distilled from the executive committee's recommendations, to each advisory team member for that person's notes and suggestions. Some of the producer's executive and advisory team will have multiple experiences with the directors on this list and will render exceptional counsel relative to the consideration, approach and eventual relationship with the director.

After checking each director's availability, the producer next prepares a final priority list of directors, considering advisory team input, additional creative research, and discussions with other producers who have experience with these directors.

Then the producer prepares correspondence for the U.S. studio and each foreign territory greenlit distributor, confidentially revealing the directors being considered, in their order of priority, and requesting each distributor's preferences and comments. Typically, this letter is presented in person to the U.S. studio, and, if it is close to a film sales conference, also to the foreign distributors. If appropriate, a demonstration reel is prepared that accompanies each distributor's letter.

Tempered by distributor responses, the producer creates a final priority list of directors.

It is rare that the producer's decision will match every distributors' first choice. This being so, the producer's letter to each participating distributor usually includes an explanation of why the final three director candidates were selected in the particular order they were. This letter also states that the producer is now proceeding to attach the picture's director.

As reviewed in Chapter 8, producers must meet about the story with the director before talking about compensation. Most directors comfortably accommodate these initial creative meetings, since they may have their own production companies and business-wise, are negotiating their own agreements and using their attorneys and agents primarily for documentation and counsel.

It is during the initial creative meetings with the three leading directors that it often becomes apparent who should direct the picture, because of the director's affinity for the story and the director and producer's natural ability to communicate and respect each others' position, relative to developing and producing the picture.

After the producer reviews the creative meetings' events with the advisory and executive teams, a director decision is made and offering parameters are approved. A negotiation meeting is then set with the director and the director's entourage. If the director's attorney has been asked to participate in the negotiation, the producer's attorney should also participate.

As presented in Chapters 7 and 8, the director's relationship should be negotiated and documented. Part of this negotiation should include this relationship's press announcement.

The U.S. studio and foreign distributors are then notified of the successful attachment of the director, followed closely by a jointly coordinated press release and paid trade announcement in the entertainment trades.

The Producer/Director Relationship

The producer is the ultimate parent of the picture. The producer discovers the story, holds the initial vision of it as a motion picture, provides the environment and resources for the picture to be developed and produced, and even selects the director. However, the producer has simultaneous multiple-picture responsibilities. The final preparation and actual production of the picture is so intense that one person must be exclusively focused on each picture: the director.

The producer sustains the ultimate authority and power throughout the process. It is important that the producer exercise this authority only with the director. The department heads and all other production participants are accountable to the director, not the producer. When the producer works directly with any of the team reporting to the director, it is done only as an adjunct to the director, not as an authority superior to the director. The director must sustain position integrity with the production team as its ultimate voice. It is standard operating procedure, and everyone knows the director works for the producer. All should also understand that the director has complete power to produce the picture on behalf of the producer.

Most producers are *very* involved in each picture's development and production. Particularly when it comes to script development, talent attachment, story board creation, location selection, and the final post production and sweetening. Even after the producer reviews the dailies, the director may receive a call requesting reshoots, rewrites, and other major alterations. But this is between the director and the producer.

It is always in the best interest of the picture that the producer and director sustain this relationship integrity. To all who work on the picture, the producer creates an aura of respect for the director as the development and production chief of the picture. The director listens and responds to the producer who is, after all, the picture's creator and ultimate authority.

This is a fairly easy concept in discussion, but, typically, it can be challenging for both directors and producers to sustain during the intense heat of time and financial pressures that almost always attend development and, especially, production. As producers and directors often remind each other, it isn't the first development or production challenge and its accompanying burdens that test and tax the relationship, it is the 10th or 20th. It is at the time that neither party can recognize the picture's original schedule or the budget targets.

The truth of this working relationship is that most producers cannot direct every picture they produce. They must use directors. If the picture is going to be infused with the life it needs, the director must feel the creative freedom and the leadership control over all aspects of the picture. Directors must respect that the ultimate creative and financial ownership and responsibility belongs to the producer. The director is allowed the opportunity to create the picture, because the producer has put it in the director's hands. The producer is ultimately responsible for the picture's creative and financial success. Consequently, regardless of the extensive genius and energy directors pour into their pictures, the director should respect the producer's position and respond to requests even if they seem unreasonable.

Steven Spielberg produced and Richard Donner directed *Goonies*. These two powerful, gifted creators labored together under increasingly intense pressures as the picture progressed. Each respected the other's position. Challenging demands and decisions were made by both of them in their respective stewardships. Peace was maintained, and an excellent picture was delivered. More recently, James Cameron created the landmark achievement picture, *Titanic*. Tom Sherek at Twentieth Century Fox made suggestions. Cameron listened, considered, and responded. Each was under intense creative, time and financial pressure. Cameron later credited Sherek with the suggestion for what Cameron said was a better ending for the picture. In the final analysis, it isn't who has the greatest power, but rather how well the creative team works together to deliver the most creative and financially successful picture.

Shooting Script

The core development team now is composed of three members, the director in the primary position, along with the producer and the development manager. The producer still has the ultimate control, but the director is rightly the head of this core team, as the director is the only member of the team who is exclusively associated with this single picture.

The first focus of the core team is the story. The picture must have a first-draft shooting script prior to the intricate and intense planning and budgeting that are essential for its creation. The story will go through further rewrites as other key collaborators are attached, but the basic story will be recommended by the director and finally decided upon by the core team, tempered by executive team review and comment. This review is a key contribution to the picture's success.

Often the director is a writer and may participate in the writing of the drafts leading to the shooting script. Even if this is so, it is best to enter a multiwriter step deal, as presented in Chapter 7. This will ensure the greatest probability for the script's predictable on-schedule completion and the creation of the strongest shooting script.

Typically the director and producer will insist on having the first-draft shooting script before they approach the potential lead cast talent.

Lead Cast Attachment

The producer and development director will have drawn up a proposed list for the lead cast before the director is set. The director and producer will use this list and the director's considerations to prepare a collaborative list that is presented to the advisory team. This committee's recommendations, then, and the collaborative list will be presented to the executive committee. With the director, this team will prepare the final list of lead actors under consideration.

Following much the same process as the director selection, the U.S. and foreign distributors are contacted, their responses are weighed (considering the TVQs and marketing values of each performer in the various markets), and a final actors priority list is prepared.

The actors are approached as presented in Chapter 8, and negotiation and documentation occurs. After all that, distributor notifications are sent out prior to press releases and paid trade announcements.

Preparing for Physical Production

Once the first draft of the shooting script is completed, physical production preparation commences in earnest. This includes attaching the picture's UPM, or line producer. The UPM now becomes the central participant in the physical production process. This person will create the original and the many permutations of the picture's production breakdowns, schedules, and budgets. Various portions of these materials, along with the shooting script, will be studied and used by department heads and others in their individual planning and performance.

Production department heads will be recommended by the director and reviewed by the producer, and a final review and acceptance are made by the advisory and executive teams. The key department heads will be approached through creative discussions that will expand into negotiations and then attachment to the picture.

Creative collaboration from the newly added genius pool of the department heads will deepen the color and dimension of the picture, further perfecting the script and bringing the picture into clearer focus.

Development of physical production now begins in earnest, with locations being determined, departments making staff arrangements, the balance of the cast being attached, and, of course, the continual enhancement of the script in response to the reality of these elements.

Maturing Marketing Materials

As talent is attached to the picture, so are their representative reels, including those from the director, actors, cinematographer, production designer, and composer. Through many of the excellent film commissions, reels are even provided on the picture's locations. The compilation of these elements, together with print elements, combines for a rich resource to create the picture's print, film, and video presentations for the major markets. When these are presented to participating distributors, they use them to promote the picture within their respective territories.

Preparing the Production Bank Financing Facility

Since the completion bond advisor's company usually bonds all of the production company's pictures, and the bank advisor's bank finances most of the pictures, each of their companies are regularly brought up to speed on the picture's progress. In addition to the referenced advisory meetings, at least two additional meetings with documented picture plans should be set up prior to placing bonding and lending requests with these institutions.

Typically five to nine months pass between the story acquisition and the placement of the production loan request with the bank. During this time, the most aggressive distributors for the picture become apparent. (All distributors should be aggressive, but some are more than others.) Also, conditions within these territories change from the time of the first greenlight. Mergers, acquisitions, and changes in the economy are largely responsible for these shifts.

Because of these phenomena, the global rights manager should revise the picture's liquidation breakdown at least monthly, and again just prior to preparing the picture's presale plan and bank loan analysis. The presentation of how to prepare the plan and analysis is in Chapters 3 and 5.

The UPM then prepares a fresh budget for use with the preparation of this documentation.

Once the bank loan analysis is prepared, it is presented, along with the presale plan, to the executive committee for approval. Following its approval, the bank loan memorandum, as described in Chapter 5 and the completion bond memorandum, as described in Chapter 6, are prepared by the production company's finance vice president. The bond memorandum is prepared and presented first, since the completion bond company's intent will accompany the bank memorandum.

Each of these memoranda are mature intent documents. Their purpose is to receive a contingent commitment from each participant, so that when the producer provides the imminent elements declared in the memoranda, each respective entity will participate in the picture's production funding. The production company must be bondable to engage the production bank loan, and the bank loan facility must be available to draw the picture's pre-sales into it.

The producer meets with the bonding organization and receives the completion bond contingent commitment first, then meets with and receives the bank's contingent commitment.

The U.S. Studio Distribution Agreement _____

As thoroughly reviewed in Chapter 2, this agreement affects all other rights relationships and earnings and is central to the picture's global success. This is the time when producers should obtain their picture's U.S. theatrical distribution.

As suggested previously, the studios are excellent marketers as well as negotiators. They understand the value of a picture, and, as they have global liquidation power, they prefer to acquire all global rights.

Fortunately, there are ten competitive U.S. studios. These studios have become very open to a broad spectrum of distribution relationship configurations. Each wants the valuable inventory, the product with substantial earnings power.

As reviewed in Chapter 2, U.S. theatrical distribution rights are usually more of a liability than an asset. Typically the producer plans a studio distribution relationship that is a combination of U.S. theatrical (the right with the least earnings potential) and U.S. video (the right with the greatest earnings potential). Each is an excellent offset to the other. Also, the timing of these two distribution windows is very close, with video earnings primarily driven by the picture's theatrical campaign.

Though the U.S. theatrical and video distribution rights bundle is the most common studio relationship approach, as the picture matures through development, the U.S. studio may become much more aggressive in negotiating for specific or all foreign rights, as well as for specific or all ancillary rights. Many of these distribution proposals are extremely competitive with those the producer has developed throughout the picture's development and preproduction. The producer should analyze the studio proposal and compare its gross potential, distribution fees, and costs, as well as the producer's internal costs, against these factors in the existing relationships. Then, with the counsel of the advisory and executive teams, the producer must decide the best financial course of action. The studio offer would need to perform substantially greater before it should be considered over the existing distribution relationships.

To clearly compare the offers, producers must also recalculate the picture's bank financing worksheet. The studios do not provide a bank letter of credit, so their contract will receive a larger bank discount than the foreign presale collateral, as reviewed in Chapter 5.

The Presales _____

The presales are entered into with those licensees discovered during the presale analysis, and they usually include at least one major foreign territory (often two or three), and frequently U.S. premium cable and/or network television.

The foreign license strategy and approach is presented in Chapter 3 and the premium and network television rights in Chapter 4.

When motion picture development becomes this mature, the picture is a familiar name among trade participants in the major territories and in the U.S., and more often than not, consumer press has begun.

By this time the producer has been approached by other foreign distributors who compete with the participating greenlight distributors. The producer maintains the integrity of the participating distributor relationships; however, the competing distributors will become increasingly interested in engaging license rights for the picture.

The producer prepares and presents a preferential license opportunity to the proposed presale licensees. In the licensee presentation meeting, the producer first reveals the name of the bank providing the picture's production funding and the completion guarantor providing its bond. Next, the producer presents the plan for this particular distributor to obtain the rights to the picture for its territory by entering a presale license agreement. This license calls for a traditional license advance, paid against the producer's share of a revenue-sharing relationship with the licensee. The differences in this license are (1) that the advance amount is discounted by approximately 20 percent compared to what they would be expected to advance after the picture is completed (most often this is only 5 to 12 months away); and (2) that only 10 percent of the license advance is due at the license signing; the balance is not due until the licensee has access to the picture and its associated elements.

The producer only makes this offer to the distributors that are part of the presale plan. The offer is made at the time when these producers should be especially motivated to secure the picture's rights, and to receive the financial advantage associated with the license advance discount. This is good business for both the distributor and the producer.

The appeal for this relationship is heightened by the licensee's advance amount typically being no more than the lowest amount the licensee may earn from the rights being purchased.

If there are U.S. ancillary presales, these are offered in much the same manner, with similar discounts, as discussed in Chapters 1, 4, and 5.

Engaging the Completion Bond

The completion bond is necessary for the bank loan and is formally requested immediately following the securitization of the presale documentation.

The request for the completion bond is made in writing with the most recent shooting script, production budget, and supporting documentation.

Engaging the Production Bank Loan

The collateral and completion bond are presented to the bank to engage the production loan. Processing the loan includes conforming the letter of credit(s) language to language that is acceptable to the bank. This process may take five to ten working days.

At this time, the producer forms the picture's producing company as a corporation or LLC. As presented in Chapter 9, this organization is a wholly owned subsidiary of the production company and will produce and own the picture. After the production line of credit is open, the production company begins making the several advances to the producing company as it will continue to do throughout the completion of the picture.

The first expense of the producing company is the purchase of all rights, title, and interest of the picture from the development company, according to the production company's purchase agreement with the development company.

Final Preproduction

During final preproduction the producer:

1. Closely participates with and supports the director. As frenetically paced as this time is, this is the last sane time the producer can participate with the director until principal photography wraps. The creative look of the picture is substantially established during this period. The script receives special producer scrutiny for the apparent creative reasons, as well as special needs that include writing, planning, and budgeting for foreign territory and ancillary media cover shots.

2. Sets the picture's novelization relationship with a publisher, even if the story has been or currently is in release, as explained in Chapters 1 and 4.

3. Pursues potential premium tie-in and product placement relationships. To accomplish this, the global rights and advertising VPs combine their efforts in preparing the presentations, setting the meetings, and negotiating the relationships, as reviewed in Chapter 4.

4. Prepares, in cooperation with the U.S. and foreign distributors, the picture's ramp-up consumer PR and advertising; the print, TV commercial, and trailer title, look, teaser, and long-form element list; layouts; boards; title research, and treatment; along with related activities. Some of this is for release soon after principal photography begins, and the rest is for the several releases that will escalate as the picture approaches the global marketplace.

Principal Photography

As principal photography commences, primary location accommodations are made for special production guests, including development company partners, U.S. studio representatives, pre-buy participants, foreign territory greenlight participants, and trade and consumer press. Appropriate invitations are sent to these guests, and as they respond, their individual arrangements are made.

The producer reviews all the picture's dailies, consulting with the director relative to the picture's creative progress, and informing the director about the picture's distribution and marketing. The producer will be on location from time to time, as well as with the picture's post production team, which most often begins assembling the picture within two weeks from the beginning of principal photography.

The initial consumer press releases are staged and rolled into the U.S. and global territories. Trade press and paid announcements are released.

As the picture is produced, the marketing reel expands; the teaser trailer is assembled and released to the theatrical distributors; the primary trailer(s) start and continue to assemble; and promotional coverage is captured, assembled, polished, and released, according to the marketing plan. Copies of all press releases and promotional materials are sent to the major distribution participants.

The picture's up-to-the-minute promotional reel is exclusively exhibited in the appropriate global markets.

Post Production

The director is usually the post-production supervisor. As this process begins, soon after principal photography commences, assemblies are sent to the director for review. The digital post-production process, Web use, and digital phone transfer have been extremely useful in *fixing it in principal photography*, which is most often much better and less expensive than the traditional fixing it in post.

In addition to more traditional post production duties, the producer supervises in-house produced trailers and ad spots. The producer also reviews the preparation and audience testing of distributor and trade specialist produced trailers in two or three versions, and television commercials in four or five versions. If the picture's title is in question (this process is often excruciating), it will also be market and audience tested, before it is eventually decided.

As post production is completed, foreign sales substantially heat up, and the U.S. and major foreign distributors deepen their marketing preparation.

The Picture's U.S. Branding

The picture's total U.S. audience size and earnings are substantially determined by the effectiveness of the picture's branding during its theatrical release. The picture's total earnings are not determined so much by the picture's theatrical gross, as they are by the power of the picture's campaign, the reach and frequency of its media buy to its target audiences, and the word-on-the-street among the picture's targets. Box office grosses can also be negatively affected as much as one-third by marketplace anomalies including picture release glut, weather, spectacular national news, or sports events.

The producer is never busier than during a picture's post production and pre-theatrical release. In fact, it is not enough to make an outrageously fine motion picture. Audience reactions to a picture's early trailers are excellent indications of the content and texture that should be used in the picture's strongest television commercials, as well as its trailers that will be shown closer to the picture's release and the clips shown during celebrity show visits.

At the time the television campaign begins (about three weeks prior to the first theatrical street date), the picture's novel should be flooding check-out stands with the picture's one-sheet on their covers. The publisher will want to correlate the timing of the paperback release with the timing of the television campaign.

If the premium brand tie-in(s) were entered into six to nine months previously, these brand-partner commercials will begin airing immediately before and then into the picture's theatrical release.

The week the picture opens, the PR and advertising departments at the studio are at full throttle. Theatrical premieres, entertainment, morning, news, and other television shows are sporting celebrity and picture highlight segments; entertainment and other publications have eye-grabbing photos and articles about the picture, and literally every other promotional and purchasable device is employed to establish and turn up the heat on making the picture a living legend.

The Global Territories and Ancillary Markets

Once the picture is completed, then lab access letters are delivered to pre-buy distributors and special screenings are set for the other foreign greenlight distributors, as discussed in Chapter 3, and for major ancillary rights media, as presented in Chapter 4. This is the completion of the primary cycle of discovering, producing, and bringing a picture into the market. A checklist of the entire cycle follows below.

Summary

Before the production company begins the process of developing, producing, and liquidating its motion pictures, the operating plan and the team that will run it should already be prepared and in place.

This team and their organizations establish and finance the development companies, discover, qualify, and develop the stories, begin and manage the marketing of the pictures, fund the production of the pictures, produce the pictures, mature their marketing, and manage the global distribution of the pictures. These are seven individually critical processes of assuring that the production team produces the pictures it wants, and that each picture individually has the greatest opportunity for artistic and financial success.

Producers must understand how all the pieces fit together and how the team accomplishes the work and sustains the critical checks and balances during the process. Thoroughly understanding the whole process and preparing for its successful operation are essential to achieving team objectives.

Motion Picture Development and Production Checklist

1. Story search
2. Begin development company's design and deal preparation and assemble or tune the team
3. Conduct a successful Greenlight for the 1st picture
4. Produce the development company investment offering
5. Subscribe the development company partners
6. Begin and continue partner communications
7. Work the development plan
8. Story review and selection
9. Pre-director picture development
10. Director search and attach
11. Cause the first draft shooting script to be created
12. Attach the lead cast
13. Physical production preparation
14. Prepare and mature the picture's marketing materials
15. Prepare the bank financing facility
16. Enter the U.S. studio agreement
17. Design and enter the picture's presales
18. Engage the completion bond

19. Engage the bank loan
20. Complete the final preproduction
21. Principal photography producer's duties
22. Post production producer's duties
23. The picture's U.S. branding
24. Selling the open global ancillary markets and foreign territories

Chapter 13

The Producer's Business

This chapter presents the producer's role in the process of multiple picture production, the establishment of the production company brand presence with the
global entertainment trade and consumers, the balancing act between business,
artistic and personal objectives, the management of library pictures, and the
advancement of team vitality and allegiance.

Multiple Picture Management

As demonstrated in the previous chapter, shepherding a single picture through the
complete cycle, from discovery and development through production and distribution, is a wonderfully complex process. When producers plan multiple pictures,
their activity projection reveals the super-challenge of simultaneously managing a
picture in post, starting another's principal photography, moving another picture
through greenlit development, and reviewing new stories.

The single picture activity and cash flow planning that is reviewed in Chapter 12
must be done for each picture proposed in the producer's multiple picture development plan. Each picture must be considered separately, yet with the full consideration of both the distractions and the time and expense benefits that each picture
in the development plan has on the others.

The capacity to manage multiple pictures is directly related to how well the
producer understands the entire development/production/distribution process. It
also depends on the planning and work ethic of the individual. Juggling is an useful
analogy to this process. Each juggling rotation has its unique arc and rhythm. A
good juggler sustains the integrity of each individual rotation, while focusing on the
balance between the three rotations. Similarly, producers must sustain the indi-

vidual creative and business integrity of each picture, while they focus on the creative and business balance among all the pictures.

Seasoned producers adhere to the most successful processes of multiple picture development and production by thoroughly planning for the needs and timing of each picture, and focusing on the pictures as a group, in such a fashion that each picture actually benefits the other.

Time and Budget Economies

Investors are not the only parties pressing the producer to be engaged in multiple pictures. Most of the producer's primary relationships, such as licensees, agents, bankers, and sales teams, are more supportive when the producer has several pictures in process.

Studio Relationships

Licensees are motivated in their relationships with producers who both deliver pictures that perform strongly and provide a regular high volume of pictures. It is a combination of these two qualities that determines a producer's value to each licensee.

During a meeting with studio licensees, a producer may pitch a new picture for studio greenlight, review cast considerations for another picture and deliver marketing elements for another. The greater the number of significant pictures delivered by a producer, the stronger the producer's relationship is with licensees.

Agents

As presented in Chapter 8, most agencies have packaging agents, who combine internal story and performing elements with other creative elements represented outside their agencies in order to motivate the making of pictures that substantially include their clients.

The most organized production companies are those that are the most sought after by agency packagers. These agencies are pleased to meet and assist such producers on their pictures, as well as use the opportunity to approach them with agency packages. And multiple picture production necessitates regular agency meetings. This keeps the producer's operating style and integrity fresh and vital with these firms.

Banks and Completion Guarantors

Some pictures will develop and produce in a smoother fashion and achieve greater income performance than others. Bankers and insurers tend to have a greater sense of balance and stability with those producer clients who are driving multiple pictures. Further, a slate of pictures allows the producer to offer offsetting guarantees among these pictures to banks and bonding companies. Such cross-collateralized relationships must be entered into within the bounds of the agreements set forth with the several profit participants associated with each picture. This often establishes a substantially deeper deal stability and relationship confidence with insurers and banks that is unique to multiple-picture production.

Sales Events

Though independent producers' pictures are normally represented by domestic studios at U.S. theatrical and video events, the producers or their representatives usually represent their pictures with the six major territory greenlit distributors and at foreign territory sales conferences. Similar to the U.S. studio relationship, having multiple pictures strengthens foreign territory relationships. Additionally, multiple pictures allow the producer to amortize these significant expenses over several pictures.

Establishing the Production Company Brand Presence

Especially new production companies must establish and then advance the heat of their company's global trade brand presence, as has been emphasized throughout this book. The importance and relative business value of a production company's brand reputation among the global industry cannot be overemphasized. Appropriately, this reputation is almost entirely established and sustained by the performance of the producer's pictures in the global marketplace. In fact, the *trade* brand respect for a production company is chiefly a mirror for the global *audience* respect for the producer's pictures.

Who we are always speaks more loudly than who we say we are. Likewise, a production company is substantially known by its pictures rather than its mission statement. Understanding this basic reality, producers who want to establish their production company brand with its audiences will be benefited by correlating their picture selections with their mission statements. If a producer becomes committed to produce a picture that is outside the scope of the company's creative charter, but wants to sustain the company's brand presence, then perhaps the producer should create another production entity for that picture.

Because each motion picture's campaign is necessarily intense and focused on that picture, little campaign emphasis is typically given to the production company or the studio. Further, it is almost unheard of for production companies or studios to launch a campaign exclusively on themselves, or even a campaign where they are the dominant focus. This is the prevailing notion in the current culture of the motion picture industry. Like many cultures, this practice is not necessarily the most effective way to drive audiences to pictures delivered by the production company and the studio. It may be a profitable exercise for producers and studios to consider if there may be motion picture marketing advantages associated with a production company's name becoming an icon to audiences.

There are lessons to be learned by other global consumer brands and the way in which they are marketed. Nike, IBM, Microsoft, and many other brands have specific product commercials, as well as primarily brand commercials that, in turn, drive consumer response to their individual products. If the new product release (which every nonfranchise motion picture is) is driven by a brand name that has consumer confidence, the new product's reception and success are substantially more predictable. For their target consumers, Nike's new basketball shoe, BMW's new roadster, and McDonald's new kid's meal are all "must-have" purchases. Their target consumers are all substantially motivated to buy because of their perception of the brand.

From an audience perspective, Disney is currently the only studio/production company with a brand reputation for delivering a specific kind of motion picture entertainment. The U.S. studios have a general reputation for delivering high quality entertainment, but not necessarily delivering a certain style of entertainment. Associated with their style, U.S. studios are not known for skewing to any particular target audiences.

Consider the similarities of the motion picture industry to the fashion industry. Just as there are high-, medium-, and low-profile department stores, there are flagship, medium- and low-profile multiplex theaters. Just as high-end department stores offer greater perceived quality and more sought-after brands and other department stores commonly offer lesser or unknown brands, so do the finest multiplexes offer the strongest pictures at their earliest release, while the other theaters deliver lighter or more eclectic fare, and/or pictures at later release dates.

Most brands are known by their style rather than their product categories. For instance, Ann Klein provides a broad range of consumer products, but each product has this brand's quality and style associated with it, and consumers know that brands such as Ann Klein are offered in higher-profile retail stores. The brand is sold in large measure because of product integrity, and specific new products are successfully launched, substantially benefited by the strength of the brand presence with its targeted consumers. It is a well exercised retail concept, but one little used in the motion picture industry.

Pictures by Spielberg and Lucas have a consumer-brand presence. They owe this primarily to audience satisfaction of their prior pictures, but also because of their respective companies' continual and highly effective promotion and public relations output. But what of Imagine, Castlerock, and even Dreamworks? These companies are well known names within the trade, but they are largely without product definition to audiences.

Production companies who create a strong consumer brand presence will deliver a powerful marketing advantage for their pictures. This important marketing edge will render their pictures easier to sell and, consequently, more valuable to global licensees.

Production companies committed to becoming audience icons will refocus their companies' motion logo, include new brand marketing language in their distribution agreements and increase their company brand strength in their pictures' advertising and promotion campaign.

Sustaining Business, Artistic and Personal Objective Balance _____

As independent producers review their responsibilities, and more pointedly, as they perform them, it becomes inescapably apparent that unless managed well, a producer's life can easily be consumed entirely with motion picture activities.

Producing well is an exceptional accomplishment and immensely satisfying. But for most of us, it is essentially important to participate in the lives of our family members. Further, to be whole, balanced, and prepared, it is beneficial for us to study ancient and New Age thought, to meditate, and to discover ourselves and life anew through such acts as caring for a child. We need to advance our understanding of new technologies, to participate in and be nourished by the arts, to keep and occasionally review a personal journal. Additionally, we can balance ourselves by caring for those less able than us, and perhaps even by planting and caring for a garden.

Work is the lubricant of life. When we cease to be productive, we tend to lose our purpose and place. But it shouldn't consume us. We must plan for *seasonings* of our life, or ours will be bland, lacking full symmetry and fulfillment. Family, contemplation, study, the arts—these are the desserts of life. Without them, we will wake up one day and find ourselves separated from our central motivators.

In the words of historian Will Durant, "To seize the value and perspective of passing things, we want to know that the little things are little and the big things big, before it is too late. We want to see things now as they will seem forever, in the light of eternity." To strike balance in our lives between the big and small, but important things, is not as impossible as it might seem. It is largely a matter of perspective, planning, and performance.

The most effective and productive leaders I know in the entertainment industry have written their short- and long-term life objectives, which they frequently revise. Doing so allows them to temper their passionate, classically well planned filmmaking commitments. They use their written objectives to develop a detailed written plan in which they pencil in specific appointments for their daily, weekly, monthly, and annual schedules. Yes, they actually schedule personal time with family, along with times for service, reading, study, and even (perhaps especially) play.

The power of scheduling these activities provides for balance in their lives and even gives them occasion to respond, "I'm sorry, I am booked then, but we can get together . . .". By keeping as faithful to their schedules as possible, these people prosper in their family relationships, thrive as teachers and learners, and experience the truly good things of life, each of which keeps them happier, more productive, and by their admission, more creative.

In the main, producers love their work and immerse themselves in it. This is essential to achieve their finest pictures. But if this is done to the exclusion of other rich aspects of life, they may become personally weak, even in motion picture production.

Managing Library Pictures

As reviewed in earlier chapters, motion pictures premiere in each major distribution window. Then they become library pictures, continuing their audience and earnings life primarily in global television syndication.

A wonderful phenomenon of this industry is continual audience evolution. Some television syndicators constructively measure audience evolution in seven-year cycles. Whatever the year of the picture's television premiere, in seven years, newborns will be 7 years old and are a new kids audience. Seven-year-olds grow to be 14 and become a new youth audience; 14-year-olds become 21 and thus a new young-adult audience. By the time 21-year-olds become 28 and have started families, they view entertainment from a substantially new lifestyle perspective.

Because of audience evolution, pictures should be reanalyzed by their target audiences every five years. Some pictures will warrant a more aggressive rerelease strategy than others. A picture's reanalysis will assist the producer in an accurate valuation for new television syndication licenses. Other pictures may justify rerelease strategies that include release through higher distribution windows, creating new advertising and public relations campaigns, negotiating campaign tie-ins with other consumer brands, and novelization rerelease, among others. Motion pictures, which are the producer's inventory, should be regularly and thoroughly evaluated, kept fresh and valuable to prior audiences, and marketed to new target audiences with reasonable aggression.

Theatrical Rerelease

Most motion pictures play very well on in-home media, especially as television screens enlarge, increase in clarity, and have sound advances that bring them close to theater grade. But most motion pictures are produced to be experienced on a large theater screen, with pristine, powerful sound. No lights, no phones, no commercials—just pure, undiluted audience-story absorption.

Newly evolved audiences may prefer to experience rereleases in the theater. Recent rereleases of *Star Wars* and *Gone With the Wind* have demonstrated this, especially for epic pictures. It appears that there may also be new audiences and income for many other audience-proven pictures. A ridiculously short list of these examples include *Ferris Bueller's Day Off, Superman, City Slickers, Robin Hood: Prince of Thieves, A Room With a View, Dances With Wolves, On Golden Pond, Toy Story, Ghost, Home Alone,* and *Karate Kid.*

It should be considered, as reviewed in Chapter 2, that each picture's campaign and media buy almost exclusively determines the success of its opening week. If the distributor is not committed to an aggressive rerelease, the picture will most likely fail. Market data and original-picture release data combine to make a strong argument in favor of the likelihood that several major motion pictures will potentially perform well if rereleased, either in theaters, on video, on premium cable, and/or on network television.

Currently, Buena Vista is the only studio that boldly exploits their pictures in this way, and only those pictures which primarily exploit the kids (5 to 11) audience. And they do it well. A review of the theatrical grosses of these rereleases provides a clear confirmation of the power of rereleased pictures with new-evolution audiences. *101 Dalmatians* was rereleased theatrically during the 1985 Christmas holidays, earning $31 million, and again, almost six years later in the summer of 1991, earning almost $61 million. *Snow White* was rereleased in the summer of 1987, earning $46.6 million, and in the summer of 1995 this picture earned $41.6 million.

Advancing Team Vitality and Allegiance

The production and development company team is best served by the producer who analyzes and directs from the perspective that the process they are engaged in is a whole and living entity. The team is responsive to everything that affects it, thereby increasing or decreasing in its health, vitality, and productivity. Producers who understand this regularly evaluate and revitalize the team.

Much like a fruit tree, healthy teams produce appealing, good fruit, in the form of pictures and related products. And like that fruit, both products and people leave the company in their seasons, and this is a healthy sign of productivity. Some team members progress beyond the capacity of the production team, while others may not be able to sustain the team's performance integrity. For either of these reasons, it is best for them to go.

Also, just as trees become burdened with unproductive growth that needs to be trimmed, so production teams may have members who are more like anchors than sails. Though this process is most often uncomfortable, pruning provides for the best growth, both for these individuals and the team. Between these two extremes exists the necessity of caring for the team. This can only be sufficiently accomplished when team members are individually and regularly reviewed (twice per year is optimal).

Producers strengthen their team members when they seek for opportunities to help expand their experience, education, and stewardship. This can be effectively done through providing team members with both the means (such as expenses for classes in Web design, digital special effects, and foreign languages) and motivation (promotion, prizes, perks, bonuses, and/or pay increases for successful achievements). Providing team members with the means and the motivation results in a team that is continually expanding its performance capacities and deepening team commitment and solidarity.

Sustaining business, artistic, and personal objective balance applies to all members of the team, not just the producer. Producers can provide a broad range of benefits to their teams, which, in return, can create the greatest success attainable. These benefits begin with each team member understanding and performing in harmony with the company's mission statement, and encompass spouse and family travel accommodations and office environment perks, including exercise rooms, nursery care, a well stocked kitchen, and a library.

Summary of the Producer's Business

Dream expansively, plan comprehensively, work valiantly, and live completely.

Reports, Data, and Producer's Principles

This chapter presents and analyzes industry data particularly useful to independent producers, presents information sources enabling producers to keep current on this data, and brings together in a list, the cornerstone principles presented in this book that form the independent producer's most predictable foundation for success.

Entertainment Industry Statistics and Reports

One resource that can powerfully assist producers in sustaining a clear and balanced perspective among each picture, its respective global audiences, and its potential earnings are comprehensive entertainment data and the reports derived from this data. Accessing and regularly reviewing this information lends a critically important advantage to the producer's companies and pictures.

Barry Reardon retired as Warner Bros. distribution president March 19, 1999, after serving the studio in this position for 17 years. Reardon exercised his excellent natural audience sense and deep distribution experience in the release of scores of successful pictures. This sustained Warner Bros. for 16 years as one of the leading three studios—eight of those years in first position, and five of those years in second position. In his 31-year career, he participated in and, more often, was the lead innovator in the way motion pictures are distributed.

Reardon amplified his natural marketing savvy by using a powerful studio distribution database that tracks all major releases, not just those of Warner Bros. This database was substantially developed by Reardon and continues to assist the studio in making the most predictable decisions regarding high-impact, motion picture distribution.

Every picture, regardless of its earnings, provides a lesson for its producers and distributors. There are so many elements that affect a picture's earnings, including (1) the power of the picture's inherent campaign elements, (2) the capacity of the created campaign, especially the picture's trailer and television commercials, but also its radio, print, outdoor and PR, to drive the target audience, (3) each type of media's reach and frequency of target audience, (4) the theatrical release pattern (including which theaters are booked and how many), (5) the time the picture is released (not so much the time of year as much as the competing pictures released during the same period), and, of course, (6) the picture's audience satisfaction for each target and (7) critical reviews.

Consequently, all of these seven aspects are important tracking considerations in analyzing why pictures succeed or fail to the extent they do. These aspects should be considered during all of the phases of development, production, distribution planning, and execution of each picture.

In addition to the above aspects, producers are well served, when tracking other story and production-related elements that affect both grosses and profits, if they are aware of (1) each picture's target audiences, their sizes, and consumption profile for each major distribution window, (2) the use of star power for their earnings effect, compared with the star cost, (3) the overall earnings effect of using a major director as compared with the director's cost, (5) the effect, if any, of a picture's genre, (6) its rating, and (7) even the effect of running time of a picture.

Data on several pictures, side by side, tell a story that can wonderfully halt speculation. Knowledge really is power, and, to know each picture's inherent strengths and weaknesses, allows both producers and distributors to mount an approach in which they can view each picture's several audiences for maximum success patterns.

The Most Successful Motion Pictures Ever Released in the U.S.

A limited profile of some important characteristics of the 35 most theatrically successful motion pictures ever released in America follows. To measure these pictures fairly, each picture is positioned according to the quantity of theatrical admissions, since a theater ticket in 1949 was about $.39, compared with 1999 ticket prices that average approximately $4.78.

As pictures on this list range from 1937 to 1999, our evaluation should be tempered by the vast changes in the entertainment universe during this time. In 1937, television was not a theatrical competitor, whereas, in 1999, 99 percent of U.S. households had at least one color TV. VCRs did not reach 50 percent U.S. household penetration until 1986, and, by 1999, they were at 85 percent penetration. Basic cable television with its broad channel selection didn't reach 50 percent U.S. household penetration until 1987, and, by 1999, was at 70 percent. On the other hand, the U.S. population has grown well over 50 percent during this period of time, to 100 million households in 1999.

Although there are several important revelations to be discovered in analyzing this document, we will consider a few that are most helpful to producers and distributors.

Figure 14.1
The Most Successful U.S. Motion Picture Releases of All Time

++ Includes re-releases, using ticket prices current during each release.
* Grosses estimated from film rental
^ Marquee Star at the time of original release.

Position	Picture	Symbol	US GBO Adjst'd to '98	Prdctn Bdgts Adjst'd to '98	Prdctn Bdgt To GBO Ratio	US Studio	Producer	Director	Star Power^
1	GONE WITH THE WIND	++	$959.8	$45.3	21	MGM	David Selznick	Victor Fleming	Clark Gable, Vivian Leigh
2	STAR WARS	++	$835.3	$29.0	29	FOX	George Lucas	Geaorge Lucas	
3	THE SOUND OF MUSIC	++,*	$667.9	$41.2	16	FOX	Robert Wise	Robert Wise	Julie Andrews, Christopher Plummer
4	E. T.	++	$637.8	$16.8	38	U	Stvn Speilberg	Stvn Speilberg	
5	THE 10 COMMANDMENTS	*	$614.4	$80.2	8	PARA	Cecil B. DeMille	Cecil B. DeMille	Charlton Heston, Yul Brynner
6	TITANIC		$613.7	$203.2	3	FOX/PARA	James Cameron	James Cameron	
7	JAWS	++	$600.7	$35.4	17	U	Richard Zanuck	Stvn Speilberg	Roy Scheider, Richard Dreyfuss
8	DOCTOR ZHIVAGO		$513.7	$56.7	9	MGM	Carlo Ponti	David Lean	Julie Christie
9	SNOW WHITE		$511.2	$16.9	30	BV/RKO	Walt Disney	David Hand	Animated
10	MARY POPPINS	++,*	$505.0	$26.3	19	BV	Walt Disney	Rbt Stevenson	Julie Andrews, Dick Van Dyke
11	101 DALMATIONS (Original)	++,*	$493.4	$0.0	n/a	FOX	Walt Disney	Geronimi / Luske	Animated
12	THE EMPIRE STRIKES BACK	++	$460.1	$34.2	13	FOX	George Lucas	Irvin Kershner	Mark Hamill, Harrison Ford, C. Fisher
13	BEN-HUR	++,*	$459.6	$83.6	5	MGM	Sam Zibalist	William Wyler	Charlton Heston
14	RETURN OF THE JEDI	++	$459.5	$52.6	9	FOX	George Lucas	Richard Marquand	M Hamill, H Ford, C Fisher
15	THE STING	*	$427.8	$19.1	22	U	Tony Bill, &	George Roy Hill	Paul Newman, Robert Redford
16	THE PHANTOM MENACE		$422.0	$115.0	4	FOX	McCallum & Lucas	George Lucas	Liam Neeson
17	THE EXORCIST	*	$409.4	$42.6	10	WB	Wlm Ptr Blatty	Willam Friedkin	Ellen Burstyn, Max von Sydow
18	RAIDERS OF THE LOST ARK		$408.9	$34.9	12	PAR	George Lucas, &	Steven Speilberg	Harrison Ford
19	THE ROBE		$408.0	$30.5	13	FOX	Frank Ross	Henry Koster	Rchrd Burton,Jean Simmons,V Mature
20	JURASSIC PARK		$404.2	$70.8	6	U	Stvn Spielberg,&	Stvn Spielberg	
21	THE GRADUATE		$401.3	$0.0	n/a	AVCO	Mike Nichols	Mike Nichols	Anne Bancroft, Dustin Hoffman
22	FANTASIA	++,*	$389.5	$26.5	15	BV	Walt Disney	Algar/Armstrong	Animated
23	THE GODFATHER	*	$372.2	$23.1	16	PAR	Albert Ruddy	Francis Coppola	Marlon Brando, Al Pacino
24	BAMBI	++	$371.7	$0.0	n/a	BV	Walt Disney	David Hand	Animated
25	FOREST GUMP		$369.9	$58.0	6	PAR	Wndy Fineman, &	Robert Zemeckis	Tom Hanks
26	THE LION KING		$351.0	$46.5	8	BV	Don Hahn	Allers, Minkoff	Animated
27	GREASE		$335.0	$14.5	23	PAR	Un Carr, Rbt Stigwoo	Randal Kleiser	John Travolta, Olivia Newton John
28	GHOSTBUSTERS		$333.0	$49.8	7	COL	Ivan Reitman	Ivan Reitman	Bill Murray,Dan Aykroyd,Sigmy Weaver
29	BEVERLY HILLS COP		$327.7	$21.8	15	PAR	Bruckheimer,Simpson	Martin Brest	Eddie Murphy
30	PINOCCHIO	++,*	$326.5	$30.2	11	BV	Luske, Sharpsteen	Luske, Sharpsteen	Animated
31	INDEPENDENCE DAY		$324.8	$77.5	4	FOX	R. Emmerich	Dean Devlin	
32	HOME ALONE		$317.5	$21.4	15	FOX	John Hughes	Chris Columbus	
33	BUTCH CASSIDY & THE SUNDANCE KID		$317.1	$43.5	7	FOX	John Foreman	George Roy Hill	Paul Newman, Robert Redford
34	CINDERELLA		$310.9	$0.0	n/a	BV	Walt Disney	Geronimi,Jackson	Animated
35	BATMAN		$295.3	$52.0	6	WB	Ptr Guber, Jon Peters	Tim Burton	M Keaton, J Nicholson, Kim Bassinger

Figure 14.1 continued
The Most Successful U.S. Motion Picture Releases of All Time

Kids: 5-11
Youth: 12-17

Position	Picture	Target Audiences	Genre	US Rating	Opened US Theatrical	Running Time In Hours	Tagline
1	GONE WITH THE WIND	Women, men	Romantic drama	G	12/15/39	3.7	The most magnificent picture ever!
2	STAR WARS	Youth,kids,men,wmn	Ac Adv, Sci Fi	PG	5/25/77	2.0	A long time ago in a galaxy far, far away . . . .
3	THE SOUND OF MUSIC	Women,men,families	Mscl Rmntc drma	G	3/2/65	2.9	The happiest sound in all the world!
4	E.T.	Kids, youth,men,wmn	Adv, Drama, SciFi	PG	6/11/82	1.9	He is afraid. He is alone. He is 3 million light years from home.
5	THE 10 COMMANDMENTS	Women, men, families	Drama	Not Rated	11/9/56	3.7	The greatest event in motion picture history.
6	TITANIC	Youth, women, men	Rmntc drma, Ac	PG-13	12/19/97	3.2	Collide with destiny.
7	JAWS	Men, youth, kids	Ac, Thrllr, Horror	PG	6/20/75	2.1	She was the first.
8	DOCTOR ZHIVAGO	Women, men, youth	Romantic drama	PG-13	3/6/4	3.3	A love caught in the fire of the revolution
9	SNOW WHITE	Kids, Families	Ani Chldms Fntsy	G	12/21/37	1.4	Walt Disney's first full length feature production
10	MARY POPPINS	Kids, families	Chldrns Mscl Cmdy	G	8/29/64	2.3	It's supercalifragilisticexpialidocious!
11	101 DALMATIONS (Original)	Kids, families	Anim Chldms Adv	G	1/25/61	1.3	It's 'arf comedy...'arf mystery...and it's howlarious!
12	THE EMPIRE STRIKES BACK	Youth,kids,men,wmn	Ac Adv, Sci Fi	PG	5/21/80	2.1	The adventure continues...
13	BEN-HUR	Men, youth, women	Ac Adv Drama	G	11/19/59	3.5	The world's most honored motion picture.
14	RETURN OF THE JEDI	Youth,kids,men,wmn	Ac Adv, Sci Fi	PG	5/25/83	2.2	The Empire falls....
15	THE STING	Men, youth, women	Crime Drma Cmdy	PG	12/25/73	2.2	All it takes is a little confidence!
16	THE PHANTOM MENACE	Youth,kids,men	Ac Adv, Sci Fi	PG	5/23/99	2.3	Every generation has a legend. Every journey has a first step. Every saga has a beginning.
17	THE EXORCIST	Men, youth	Horror	R	12/26/73	2.0	
18	RAIDERS OF THE LOST ARK	Youth,men,kids,wmn	Action Adventure	PG	6/12/81	1.9	Indiana Jones-the new hero from the creators of Jaws and Star Wars
19	THE ROBE	Men,women,families	Drama	Not Rated	9/16/53	2.2	The modern miracle you see without glasses!
20	JURASSIC PARK	Youth,men,kids,men	Ac,Ad,SciFi, Thrlr	PG-13	6/11/93	2.1	An adventure 65 million years in the making
21	THE GRADUATE	Women, men	Romantic Drama	R	3/8/4	1.8	This is Benjamin. He's a little worried about his future.
22	FANTASIA	Kids, families, youth	Anmtd Mscl Fntsy	G	11/13/40	2.0	Walt Disny's technicolor FEATURE triumph
23	THE GODFATHER	Men	Crime Drama	R	3/15/72	2.9	
24	BAMBI	Kids, families	Cldm Anim Fntsy	G	8/13/42	1.1	A great love story.
25	FOREST GUMP	Men, women, youth	Drama,Rmnc,Adv	PG-13	7/6/94	2.4	The world will never be the same once you've seen it through the eyes of Forest Gump
26	THE LION KING	Kids, families, youth	Anim Mscl Fntsy	G	6/15/94	1.5	
27	GREASE	Youth,wmn,kids,men	Mscl Cmdy Rmnc	PG	3/19/4	1.8	Grease is the word.
28	GHOSTBUSTERS	Youth,men, women	Comedy, Horror	PG	3/25/4	1.8	They're here to save the world.
29	BEVERLY HILLS COP	Men, youth, women	Ac Crime Cmdy	R	3/25/4	1.8	The heat is on!
30	PINOCCHIO	Kids, families	Chldrns Anl Fntsy	G	2/9/40	1.5	For anyone who has ever wished upon a star.
31	INDEPENDENCE DAY	Men, youth, women	Action SciFi War	PG-13	7/3/96	2.4	EARTH Take a good look. It could be your last.
32	HOME ALONE	Kids, youth, families	Comedy, Drama	PG	11/16/90	1.8	A family comedy without the family.
33	BUTCH CASSIDY & THE SUNDANCE KID	Men, women, youth	Ac Wstm Cmdy	PG	3/10/4	1.8	Not that it matters, but most of it's true.
34	CINDERELLA	Kids, families	Chldms Anl Mscl	G	2/15/50	1.2	A love story with music for all the world to love
35	BATMAN	Youth,kids,men,wmn	Ac Fntsy Adv	PG-13	6/23/89	2.1	

In order of prominence, the data sources are from Exhibitor Relations Company, the National Association of Theatre Owners(NATO) Encyclopedia of Exhibition, Internet Movie Data Base, and the Motion Picture Association of America (MPAA).

Box Office Weighted by Gross Profit Figures

This report, in keeping with the industry standard of ranking each picture by its box-office dominance, places *Gone With the Wind* in first position. For producers, this report would be misleading if it did not also show each picture's negative cost, and its box-office-to-production-cost ratio, adjusting these budgets to a 1998 currency value. Using this gross-profit perspective, *E. T., Snow White,* and *Star Wars* are the leading three pictures, with *Gone With the Wind* slipping to seventh position.

One very important element is readily evident here: that a picture's earnings capacity does not increase with its production cost. *E.T.* yields stunning box office earnings that are 38 times its negative cost. *Titanic* yielded a very similar gross, but it yields a comparatively sparse three times its negative cost. What is to be learned here? Certainly not that *Titanic* overspent. It should be assumed that the cost of this highly successful picture was approximately correct for its story. What producers can learn is that, unlike most other consumer products, motion pictures are valued by the dynamics of their stories and that of two stories with equal entertainment power, one may be substantially less expensive to produce than the other. Respecting this phenomenon may motivate producers to establish negative-cost-to-earnings parameters as part of their pictures' internal greenlight criteria.

The Studios

Seven of the ten major studios are represented in the report, plus Avco and United Artists. Fox has more pictures represented than any other studio, with nine (including its shared credit with Paramount for *Titanic*), followed closely by Buena Vista with eight pictures, and Paramount with seven.

It should be remembered that throughout this period, the studios, as a group, released 200 to 500 pictures each year. These 35 are a small sampling and do not represent the dominance in studio earnings. For instance, as referenced above, Warner Bros. has sustained a leading earnings position among the studios during this period, although it has just two pictures represented on the list.

Producers and Directors

This is one of the most telling aspects of the report. The producers and directors responsible for these pictures are the powerhouse icons of their time. Walt Disney produced seven of the eight Buena Vista pictures listed, George Lucas produced four pictures and directed one, and Steven Spielberg produced two pictures and directed four. Most of these producers and directors, even if only listed once, are unquestionably industry legends.

A great lesson here is to see the close correlation between the greatest pictures ever made and the most skilled producers and directors in the industry. This is clearly the single most consistent element among the successful pictures.

Star Power

There is a strong argument for looking at a star-caliber cast when examining such pictures as *Gone With the Wind, The Ten Commandments, Ben Hur,* and *The Sting.* On the other hand, 10 of the 35 pictures, including *Star Wars, E.T.,* and *Titanic,* use no "A-list" actors. Clearly, many leading producers and directors use talent that lend themselves to the picture, rather than primarily attaching star power for the sake of the marquee.

Target Audiences

Understanding each picture's target audience and its characteristics in each major territory is essential to grasp the earnings potential of the picture.

Studying the picture's target audience reveals some compelling and valuable characteristics. By number of target audiences, 25 of the pictures have three or more target audiences. Producers discovering pictures with three or more primary target audiences should be encouraged with these pictures' higher earnings potential.

Number of target audiences	Number of pictures
1	1
2	9
3	16
4	9

The pictures are closely divided between their most significant target audiences, with kids, youth and men dominating ten pictures each.

Most significant target audience	Number of pictures
Kids	10
Youth	10
Men	10
Women	5

The most prominent target audience appealed to in these films is men, with women and youth close behind.

One of the target audiences	Number of pictures
Men	25
Women	23
Youth	23
Kids	19
Families	11

Genre

"Sci-fi is in and cop shows are out." Commentary on this and every other combination of genres continues to be bantered about as if genre is a crucial picture-selection criterion for audiences. For these pictures, *action* is the most dominant genre category, and *drama* is the next most prominent genre category. A solid story driven with action is the dominant genre mix of these most successful pictures.

Genre	Number for which it is lead genre	Number for which it is one genre used
Action	12	13
Drama	3	12
Adventure	1	9
Romance	4	7
Animation	4	7
Comedy	2	7
Children	4	6
Science fiction	0	6
Musical	2	5
Fantasy	0	5
Crime	2	3
Horror	1	3
Thriller	0	2
War	0	1

MPAA Rating

One can clearly see from the large television-audience shares of motion pictures that have a *restricted audience* rating during their theatrical release that they appeal to the audiences who are restricted from viewing them at theaters and renting them from their video stores. Nevertheless, because of this restriction, all of the kids, most of the youth, and most of the family audience earnings are lost during the theatrical, video, and most of the premium-cable distribution windows. This reduces profits as evidenced by the sparse four *restricted-audience* pictures on this list. The 11 *general-audience* pictures are primarily pictures for kids or kids and family.

MPAA rating	Number of pictures
G	11
PG	11
PG-13	6
R	4
Not rated	3

Theatrical Release Date

So, do these pictures evidence a particular film industry golden age? On the contrary, the industry has been graced with great filmmakers throughout its brief history. There were two pictures in the 1930s, three in the '40s, five in the '50s, six in the 60s, six in the '70s, seven in the '80s, and six, so far, in the '90s.

And what about releasing pictures in off-season? For these pictures, as with most others, there is never a bad time to release a great picture. Some of these pictures were released in the traditionally off-season months of January, February, March, August, and September.

Year of release	Number of pictures	Year of release	Number of pictures
1937	1	1973	2
1939	1	1975	1
1940	2	1977	1
1942	1	1978	1
1950	2	1980	1
1953	1	1981	1
1956	1	1982	1
1959	1	1983	1
1961	1	1984	2
1964	1	1989	1
1965	1	1990	1
1966	1	1993	1
1967	1	1994	2
1969	1	1996	1
1972	1	1997	1

Running Time

The average running length for these pictures is 2 hours and 12 minutes. This includes five pictures running over three hours and four under one-and-a-half hours. Though longer pictures tend to have a higher production cost, there is no correlation between a picture's time and its grossing capacity. Consider the stronger earning *E.T.* at a sprightly 1 hour, 55 minutes, compared with *Titanic* at 3 hours, 17 minutes, or *The Ten Commandments* at 3 hours, 40 minutes.

Running-time category	Number of pictures
3 hours or more	5
2:30–2:59	2
2:00–2:29	14
1:30–1:59	10
1:00–1:29	4

Tagline

The taglines often capture a sense of the theatrical release campaign used by the studios. These can be useful in developing a sales strategy for pictures with similar audiences and stories.

Theater Attendance and Earnings by Target Audience _____

This report is on the following page and is essential for balanced producers. This report efficiently reveals the audience universe using the four major targets.

Figure 14.2
Theater Attendance and Earnings by Target Audience
1997

Attendance Percentages of Target Audiences					
Audience	1 Per Month	2 - 6 / Year	1 / Year	Never	Totals
Kids 5 - 11	N o t R e p o r t e d				
Youth 12 - 17	42%	44%	7%	5%	98%
Men 18 +	28%	36%	8%	27%	99%
Women 18 +	25%	32%	11%	32%	100%

Populations of Target Audiences, in Millions					
Audience	1 Per Month	2 - 6 / Year	1 / Year	Never	Totals
Kids 5 - 11	N o t R e p o r t e d				27.7
Youth 12 - 17	9.8	10.3	1.6	1.2	23.3
Men 18 +	27.2	34.9	7.8	26.2	97.0
Women 18 +	26.0	33.3	11.4	33.3	104.0
Total Target Audiences Populations					252.0

Annual Admissions of Target Audiences, in Millions					
Audience	1 Per Month	2 - 6 / Year	1 / Year	Never	Totals
Kids 5 - 11	N o t R e p o r t e d				297.0
Youth 12 - 17	117.4	41.0	1.6	0.0	160.1
Men 18 +	325.9	139.7	7.8	0.0	473.4
Women 18 +	312.0	133.1	11.4	0.0	456.6
Total Target Audiences Admissions					1,387.0

Approximate Box Office Earnings of Target Audiences, in Millions					
Audience	1 Per Month	2 - 6 / Year	1 / Year	Never	Totals
Kids 5 - 11	N o t R e p o r t e d				$1,363.2
Youth 12 - 17	$539.0	$188.2	$7.5	$0.0	$734.7
Men 18 +	$1,496.0	$641.1	$35.6	$0.0	$2,172.7
Women 18 +	$1,432.1	$611.0	$52.5	$0.0	$2,095.6
Total Target Audiences Admissions					$6,366.3

The data sources for this report are from Motion Picture Association of America,
the National Association of Theater Owners (NATO), Exhibitor Relations Company, Inc.
and the US Census.

Attendance Percentages

Youth are 50 percent more frequent in their regular attendance than their closest
target, 18-plus men. Youth are more involved attendees of movies as a group, with
only five percent never attending, compared with 27 percent men and 32 percent
women.

Populations of Target Audiences

As population numbers are considered in the analysis, the audience and commensurate earnings potential slips away from youth. By shear size, adult men and
women are the largest theater attendees.

Annual Admissions

Men slightly lead women in tickets purchased, and together, they spend over five times more than the youth audience.

Box Office Earnings

Each target audience demonstrates an impressive earnings vitality. However, the production of pictures that strongly appeal to all three of these targets represents the ultimate wisdom.

Information Sources

As business owners and creators, producers must keep current on creative, business, technology and related information. This information allows them to more effectively weave and bob along with the changing industry landscape, taking advantage of opportunities and avoiding the new challenges that appear with ever-greater regularity.

Fortunately, data have never been more available and convenient to access. Many sources are available over the Web, and that information which is not available can be had by e-mail or fax.

Listed below are some of the most respected sources used by entertainment executives:

> Exhibitor Relations Company, Inc.
> 116 North Robertson, Suite 606
> Los Angeles, CA 90048
> 310-657-2005

This is one of the oldest and most used sources in the industry, providing historical and weekly box office information, trade screening reports, development and production reports, and many special statistical and narrative reports, including (1) weekly box office/trade screening/CARA (Classification and Rating Administration) rating/special report updates, (2) bimonthly motion picture release schedules for all major and minor studios, by picture, showing primary cast, director, and release date (there is an e-mail version of this sent weekly that includes release patterns), (3) reports on motion pictures in development, including their relative detail, (4) reports on pictures in production, with creative and distribution detail, (5) reports on pictures in production without distribution, (6) the "Alpha List," which details pictures in comatose development, active development, and production, and (7) special research on demand.

> *NATO Encyclopedia of Exhibition*
> 4605 Lankershim Boulevard
> North Hollywood, CA 91602
> 818-506-1778

This book is published annually and contains several extremely helpful reports. These are not always in the ultimate final form for analysis by producers, and are for the pictures released a year prior to the one just ended, but the data are accurate and, in the main, complete.

Consider the information below, combined from two of these reports, which reveals CARA-rated motion pictures that received no U.S. theatrical distribution. Various estimates from festivals and other sources indicate that there are five to ten times more feature length pictures that are not rated, and so do not appear on these reports. If that is true, that increases the annual number of produced but unreleased pictures to more than a thousand. This is a terrible waste of resources and sobering motivation for producers to collaborate with global distributors from the earliest beginnings of their pictures.

Year	CARA-rated pictures	Pictures released by all U.S. distributors	Pictures not distributed
'90	570	385	185
'91	614	423	191
'92	616	425	191
'93	605	440	165
'94	635	410	225
'95	697	370	327
'96	713	420	293
'97	673	458	215
'98	686	509	177
'99	677	461	216
2000	762	478	284

The NATO Encyclopedia annually reports on the number of theater tickets sold, total box office take, average ticket prices, average major motion picture production costs (which were $52.7 million average per picture in 1998), average studio theatrical release print and advertising costs (which were $25.3 million average per picture in 1998), a report on each studio's theatrical grosses by picture, among several other excellent reports.

> Nielsen Media Research
> 11150 West Olympic Boulevard, Suite 1000,
> Los Angeles, CA 90064,
> 310-966-4900

This is perhaps the most complete and accurate source for television-viewing information, in a broad array of published reports and custom-designed research.

> Daily and Weekly *Variety* at variety.com

> *The Hollywood Reporter* at hollywoodreporter.com

These provide daily news and maintain archives on everything entertainment in the industry. They each also have research capacities.

> National Cable Television Association
> 1724 Massachusetts Avenue, NW
> Washington, DC 20036
> 202-775-3550

This is the best initial source for understanding the 100-plus cable television network landscape. Their *Cable Television Developments* book lists all the networks, their primary executives, contact information, programming reviews, and homes reached.

> Lone Eagle Publishing at loneeagle.com
> 2337 Roscomare Rd, Suite 9
> Los Angeles, CA 90077
> 310-471-8066

This is one of the oldest and most respected motion picture production talent information sources. They publish written reports, and their eagle eye Web site service is easy to navigate.

> Paul Kagan Research at pkbaseline.com

This is one of the most respected and reliable entertainment industry research firms. They publish reports and perform sophisticated research and analysis.

> Internet Movie Database at imdb.com

This is a powerful, user-friendly, free motion picture information Internet service.

> Showbiz Data at showbizdata.com

This data resource has an especially useful, free weekly Internet news update that reports the prior week's box office figures for the top 20 pictures, tracks the top ten U.S. pictures for the year, updates the ten U.S. studios by their grosses, and summarizes some of the week's top stories. The site also offers a paid service for U.S. and foreign box office data and other industry information.

Producer Success Principles

These principles are especially for motion picture producers, but they are also profitably applied by producers of television narrative and documentary programming, commercials, and even student film productions.

1. Story. Discovering, developing, and producing quality stories is the central focus. Story is the single most essential, important, and powerful asset.

2. Target Audiences. Every story appeals to specific target audiences more than to others. Producers should know who these audiences are, where they are, how many there are, what their entertainment consumption profile is, and what drives their motion picture passions. With the majority of audiences and income sourced outside the U.S., this audience understanding should also be understood for, at least, the six leading foreign territories. Where appropriate, cover shots should be produced to deliver seamless pictures to these markets. The audience is the most important participant in the industry. Cater to them.

3. Balance. Sustaining a balance between each picture's story, targeted audiences, and potential profit (negative cost to producer's gross relationship) is the most predictable approach to ensure each picture's development, production, and global distribution.

4. Talent. The strongest evolution of producer/talent relationships begins with meetings that allow each to test the other's creative affinity for the story, then continues with deal-making meetings involving the talent's agent and/or

attorney. The producer's research, planning, and preparation all help render talent attachment a predictable and even pleasant experience.

5. Global Distribution. Producers should exclusively develop and produce motion pictures for which they have first received at least preliminary distributor greenlights from the U.S. and at least five of the six major foreign territories. Distributors do what producers cannot do. They make each unknown picture a household name to their target audiences. They set up and manage each picture in the marketplace. They do the impossible. They sometimes even make mistakes. In any case, they are the independent producer's inseparable partners.

6. Development. Producers should plan and finance each picture's development in a fashion as well defined and complete as the manner in which they plan and finance each picture's production.

7. Financing. Producers should never accept private financing for production with the exception of motion pictures for which there are existing bankable distribution contracts in at least the amount of the picture's negative cost. Producers should use banks as their primary production financing source. Accordingly, producers should understand entertainment banking sufficiently to submit exclusive funding requests that they know will be accepted.

8. Entertainment Law. The development, production, and liquidation of motion pictures consistently engage the producer in the process of representation, negotiations, and documentations. Contract language does not always correlate with contemporary language interpretation. In negotiations, producers should be decisive, but *always* agree on basic terms only, with these being subject to their attorney's review.

9. Production Company Team. A producer's sustained solidarity is largely assured by the production company team. These members must be skilled, dedicated, and largely self-managed. Consequently, they must be carefully selected, refined, empowered, advanced, and allowed to monetarily participate in the team's successes.

10. Living a Full Life. In addition to skilled imagineering, producing, and releasing successful motion pictures, producers need the full symmetry of participation with their family, use of contemplation and study, and participation in the arts. If these are kept in mind as producers plan and schedule their time, they will enrich and fulfill their lives.

Index

A

Acquisition, literary rights option, 80–82
Activity projections, preparing, 107–12
Admissions, annual, 162
ADR (Alternative Dispute Resolution), 85
AFM (American Film Market), 35
AFMA (American Film Marketing
    Association), 40–41
Agencies, 89–95
Agents, 89–95, 146
    attorneys as, 92
    as creative resources, 94
    meetings with talent and, 91–92
Agreements
    letter, 82–83
    U.S. studio distribution, 139
American motion pictures, global popularity
    of, 31–35
Ancillary audience characteristics, 47–50
Ancillary earnings, producers rely on, 50–51
Ancillary markets, 143
    and rights, 45–58
Ancillary media and licenses, 14
Ancillary rights, miscellaneous, 55–58
Ancillary windows, 51–55
    free television syndication, 54–55
    network television, 53–54
    premium cable television, 52–53
    video distribution, 51–52
Arcade games, 57–58
Artistic balance, sustaining, 148–49
Attendance
    percentages, 161
    theater, 160–62
Attorneys, 73–87
    as agents, 92
    as counsels, 84
    participation of producers', 95
    producers performing as, 74–75
    and their firms, 73–74

Audience characteristics, ancillary, 47–50
Audiences, 1–4
    distributor pitch preparation, 3–4
    earnings by target, 160–62
    initial feasibility analysis of internal
        greenlight, 2
    orientation of, 3
    populations of target, 161
    sizes in major windows, 46–47
    target, 158

B

Balanced producers, 10
    development and production approach,
        10–11
Bank financing facility, preparing pro-
    duction, 138
Bank loan, engaging production, 140–41
Banking
    business, 59–60
    entertainment, 59–66
        approaching banks, 65–66
        banking business, 59–60
        basis of lending decisions, 60–63
        gap financing, 65
        loan approval process, 63
        production financing worksheet, 63–65
        types of loans, 65
Banks
    approaching, 65–66
    and completion guarantors, 146
Bonds, completion, 69–70, 140
Box office
    earnings, 162
    statistics
        foreign, 32–35
        global, 32–35
    weighted by gross profit, 157

Brand presence, 5–6
  establishing production company,
    147–48
Branding, picture's U.S., 142
Brands
  establishing each picture's, 5
  major consumer, 14–15
Budget economies, time and, 146–47
Business
  balance, 148–49
  producer's, 145–51
    advancing team vitality and
      allegiance, 150–51
    managing library pictures, 149–50
    multiple picture management, 145–46
    production company brand
      presence, 147–48
    sales events, 147
    sustaining artistic balance, 148–49
    sustaining business balances, 148–49
    sustaining personal objective
      balance, 148–49
    time and budget economies, 146–47

C

Cable distribution, premium, 24–25
Cable television, premium, 52–53
CARA (Classification and Rating
  Administration), 162
Cash flow projections, preparing, 113–14
Cast attachment, lead, 137
CCI (Cinema Completions International), 67
Communications, investment in partner, 130
Companies, 98–99
  defining and establishing production, 126
  development, 99
  forms of, 101
  funding development, 114–15
  interrelationships of, 99
  producing, 99
  production, 98–99
Company financing, development, 100–101
Company structures
  power of, 97
  producing, 97–102
Completion bond
  engaging, 140
  package, 69–70
Completion guarantees, function of, 67–68
Completion guarantors, 67–71
  banks and, 146
  producers' value of, 68–69
Completion insurance
  costs, 70–71
  relationships, 69

Consumer brands, major, 14–15
Contracts, long form, 82–83
Coproduction company financing, 107
Corporate structure, 118–19
Cost, completion insurance, 70–71
Counsels, attorneys as, 84
Creative protectionist producers, 8–9
Creative resources, agents as, 94
CRI (color reverse internegative), 21

D

Data, 153–65
Dates, theatrical release, 159–60
DDE (direct distribution expenses), 23
Deal
  memos, 82–83
  reviews, 83–84
Deal documentation, producers preparing, 83
Deals
  planning, 92
  preparation of fair, 94
  step, 78–80
Development, 97–102
  companies, 99
    emphasis of, 127–28
    financing, 100–101
    funding, 114–15
    teams of, 122
  essential power of funded, 103–4
  financing, 103–15
    process of securing, 107–15
    raising, 129–30
  funding sources, 104–7
  negotiations, 92–93
  pre-director picture, 134
Development plan, working, 130–33
Development team and advisors,
  selecting, 114
Director attachment, 134–35
Director relationship, producer, 135–36
Directors
  producers and, 157
  See also Pre-directors
Dispute resolutions, 85
Distribution
  network television, 25–27
  premium cable, 24–25
  subcontractors, 14
  theatrical, 23
  units, 19
  video, 24, 51–52
  windows, 12–13
Distribution agreement, U.S. studio, 139
Distribution-only relationship, 21–22
Distribution relationships, foreign, 37–38

Distributors, 4–7
    establishing each picture's brand, 5
    major and minor, 17–18
    operating perspective, 6–7
    producer relationships with foreign, 35–37
    studio integrity, 18–19
    studio operating perspective, 5
    U.S. theatrical, 17–29
        critical effect of U.S. studio
            attachment, 29
        major and minor distributors, 17–18
        producer relationship comparisons, 22–27
        split negative pickup relationships, 27
        studio acquisition of renegade
            pictures, 27–29
        studio relationships with independent
            producers, 20–22
        three studio arenas, 19–20
    U.S. theatrical, three studio arenas
        distribution units, 19
        production arena, 20
        studio executives, 19
Documentation
    license, 40–43
    preparing investment's, 114
    producers preparing deal, 83

E

Earnings
    box office, 162
    producers rely on ancillary, 50–51
    by target audience, 160–62
Economies, time and budget, 146–47
Entertainment banking, 59–66
Entertainment industry statistics and
        reports, 153–60
    box office weighted by gross profit, 157
    genre, 158–59
    most successful motion pictures
        released, 154–56
    MPAA (Motion Picture Association of
        America) rating, 159
    producers and directors, 157
    running time, 160
    star power, 157–58
    studios, 157
    taglines, 160
    target audiences, 158
    theatrical release dates, 159–60
Entertainment law, 73–87
Events, sales, 147
Executive committee, 121
Executives, studio, 19

F

Fair deals, preparation of, 94
Financing
    coproduction company, 107
    development, 103–15
        development funding sources, 104–7
        essential power of funded
            development, 103–4
    development company, 100–101
    gap, 65
    investor, 105–6
    participants, 14
    process of securing development, 107–15
        developing plans, 107
        formulating investments, 114
        funding development company, 114–15
        making presentations, 114–15
        preparing activity projections, 107–12
        preparing cash flow projections, 113–14
        preparing investment's
            documentation, 114
        selecting development team and
            advisors, 114
    production company, 104
    raising development, 129–30
    studio, 105
Financing facilities, preparing production
        bank, 138
Financing worksheet, production, 63–65
Foreign box office statistics, 32–35
Foreign distribution relationships, 37–38
Foreign distributors, producer relationships
        with, 35–37
Foreign territories, 13, 31–44
    establishing new foreign distribution rela-
        tionships, 37–38
    foreign trends, 44
    global popularity of American motion
        pictures, 31–35
    license documentation, 40–43
    license timing, 39–40
    managing global relationships, 43–44
    nurturing relationships, 38–39
    producer relationships with foreign dis-
        tributors, 35–37
Foreign trends, 44
Funded development, essential power
        of, 103–4
Funding development company, 114–15
Funding sources, development, 104–7

G

Game sales, retail, 57–58
Games, arcade, 57–58

Gap financing, 65
Genre, 158–59
Global box office statistics, 32–35
Global popularity of American motion
        pictures, 31–35
Global relationships, managing, 43–44
Global territories, 143
Greenlight review, literary, 80
Greenlights, initial, 133–34
Gross profit figures, box office weighted
        by, 157
Guarantors
    banks and completion, 146
    completion, 67–71
    producers' value of completion, 68–69

H

Hotels and motels, 58

I

In-flight, 58
In-house studio production, 20
Independent producers, 7–11
    studio relationships with, 20–22
Indian reservations, 58
Information sources, 162–64
Internal greenlighting, 2
Insurance cost, completion, 70–71
Insurance relationships, completion, 69
Investments
    documentation of, 114
    formulating, 114
    memorandums, 129
    offerings, 128
    in partner communications, 130
Investor financing, 105–6

L

Law, entertainment, 73–87
Lead cast attachment, 137
Legal aspects relating to stories
    vital, 77–83
        literary greenlight review, 80
        literary releases, 77–78
        literary rights option/acquisition, 80–82
        step deals, 78–80
Lending decisions, basis of, 60–63
Letter agreements, 82–83
Library pictures, managing, 149–50
License documentation, 40–43
    territory differences of, 43
License timing, foreign territories, 39–40
Licensed media, and retailers, 11–13
Licenses, ancillary media and, 14

Literary greenlight review, 80
Literary releases, 77–78, 86–87
Literary rights option/acquisition, 80–82
LLCs (Limited Liability Companies), 99,
        101, 118
Loans
    approval processes of, 63
    engaging production bank, 140–41
    types of, 65

M

Management, multiple picture, 145–46
Marketing materials, maturing, 138
Markets, ancillary, 45–58, 143
    motion picture effects on other
        windows, 45–46
    theatrically released motion
        pictures, 45–46
Media
    ancillary, 14
    retailers and licensed, 11–13
Memos
    deal, 82–83
    producing investment, 129
Merchandising, toys and, 57
Military, 58
Motels and hotels, 58
Motion picture industry
    functions of, 1–16
    participant categories and functions, 1–16
        ancillary media and licenses, 14
        audiences, 1–4
        brand presence, 5–6
        distribution subcontractors, 14
        distributors, 4–7
        financing participants, 14
        foreign territories, 13
        independent producers, 7–11
        major consumer brands, 14–15
        production talent and subcontractors, 14
        retailers and licensed media, 11–13
    participant category summary, 15
    story, 15–16
Motion pictures
    effects on other windows, 45–46
    global popularity of American, 31–35
    output relationships, 28–29
    theatrically released, 45–46
Motion pictures released, most
        successful, 154–56
MPAA (Motion Picture Association of
        America), 48–49
    rating, 159
Music publishing, soundtracks and, 57

N

NATO (National Association of Theater Owners), 46, 49, 162
Negative pickup, 20–21
Negative pickup relationships, split, 27
Negotiating, 75–77
Negotiations, 73–87
    development, 92–93
Network television, 53–54
Network television distribution, 25–27
Novelization, 55

P

Participant categories and functions, 1–16
Participation, points, 93–94
Partner communication, investment in, 130
Personal objective balance, sustaining, 148–49
Photography, principal, 141
Physical production, preparing for, 137
Pickup, negative, 20–21
Picture development, pre-director, 134
Picture industry, motion, 1–16
Picture management, multiple, 145–46
Pictures
    global popularity of American motion, 31–35
    managing library, 149–50
    studio acquisition of renegade, 27–29
    theatrically released motion, 45–46
    U.S. branding of, 142
Pictures released, most successful motion, 154–56
Plans
    developing, 107
    working development, 130–33
Points participation, 93–94
Populations of target audiences, 161
Post production; See also Production; Preproduction, 142
Pre-directors, picture development of, 134
Premium cable distribution, 24–25, 52–53
Preproduction
    final, 141
    See also Production: Post production
Presales, 139–40
Presentations, making, 114–15
Prison systems, 58
Producer director relationship, 135–36
Producer relationships
    comparisons, 22–27
        network television distribution, 25–27
        premium cable distribution, 24–25
        theatrical distribution, 23

video distribution, 24
    with foreign distributors, 35–37
Producer success principles, 164–65
Producers
    creative protectionist, 8–9
    and directors, 157
    independent, 7–11
    performing as attorneys, 74–75
    preparing deal documentation, 83
    principles of, 153–65
    rely on ancillary earnings, 50–51
    studio relationships with independent, 20–22
        distribution-only relationship, 21–22
        in-house studio production, 20
        negative pickup, 20–21
Producers' attorneys, participation of, 95
Producers, balanced, 10
    development and production approach, 10–11
Producer's business, 145–51
    advancing team vitality and allegiance, 150–51
    managing library pictures, 149–50
    multiple picture management, 145–46
    production company brand presence, 147–48
    sales events, 147
    sustaining artistic balance, 148–49
    sustaining business balances, 148–49
    sustaining personal objective balance, 148–49
Producers' value of completion guarantors, 68–69
Producing
    companies, 99
    company structures, 97–102
    investment memorandum, 129
Product placements, 55–56
Production bank
    financing facility, 138
    loans, 140–41
Production companies, 98–99
Production company
    brand presence, 104, 147–48
    defining and establishing, 126
    financing; See also Coproduction company financing
    operation, 125–44
        ancillary markets, 143
        assembling teams, 128–29
        development company emphasis, 127–28
        director attachment, 134–35
        engaging completion bond, 140

engaging production bank loan, 140–41
final preproduction, 141
global territories, 143
initial green lights, 133–34
investment in partner
    communications, 130
lead cast attachment, 137
maturing marketing materials, 138
picture's U.S. branding, 142
post production, 142
pre-director picture development, 134
preparing for physical production, 137
preparing investment offering, 128
preparing production bank financing
    facility, 138
presales, 139–40
principal photography, 141
producer director relationship, 135–36
producing investment
    memorandum, 129
raising development financing, 129–30
shooting script, 136–37
story searches of, 126–27
story selection, 133–34
U.S. studio distribution agreement, 139
working development plan, 130–33
teams, 119–21
Production; See also Preproduction; Post
    production, 97–102
arena, 20
financing worksheet, 63–65
in-house studio, 20
preparing for physical, 137
talent and subcontractors, 14
Profit, gross, 157
Protectionist producers, creative, 8–9
Publishing, music, 57

R

Rating, MPAA (Motion Picture Association
    of America), 159
Relationship comparisons, producer, 22–27
Relationship evolution, 90–91
Relationships
completion insurance, 69
distribution-only, 21–22
establishing new foreign distribution, 37–38
managing global, 43–44
motion picture output, 28–29
nurturing, 38–39
producer director, 135–36
split negative pickup, 27
studio, 146
Release dates, theatrical, 159–60

Releases, literary, 77–78, 86–87
Renegade pictures, studio acquisition
    of, 27–29
Reports, entertainment industry statistics
    and, 153–60
Rereleases, theatrical, 150
Reservations, Indian, 58
Resolutions, dispute, 85
Resources, agents as creative, 94
Retail game sales, 57–58
Retailers and licensed media, 11–13
    distribution windows, 12–13
Reviews
    deal, 83–84
    literary greenlight, 80
Rights
    ancillary markets and, 45–58
    literary, 80–82
    miscellaneous ancillary, 55–58
Running time, 160

S

Sales
    events, 147
    See also Presales
Sales events; See also Presales, 147
Sample forms, 82–83, 101
Schools, 58
Script, shooting, 136–37
Sea, ships at, 58
SECs (securities and exchange com-
    missions), 105
Securities, 101
Ships at sea, 58
Shooting script, 136–37
Soundtracks and music publishing, 57
Sources, information, 162–64
Star power, 157–58
Statistics and reports
    entertainment industry, 153–60
        box office weighted by gross profit, 157
        genre, 158–59
        most successful motion pictures
        released, 154–56
    MPAA (Motion Picture Association of
        America) rating, 159
    producers and directors, 157
    star power, 157–58
    studios, 157
    target audiences, 158
    entertainment industry statistics and
    reports
        running time, 160
        theatrical release dates, 159–60

Step deals, 78–80
Stories
    motion picture industry, 15–16
    searches of production company
        operation, 126–27
    selection of, 133–34
    vital legal aspects relating to, 77–83
Studio acquisition of renegade pictures, 27–29
Studio arenas, three, 19–20
Studio attachment, critical effect of U.S., 29
Studio distribution agreement, U.S., 139
Studio production, in-house, 20
Studio relationships, 146
Studio relationships with
    distribution-only relationship, 21–22
    in-house studio production, 20
    independent producers, 20–22
    negative pickup, 20–21
Studios, 157
    executives, 19
    financing, 105
    integrity, 18–19
    operating perspective, 5
Subcontractors
    distribution, 14
    production talent and, 14
Syndication, free television, 54–55

T

Taglines, 160
Talent, 89–95
    production, 14
    reserve, 95
Talent and agents, meetings with, 91–92
Target audiences, 158
    earnings by, 160–62
    populations of, 161
Team vitality and allegiance,
    advancing, 150–51
Teams, 117–24
    advisory, 119–20
    assembling, 128–29
    compensating, 123–24
    complete, 117
    corporate structure, 118–19
    development company's, 122
    discovering, 123–24
    negotiating, 123–24
    optimizing, 123
    production company's, 119–21
        advisory teams, 119–20
        executive committee, 121
Television
    network, 53–54
    premium cable, 52–53

Television distribution, network, 25–27
Television syndication, free, 54–55
Territories
    foreign, 13, 31–44
        establishing new foreign distribution
            relationships, 37–38
        foreign trends, 44
        global popularity of American motion
            pictures, 31–35
        license documentation, 40–43
        license timing, 39–40
        managing global relationships, 43–44
        nurturing relationships, 38–39
        producer relationships with foreign dis-
            tributors, 35–37
    global, 143
Theater attendance, 160–62
Theatrical distribution, 23
Theatrical distributors, U.S., 17–29
Theatrical release dates, 159–60
Theatrical rereleases, 150
Theatrically released motion pictures, 45–46
Tie-ins, premium, 56
Time and budget economies, 146–47
Timing, foreign territories license, 39–40
Toys and merchandising, 57

U

UPMs (Unit Production Managers), 55, 68,
    89, 110, 114, 137–38
U.S.
    most successful motion pictures
        released, 154–56
    studio attachment, 29
    studio distribution agreement, 139
    theatrical distributors, 17–29
U.S. branding, picture's, 142

V

Video distribution, 24, 51–52

W

Windows
    ancillary, 51–55
        free television syndication, 54–55
        network television, 53–54
        premium cable distribution, 52–53
        video distribution, 51–52
    audience sizes in major, 46–47
    distribution, 12–13
    motion picture effects on other, 45–46
Worksheets, 22, 63–65, 108, 111

About the CD-ROM...

This companion CD to *The Producer's Business Handbook* contains several documents (most of which are in Excel format) that will help deepen your understanding of the business processes and principles presented in the book aimed to help you plan and operate your own production and development companies.

The CD features a tutorial interface that contains examples of all the documents on the CD-ROM. After completing the exercises with the sample data provided, you will be prepared to do similar analyses on your own pictures and to customize the template worksheets included herein. With sufficient practice, you will be able to generate your own documents without referring to the tutorial. Further experience will allow you to apply the basic principles taught in the tutorial to situations beyond those covered in the tutorial and book.

Before you begin, review the explanation of the interface or descriptions of the documents included in the tutorial. The interface documents are always accessible via the "Help" button located at the top of this browser window. You can also check www.EBgroup.net/ProducerResources/Updates for updated exercises and new resources. (This requires a connection to the Internet.)

System Requirements

Windows 95/Windows 98/Windows NT 4.0
- Intel(R) Pentium (or comparable) processor or higher
- Minimum 32MB available RAM
- SVGA 256-color mode (or greater)
- MS Word and Excel to access example documents

Mac OS 7.6.1 and later
- PowerPC
- 32MB available RAM, 20MB free disk space
- SVGA 256-color mode (or greater)
- MS Word and Excel to access example documents

For further information, please see Readme.txt on the CD.

Beyond providing replacements for defective discs, Butterworth-Heinemann does not provide technical support for the content of this CD; however, you may address your replacement questions via email to techsupport@bhusa.com. Be sure to reference CD-03965.